PRAISE FOR
I REFUSE TO KILL

"Francesco Da Vinci's *I Refuse To Kill* will inspire and move you deeply. This amazing true story confirms that one person, acting with courage and conviction, can successfully oppose war and help change a part of history. Francesco's story reminds us that acts of conscience are never pursued in vain."

—**Peter Yarrow**, Peter, Paul & Mary

"I Refuse To Kill is a masterpiece!"

—**Steven Starr,** The Village Voice

"I was especially moved by how *I Refuse to Kill* connects the '60s to today. The themes Francesco raises, social justice the persecution of nonviolent activists, feeltragically modern."

—**Charles Sherman**, Sculptor

"As a veteran of the Iraq War, I wish I had summoned up the same courage Francesco Da Vinci showed in opposing the Vietnam War. *I Refuse To Kill* is more than a memoir; it is a guide book on how to stand by our convictions for peace no matter what the odds."

—**Garett Reppenhagen**
Executive Director - Veterans For Peace

"Conscientious objectors, who stand up to counter perpetual war, have a heck of a lot of courage because they know they are going to be vilified. And I know that Francesco Da Vinci was one of those who willingly paid a high price in order to champion nonviolence."

—**Governor Michael Dukakis**

"Francesco Da Vinci has written a book which should be read by all people who populate the Department of 'Defense' and all in the military-industrial complex."

—**Helen Caldicott**, Physician

"Francesco's amazing story is about holding onto a dream and making it happen. That's what the Supremes did in the '60s with our music. And that's what Francesco did—he dreamt up a peace group that inspired and raised hope across the nation."

—**Mary Wilson**, The Supremes

"Francesco Da Vinci's story is the testament of a brave activist risking his own freedom to ensure the humanity and dignity of others. May this book embolden people to oppose war and violence, and muster the courage to test new alternatives."

—**Joyce Ajlouny**, General Secretary
American Friends Service Committee

"Francesco Da Vinci has written a gripping story about the Vietnam war and his stance in refusing to fight in that cruel, senseless conflict. Mr. Da Vinci's story of resistance, in which he risked everything for his moral convictions, could not be more timely as the US continues to be mired in numerous, seemingly endless, and equally senseless wars of choice."

—**Daniel Kovalik**, author of *No More War*

"*I Refuse to Kill* is well-written and compelling. Francesco Da Vinci's case as a conscientious objector set a precedent, protecting the rights of all COs who don't belong to a traditional organized religion. Francesco's strong moral stand should motivate readers to ask themselves, 'What do I stand for?'"

—**Robert Richter**, Film Producer

"I strongly support and recommend Francesco Da Vinci's historical memoir. War is not the answer. It is time that the people of this country are more offended by war and more encouraging of peace and conscientious objection. Da Vinci's eye-opening book is an important step toward that end."

—**Ed Asner**, Actor

I REFUSE TO KILL

My Path to Nonviolent Action in The Sixties

FRANCESCO DA VINCI

United States Register of Copyrights
Washington, DC
Registration Number: TX-9-073-622
February 4, 2022

Dedication

In memory of Neil Armstrong,
my friend for more than 20 years.

And to all the courageous conscientious objectors
throughout history, who suffered greatly
to champion nonviolence.

CONTENTS

ACKNOWLEDGMENTS

My heartfelt gratitude to my brilliant editor Carrie Almir. Her dependability and dedication to excellence helped make this book possible.

I would also like to thank my two main writing mentors who encouraged me despite the fact that I was unpublished at the time: the late Pulitzer Prize-winning author Frank McCourt, and the former Senior Vice President of Doubleday, Nan Talese. I will be forever grateful to them for nurturing my craft.

Beyond those friends, there are far too many people who have helped me along the way for me to acknowledge all of them here. Instead, I will personally extend my deep gratitude.

INTRODUCTION

By Peter Yarrow of Peter, Paul & Mary

An exceptional musician and activist, Peter has fought for human rights and nonviolence throughout the world.

Francesco Da Vinci's *I Refuse to Kill* will inspire and move you deeply. This amazing true story confirms that one person, acting with courage and conviction, can successfully oppose war with nonviolent action and help change part of history.

In the turbulent sixties, Francesco battled for recognition as a conscientious objector to war. He was threatened with five years in prison for following his conscience and declaring to his Virginia draft board, "I refuse to kill." Rather than keep a "low profile," as his draft attorney prudently advised, Francesco did the opposite and founded Nonviolent Action, a peace group in San Diego that stirred the conscience of America.

The positive legacy of conscientious objectors and activists like Francesco has either been omitted or distorted from most historical accounts of the sixties. COs have been unjustly labeled as unpatriotic and cowardly by many. Yet, the opposite is true. Patriotic conscientious objectors like Francesco paid a high price for their stand, one that tested their courage and their determination to hold true to nonviolence.

Following Francesco's lead, as well as other peacemakers throughout history, we can redirect our country to the democratic values upon which it was founded. Conscientious objectors urge us to question our needless military interventions around the world—often motivated by religious intolerance, racism, and greed.

Francesco's commitment to wage peace calls to mind the brave nonviolent activists throughout history who put their lives, good names, and reputations on the line working for civil rights and for peace. When leaders such as Martin Luther King, Jr. passionately advocated nonviolent change, Francesco answered the call. He convinced his fellow peacemakers that through nonviolent action, they could help end the Vietnam war. Trying to subdue an enemy through force may have been a necessity in times before our own, but in today's world, Da Vinci asserted, resorting to violence only breeds more violence. As Francesco's role model Dr. King said, "Darkness cannot drive out darkness; only ligt can do that. Hate cannot drive out hate; only love can do that."

Clearly, there were excesses in the Sixties, but we should not lose sight of the enormous positive changes that transformed our society forever. So many of the progressive advances that came about were led and directed by young, determined peacemakers such as Francesco, who willingly paid a heavy personal price to stand for social justice and peace.

It is Francesco's dear wish that his memoir will inspire today's generation to apply the power of nonviolence. A horrific cycle of violence grips the world in which we live. But through the example of Francesco and other citizen activists, the next generation can learn the importance of carrying on the civil rights and peace movements.

I Refuse to Kill has a noble objective: to embolden activists of today in their efforts to address the violence in ourselves, in America, and the world. Violence is a formidable obstacle but it must not overwhelm and immobilize us. Francesco's call for global nonviolence starts with each of us. All our efforts, great and small, add up and matter. We save one another with every act of conscience. It is up to each of us to create a more democratic, humanistic culture through nonviolent action in this divisive and challenging time.

Francesco Da Vinci's journey in the Sixties compellingly shows that the determined nonviolent individual can indeed make a difference in a violent world, and that movements of conscience and compassion are never pursued in vain.

—Peter Yarrow

AUTHOR'S NOTE TO THE READER

I Refuse to Kill is the story of my coming of age in the Sixties and how I discovered the power of nonviolence. Inspired by spiritual leaders such as Gandhi, Dr. King, and Cesar Chavez, I studied the philosophy of nonviolence and gradually became an activist. As a conscientious objector to war, I was threatened with prison and became a target of intense intolerance that regrettably spilled over to my family and fiancée.

Although *I Refuse to Kill* is a personal story, it's also a tribute to conscientious objectors throughout history. They suffered greatly to follow their conscience. For their opposition to war, they willingly gave up their freedom; sometimes their lives. What I did as a CO and activist was minor compared to their sacrifices. I simply stood on their shoulders.

It's important to ask, Why haven't we learned about the heroic history of conscientious objection in schools? I hope that *I Refuse to Kill* will help rewrite that part of American and world history.

We also need to ask, Why have the many positive aspects of the Sixties been omitted, marginalized, or distorted to fit a divisive political agenda? The youth-led, humanistic Sixties generation bravely took up President Kennedy's call to better America, risking so much to better not just America but our planet.

Today's youth, by and large, want to live up to the challenge set forth by Congressman John Lewis—to continue the unfinished revolution, namely, to fight for social justice and peace through nonviolent action.

A knowledge of Sixties history can greatly enhance our lives today and inspire us to activism. To paraphrase Neil Armstrong, by taking one small step—in this case, a step back in time—we can take a giant leap forward for humanity. Together, we can declare, "No more war" and build a new culture that puts "We, the People" first.

Ready for some time travel? Then let's go back to the Sixties, a time like no other in US history, when, against all odds, a generation of peacemakers stopped a war.

war is not healthy for children and other living things
I WANT YOU FOR U.S. ARMY
LIFE
I AM A MAN

CAST OF CHARACTERS

The Presidents

John Fitzgerald Kennedy (1961–1963)
Lyndon Baines Johnson (1963–1969)
Richard Milhous Nixon (1969–1974)

Central Characters

Francesco – conscientious objector; founder of Nonviolent Action (NVA); Jane's boyfriend
Jane – social worker; activist; Francesco's girlfriend

Additional Characters

Ben, Norie, Jim – volunteers in Francesco's peace group – Nonviolent Action
Cesar Chavez – nonviolent activist; co-founder of the United Farm Workers union
Charlie Khoury – Francesco's ninth and final draft attorney
Dr. Frank & Mrs. Louise Da Vinci – Francesco's parents
Eric – Professor of History; member of Nonviolent Action
Ernest Fears, Jr. – Virginia State Director of Selective Service
Jerry – Naval officer and Vietnam Vet; Francesco's best friend
Joyce – the clerk at Francesco's Fairfax, Virginia draft board
Martin Luther King, Jr. – civil rights leader; encouraged conscientious objection to war
Muhammad Ali – heavyweight boxing champion; conscientious objector
Joan Baez - Singer-activist
Neil Armstrong – first human on the Moon; friend to Francesco
Ralph Da Vinci – Francesco's younger brother
Senator Eugene McCarthy (D-Minnesota) – presidential candidate in 1968, ran on a peace platform
Senator Robert F. Kennedy (D-New York) – younger brother of President John F. Kennedy; presidential candidate in 1968; ran on a peace platform

*I Refuse to Kill is based on my journals from 1960 to 1971. All the scenes in this book happened but some are not in strict chronological order. Also, the names of some individuals have been changed out of respect for their privacy.

"In the course of the [Vietnam] war, there developed in the United States the greatest antiwar movement the nation had ever experienced, a movement that played a critical part in bringing the war to an end."

—Howard Zinn, ***People's History of the United States***

1

AN AMERICAN REVOLUTION

(October 21, 1967)

"My first wish is to see this plague of mankind, war, banished from the Earth."

—George Washington

The march seemed flowers against guns. As we surged toward the Pentagon, soldiers used their rifles to shove us back. I was caught up in the middle. Shouts and screams mounted. The glimpses I caught were fleeting as if I was taking split-second portraits. A protester's face would appear, mirroring panic or rage, then in an instant vanish in the maelstrom.

A girl beside me was knocked to the ground. When I leaned down to reach for her, a rifle butt slammed against the left side of my ribs. I doubled over but managed to stay on my feet. When I looked up, the girl was gone. Several people beside me fell and were trampled. Trapped in the suffocating pandemonium, there seemed no escape. Blurred havoc reigned. Someone slammed into my right shoulder, and in the next moment, I found myself on the outer edge of the clash and made my way out.

I reunited with my girlfriend Jane, who had been waiting for me at the foot of the Pentagon steps. We hugged, and I pulled back sharply as a sharp pain ripped through my ribs. Jane lifted my shirt, revealing a large ugly bone bruise.

"I guess I zigged when I should've zagged."

Unamused, Jane shook her head in weary resignation. "These marches won't do any good. No matter what we do, Johnson is going to go right on bombing the hell out of Vietnam."

"Maybe," I said, "but I've had it with sitting at home and watching the body counts on TV."

"No one is going to listen to a bunch of kids in the streets. We've got to vote the damn warmakers out."

"We can't just wait around for the next election. We've gotta keep the pressure on and keep marching."

"They're *dangerous*."

"They're a duty."

Jane motioned to a protestor with a blood-stained T-shirt. "And what do you think Middle America is going to say when they see us on TV getting our heads beat in?"

"They're going to start questioning the war."

"No way," Jane said firmly. "I'll tell you what they're going to say, and it's *exactly* what my parents would say—'They got what they deserved!'" We walked on, then paused to take one final look at the mayhem. "It's a war zone . . . the whole country is," Jane said somberly. "How did we come to this?"

I thought back to a more innocent time, a time when America wasn't so furiously divided. At the outset of the sixties, a young, charismatic president raised the hopes and dreams of the nation on his Inauguration Day—January 20th, 1961.

I was there with my camera . . .

At the dinner table, Dad announced, "We're going to watch President Kennedy's Inaugural Parade tomorrow. I booked a suite at a hotel that overlooks Pennsylvania Avenue."

"Can I bring Jerry?" I asked. Jerry, a conservative Republican, was my best buddy. I was the loyal opposition.

The night before the parade, a relentless storm deluged the nation's capital with eight inches of snow. Temperatures dropped to 20 degrees Fahrenheit. The inaugural parade was almost canceled but a task force worked night and day to clear the route for the new president.

Once my folks, Jerry, my brother Ralph, and I settled into our second-story hotel suite, Jerry and I shoved open a window, hoping to catch a glimpse of the newly elected president. How youthful and vigorous John F. Kennedy was in sharp contrast to his 72-year old predecessor, General Dwight Eisenhower. Kennedy's call for my generation to become active citizens and make the country better was a colossal change from the sleepy Fifties, which relentlessly touted conformity.

The window that Jerry and I leaned out of offered a birds-eye view of the Inaugural Parade below that included marching bands, a replica of the World War II PT-109 boat that Kennedy commanded in the Navy, tanks, and a Polaris missile.

Finally, the new president's dark blue Lincoln Continental convertible approached, flanked by two escort cars with secret service agents riding on the running boards. "The president's car is coming," I said to my parents.

My dad was pouring Virginia Gentleman into Mom's glass. "We're fine right here," Dad said. My parents toasted and laughed. I stared moodily.

Jerry tapped my shoulder. "When Kennedy gets closer, let's yell, 'Hey, Jack!' Maybe he'll look up."

My face brightened. "Brilliant!"

As the presidential limo neared, I focused my 35mm Kodak on JFK and Jacqueline and snapped off a few shots. Jackie, whom the rag trades fondly called "The Queen of Fashion," wore a beige suit and matching pillbox hat.

Jerry said, "I'll do the countdown, then we'll yell."

We leaned out the window as far as we could without inadvertently joining the parade. Jerry held up his hand. "Three . . . two . . . *one*!"

In unison, we screamed, "HEY, *JACK!!*" President Kennedy looked up with a smile, picked up his silk top hat, and waved it at us. We returned the wave and joyfully fell back into the hotel room with a loud *thud.*

Speechless, Jerry and I nodded to each other, knowing that we'd remember this day for the rest of our lives. Two things stood out in memory: First, President Kennedy waving to us. Second, Kennedy's challenge to our generation to be *active* citizens, something we took to heart more than anyone could have imagined.

I took this photo of JFK's Inaugural Parade when I was fifteen. President Kennedy & Jacqueline are in the lead car, January 20, 1961. (Photo: F. Da Vinci)

2

ALL-AMERICAN FAMILY
(The Fifties to 1961)

"The image is one thing; the human being another."

—Elvis

While President Kennedy's Inauguration inspired optimism across the nation, I was fighting depression at home. Both of my parents were alcoholics.

Growing up, I didn't understand Mom and Dad's addiction. I only knew that Dad started every morning with a shot of whiskey, while Mom's habit was a nightly tall glass filled with a lot of whiskey and a little ginger-ale. As a psychiatrist, Dad said he needed the drinks to tolerate listening to the problems of patients all day long. Mom said she needed the drinks to tolerate Dad.

From childhood on, I accumulated a maddening dam of resentments. Alienated from my folks, my teachers, and in fact from *any* authority figure, I failed ninth grade and was in danger of repeating that dubious feat the next year. No one could understand how I could be so unhappy yet seemingly have the perfect All-American family. Dad was a well-respected psychiatrist and book author; Mom was a retired nurse; we lived in a big mansion; and we were rich. That was the façade. The reality, however, was that we were at war.

The parental neglect was extreme. Mom and Dad didn't even know where my younger brother Ralph and I went to school. We weren't sons; we were boarders.

Relentlessly, I lobbied my parents to quit their drinking, but it was to no avail. I remember saying to Mom and Dad, "Maybe if parents are going to pay more attention to their drinking than to their children, they shouldn't have kids."

When Ralph hit his teens, he began to mirror Mom and Dad's addictive personalities. His focus was always on immediate gratification. Anything requiring self-discipline seemed out of the question. If he felt like eating desserts before dinner, so be it. If he wanted to blow off appointments, so what. He was the center of his universe. Everyone could orbit around him or shove off. I couldn't depend on him for anything except for being undependable. Yet, he had a spectacular sense of humor and could charm the socks off anyone he met.

Sometimes friends close to the family would recognize that I was the only one countering the self-destruction. I'll never forget one of my father's friends telling Dad, "Francesco's the one who has to pick up all the pieces."

Love in our family was confined to the self-help books that Dad steadily cranked out. The words of empathy were there on paper but the expression of love was the province of other families. As a result, Ralph and I suffered incredibly low self-esteem. We couldn't help but compare ourselves negatively to other kids who were openly adored and cherished. Occasionally, I would see parents warmly embrace their children. Since my folks never hugged or kissed me, I figured there must be something bad about me—*I must not deserve to be loved.*

The neglect would have been bad enough but it was coupled with physical abuse from Mom. Unhappy with her marriage and stay-at-home life, she made a habit of beating the living daylights out of me for seemingly no rhyme or reason. Ralph, however, was never touched. Perhaps it was because I was the thorn in Mom and Dad's side for holding them accountable for the drinking. Eventually, I got too big for the hitting, but the boyhood memories lingered . . .

I hear a terrifying sound—the rustle of Mom's skirt as she storms down the long hall of the mansion. The swish-swish sound grows louder, like an approaching storm. I stand frozen with chills running up and down my spine. Part of the terror is that her fury is random and without warning.

Mom marches into my room, draws back her strong hand, and strikes me across my face. A tooth comes loose, and I catch the blood so it won't stain the rug and make Mom even more upset. She knocks me down to the floor and starts kicking. I curl up, protecting my head. The blows come hard to my stomach. Out of pride, I won't cry. I hate my parents, but worst of all, I hate myself.

The beatings dominated my childhood and no doubt influenced my later revulsion of violence in any form.

Eventually, with the physical and emotional abuse, I realized that absolutely *no one* would intervene on my behalf. If I were ever to get past mere survival, I'd need to come to my own rescue. Reading gave me a way out. Our home library was lined floor-to-ceiling with self-help books. During his forty years of psychiatric practice, Dad had written over two dozen motivational hardbacks touting love as "the core meaning of our lives." Ironically, he failed to apply that wisdom to his own family. Instead, he myopically focused on drinking and being 'world-famous.'

But to give credit where credit is due, my father's books helped thousands upon thousands of people better *their* lives. Dad had a special gift—the ability to tell people in everyday language how to apply the power of love to transform themselves: communicating better, thinking positively, turning disadvantages into advantages, and breaking self-destructive habits. His motto seemed to be, "Do as I say, not as I do." Also, to his credit, he was a global, humanistic thinker. The entire back wall of our sun porch, for example, was a 12-foot by 8-foot map of the world. Dad would sometimes pontificate before it, describing the wars around the planet as madness. Both Dad and his father were pacifists who believed that war was never justified no matter how glorified and propagandized.

Inspired by the sound advice in his books, I became determined to put his methods of self-improvement into practice to turn my life around. By my late teens, I was on a mission, reading every self-help book I could get my hands on. The more I read, the more fortified I felt against the emotional and physical cruelty at home.

One saying in particular, from Napoleon Hill's *Think and Grow Rich,* stood out and stayed with me: You cannot be defeated unless *you* accept the defeat.

Another gem came from one of Dad's self-help books: "Take a self-inventory. Ask yourself, 'What gives me the most happiness?'"

That simple question shocked and moved me. No one had ever asked about *my* happiness.

At the top of my Happiness List was the love from my best friend in life—my Boxer, Rex. Ever since I raised him as a pup, we have been inseparable.

Second on my list was my love of writing. From childhood on I found that I simply *had* to keep a journal, not just for peace of mind, but to keep from losing my mind! Out poured a floodgate of damned-up self-expression and revelations regarding my hidden authentic self.

Third was a love of Nature. As a boy, I loved to sit by the expansive picture windows in the dining room and the living room. I would gaze out at the grand oak and maple trees and smile at the fascinating array of animals that would visit our yard from the nearby forest: birds of all kinds, squirrels, and rabbits. How I loved those animals! But others in the neighborhood killed many of them for "sport."

One day a kid stopped by with his father. They were decked out in hunting gear.

"C'mon, buddy," the kid said excitedly, "we're gonna shoot rabbits and squirrels. You don't need a gun. We'll share." He held up his rifle, and I couldn't take my eyes off it.

"No thanks," I said.

His dad looked at me with disgust and said to his son, "Your pal is a real pansy, huh? Let's go." Less than an hour later, I was in the house when I heard their shots. Every rip in the air made me shudder.

Other days I would hike in the nearby woods, marveling at the diversity of plant life and animals. In a sense, Nature took the role of nurturing grandparents, helping to heal my emotional wounds.

Next on my happiness list was the joy of stargazing. When I was eleven, I was hooked on space after witnessing a glowing golden dot called Sputnik glide across the night sky. While many Americans were threatened by it, I was exhilarated. My New Frontier was no longer just America; it was the Universe.

From then on, I habitually escaped into the backyard of the estate to check out the Moon and stargaze. Often I imagined myself freely traveling the cosmos. What a wonderful diversion from the unbearable boredom of homework and tests that required rote memorization over learning. Years later, I deeply related to the lyrics in Simon and Garfunkel's "Kodachrome": *When I think back to all the crap I learned in high school, it's a wonder I can think at all.*

Last but not least on my happiness list was photography—'drawing with light'—a hobby I eventually combined with writing for a long career as a photojournalist. In high school, taking pictures was my favorite means of self-expression. It allowed me to get over my awkward shyness. With a camera around my neck, I had an excuse to mingle with people, especially girl-people. As a photographer, I could even befriend the cheerleaders, who otherwise wouldn't have given me the time of day.

Everything on my Happiness List—my dog Rex, writing, nature, stargazing, and photography—had one thing in common—they were all powered by *inspirational dissatisfaction,* meaning—you hate something so much—in my case, my home life—that it ends up inspiring you to overcome what seems like insurmountable adversity.

As I put more time and energy into the things on my Happiness List, I became increasingly motivated to make something of my life. Finally, I had a sense of *purpose.*

Perhaps the most important by-product of my turnaround was a quality I had never previously known—self-respect. Having survived physical abuse at home and the emotional abuse of neglect, I emerged stronger than I ever would have without my adversities.

My parents, drinks in hand, c. 1955.

The family mansion in Fairfax, Virginia. (Photo: F. Da Vinci)

L-R: Me, my Mother, Ralph, Rex, and my Father, c. 1967.

Boyhood

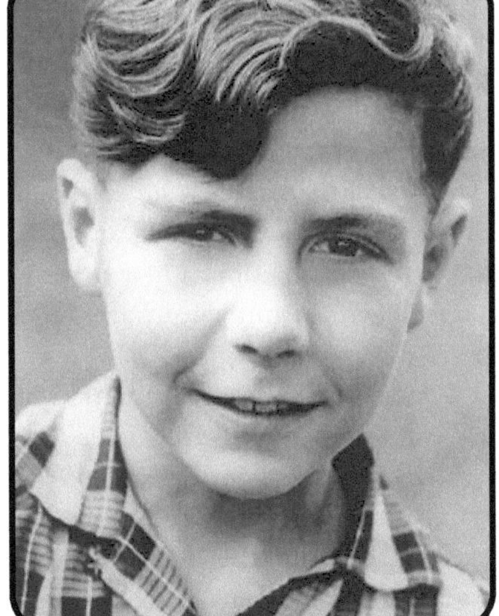

3

THE CUBAN MISSILE CRISIS

(October 1962)

"It is insane that two men, sitting on opposite sides of the world, should be able to decide to bring an end to civilization."

—President John F. Kennedy

The sky became starless as the whole world faced a full-scale nuclear war. In October of 1962, the unthinkable was at hand—Armageddon.

President Kennedy somberly addressed the nation. He announced that the U.S. was prepared to launch an all-out war with Russia over the fact that the Soviet Union was placing missiles in Cuba—only 90 miles away from the U.S. If Russia did not remove the missiles, JFK added, we would use "nuclear force."

That unnerving phrase—'nuclear force'—rang in my head, yet it was impossible to comprehend. I gave pause to a mind-boggling scenario—that modern-day humans might soon become extinct at our own self-destructive hands. Einstein's quote came to mind: *I know not with what weapons World War III will be fought, but World War IV will be fought with sticks and stones.*

Even if Kennedy did not initiate nuclear war, there was the real danger that the Soviets might launch first by concluding a first strike would be their best means of survival. History is replete with examples of wars launched due to fears of what the other side *might* do.

Preparation for a possible nuclear confrontation between the superpowers had been set in motion a year *before* the Cuban Missile Crisis. In a *Life* Magazine cover story—September 15, 1961—President Kennedy told Americans that it would be prudent to build bomb shelters in their backyards. A sense of urgency swept the country, and shelters became a fad. The Cold War was on full steam. I knew about our charges of Russian aggression but I did not know at the time that we had our missiles just outside of the Soviet Union in Turkey. Nor did I know that we had detonated a series of thirty-six atmospheric nuclear weapon tests in the Pacific Ocean from April to November 1962!

Even as early as 1955, unbeknownst to the public, Congress had a secret plan to prepare for nuclear war. President Eisenhower ordered the Department of Defense to draft emergency plans for legislators if nuclear missiles destroyed the nation's capital. Officials wanted a go-to place to maintain the continuation of the government. The secret location selected was the Greenbrier, a luxury hotel in West Virginia. It was ideal because it was close to D.C. but far enough away to supposedly be safe from a nuclear bomb. Construction of the underground bunker began in 1957 and was completed in October 1962—during the Cuban Missile Crisis!

By happenstance, the Greenbrier was one of my family's vacation spots. Periodically, during the early sixties, Dad ferried the family to the hotel for weekend getaways. Little did we realize that 720 feet beneath us was "Project X," a two-level shelter for Congress that was roughly the size of two football fields, one on top of the other.

In light of the fast-increasing threat of nuclear war in 1962, my high school began conducting duck-and-cover exercises. Blaring horns would sound at one-second intervals. By Pavlovian conditioning, we would scramble under our desks and curl up with our hands over our heads. I joined the herd and followed suit. Then one day, I asked myself, *What the heck am I doing? How can this be a "safety measure" against a nuclear blast?* As one of the high school newspaper photographers, I always had a camera with me. During one of the duck-and-cover exercises, I spontaneously decided to photograph my fellow students huddled beneath their desks, that is until a shrill voice pierced the air—"Francesco!"

I lowered my camera, facing the wrath of my disgruntled teacher. "Quick! Get under your desk and protect yourself!"

"But these desks aren't going to protect anyone. It doesn't make sense."

My teacher's eyes flared. "Francesco, get under your desk now! If the bomb doesn't kill you, *I* will!"

I complied.

The world seemed on the fast track to international suicide, or as government officials appropriately dubbed it—MAD, 'mutually assured destruction.' My biggest fear, however, was not that the world might come to an end. It was that I would never know what it was like to kiss a girl.

For thirteen eternal days, the world dreaded, almost expected, Doomsday. The Cuban Missile Crisis passed, but other nuclear close-calls occurred throughout the sixties (and beyond). For example, only three days after President Kennedy's Inauguration on January 20th, 1961, a B-52 bomber carrying a pair of atomic bombs crashed in North Carolina. Each bomb was 260 times more powerful than the nuclear weapon dropped on Hiroshima. At the crash site, responders discovered that one of the weapons had landed in a field via a deployed parachute. But the second bomb struck the ground at nearly 700 miles per hour. Three of the four failsafe switches were thrown. The last switch, however, stayed intact, thus averting an unimaginable catastrophe. Experts estimate that had the bomb detonated, the blast would have instantly killed everything within an 8.5-mile radius. The lethal fallout radiation from the blast could have traveled up the east coast and reached as far as New York.

The Cuban Missile Crisis passed but left me asking myself, *If the world suddenly came to an end, what would be the meaning of my life?* And as Dr. King prompted, *How has my life been of service to others?*

For a couple of months before our high school prom, Jerry had been seeing Melissa, so he was covered for a date. But I was too painfully shy to ask a girl to the prom. Whenever I started to work up the nerve to ask anyone out, I'd balk and say, "Never mind." As I'd back away, I'd think, *I'd love to stay and talk, but I'm too busy being a doofus!*

Thankfully, Jerry came to my rescue and suggested I ask out his sister, Linda, who accepted, maybe out of pity.

First stop on prom night was at Jerry's house to pick up Jerry and his sister. I had the obligatory corsage in hand as I entered the living room. Uneasily I greeted Jerry's Dad, a stern colonel in the Army. "Linda will be down in a minute," the colonel said.

After a few eternal minutes, Linda descended the staircase in a strapless turquoise gown. Her full dark hair was up and back, with a few tendrils framing her lovely face. She looked radiant.

An agnostic in a desperate situation, I prayed that I wouldn't have to pin the corsage on Linda in front of the Colonel and Jerry. In the middle of my meditation, Jerry's Mom appeared. She smiled hello, picked up a Kodak Instamatic, and said, "Let's take a picture of Francesco pinning the corsage on Linda!"

Dutifully, Linda stood motionless as I fumbled with the corsage just over her lovely left breast. Meanwhile, Jerry *and* his Dad were staring at me with eyes that seemed capable of firing lasers.

Finally, we were off to the prom. Dad had lent me his white El Dorado Cadillac that boasted a fire-engine red interior. Jerry and Melissa hopped in the backseat and immediately started making out.

Instead of sitting next to the passenger window, Linda sat close beside me. As we neared the prom, I looked at her gratefully, thinking, *I sure hope she doesn't mind that I don't know how to dance.* We parked in the massive lot in front of our high school and walked toward the entrance. An overhead sign read: J.E.B. STUART HIGH SCHOOL PROM—CLASS OF 1963.

As we entered the cafeteria, our heads bobbed to "Be My Baby" by the Ronettes. We danced a little, Jerry and I looking like logs in motion. The girls, however, made us look good. "Louie Louie" by the Kingsmen came on, and I no longer cared what others thought of my dancing. I was having a great time with Linda, who had a smile that lit up the room. The last song was a slow one, "Hey Paula" by Paul and Paula. "I really dig this song," Jerry said, slipping his hands around Melissa's waist. They swayed back and forth as if melting into one another.

I hesitated, wondering if Linda might not want to slow dance, but she offered her hand and said, "C'mon."

As I held her close, Jerry and Melissa looked over with smiles, seemingly pleased that Linda and I were getting on so well.

Afterward, at the punch bowl, Jerry said, "I'm starved. Let's hit the Hot Shoppes! Anybody up for burgers and fries?"

I backed into a slot at our hamburger hangout and gave everybody's order into a scratchy intercom. The exchange was so garbled I didn't know how they could decipher what we wanted, but they managed. A waitress in short-shorts roller-skated over to the top-down Cadillac with a tray of burgers, fries, and Cokes.

Melissa warned, "Everybody better take the ketchup now 'cause I'm gonna drown my fries!" We laughed, and Melissa asked, "Say, what the hell is everybody gonna do after graduation?"

Linda answered, "I'm thinking of the Peace Corps."

Jerry asked Melissa, "What are you goin' for?"

Melissa replied, "Whatever pays most!"

"Right on," Jerry laughed.

Melissa said to Jerry, "I know I don't have to ask you, babe."

"Yeah, I'm goin' Navy all the way," Jerry said.

"How about you, Francesco," Melissa asked. "You goin' Navy too?"

I shook my head no without making eye contact.

"Army?" Linda asked, tilting her head curiously. I squirmed. "Well?" she asked.

"He's anti-war," Jerry said. "Francesco thinks you can be nice to a guy like Hitler and he'll write a thank you note."

"Real funny," I said. "I want to serve, just not with a gun."

"What if you're drafted and you *have* to go in?" asked Jerry.

"I don't know."

"I get it," Melissa said, flapping her arms and clucking, "Buc, buc . . . buc, buc!"

As Jerry and Melissa had a good laugh, Linda slid away from me and pressed herself against the opposite door.

"Jerry and I have a cousin stationed in Vietnam," Linda said. "He's helping protect South Vietnam from the Communists. While you're here in your comfy Cadillac, he's putting his life on the line so you can enjoy the freedoms you obviously don't appreciate." Her eyes exuded contempt for me. "It's late," she said. "I want to go home."

With a sigh, I started the car, and we headed back in deafening silence.

With high school graduation approaching, I had no idea how or when I would serve America. Then in the summer of 1963, a month before I would go off to college, the *perfect* opportunity came my way—The March on Washington led by Martin Luther King.

While Jerry was determined to serve overseas in the military, I felt determined to serve at home. Joining marches for civil rights seemed like a good way to start. Yet, I had to admit, I was afraid of marching. I had never been in a demonstration, and I had no idea what to expect. The press had widely painted marchers as dangerous troublemakers with the potential for violence. Torn between the fear of participating and the duty to help better America, I reflected on the need to march.

Fittingly, 1963 also marked the 100th anniversary of the signing of the Emancipation Proclamation by Abraham Lincoln. We had come a long way, but there was a long way to go. The call for a March on Washington for Jobs and Freedom was the culmination of a continually expanding civil rights movement, and with trepidation, I wanted to be part of it.

Before the March on Washington, on June 12th, President Kennedy announced on television that he would begin to push for expanded civil rights legislation—the law which later became the monumental Civil Rights Act of 1964. *America is on the right track,* I thought hopefully. But the same night that President Kennedy raised hopes concerning racial harmony, tragedy struck—37-year old activist Medgar Evers was assassinated in Mississippi in his own driveway by a Klansman. His wife, Myrlie, was first to find him. The bullet from a rifle had passed through Medgar's heart, but he was still alive. He was taken to a hospital in Jackson, where he was initially refused to be admitted because he was Black. The family persisted, and he was treated. Less than an hour later, he died. Thirty-one years would pass before a conviction was made.

When I felt firm in my resolve to join the March on Washington, I faced a new fear—asking my folks for permission to join the demonstration.

I figured the best strategic time to make the announcement would be when Dad was feasting on Mom's cooking. It wouldn't be easy, though. Dad had a strict dinnertime rule—no one was allowed to talk about problems at the table. It was a Catch-22 because dinnertime was the *only* time Ralph and I saw our parents!

Nevertheless, I was determined to break Dad's rule and lobby to march in support of Dr. King's call for civil rights.

Secret Fallout Shelter for Congress, Greenbrier Hotel, West Virginia, c. 1962.

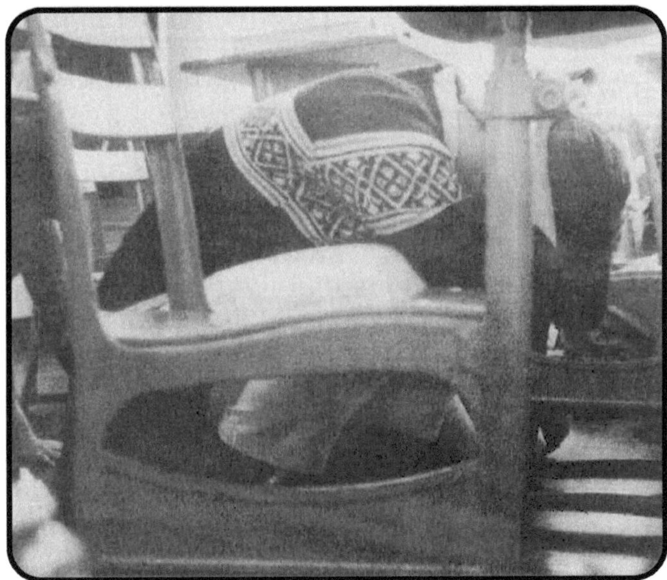

The Cuban Missile Crisis duck-and-cover drills, October 1962. (Photo: F. Da Vinci)

4

THE MARCH ON WASHINGTON
(August 28, 1963)

"I am happy to join with you today in what will go down in history as the greatest demonstration for freedom in the history of our nation."

—Martin Luther King, Jr.

Exactly one week before the March on Washington, our family gathered around the dining room table for our weekly pasta night.

Ceremoniously, Dad tucked a napkin in his shirt, bib-style, and gave his one-word dinner prayer—"Enjoy!" We dug into the feast: capellini with tomato sauce, toasty garlic bread, and an antipasto salad.

My father's wavy hair, combed straight back, was as jet black as the suspenders he wore. "Salud," Dad said, draining the proverbial half-full glass of wine in three gulps.

I tried to gauge Dad's mood, waiting for the perfect moment to bring up my burning wish to go to the march. Slowly I twirled long thin strands of capellini with my fork and spoon. Several times I began to speak, but every time laryngitis set in. Finally, I blurted, "This coming Wednesday, I'm getting up early!"

Everyone stared. At length, Mom said, "That's nice."

"I'm going to play golf at the country club, and then I'm going to the March on Washington. Can you pass the tomato sauce, Dad?"

Dad stopped chewing. "What did you say?"

"I said, 'Can you pass the tomato sauce.'"

"The part before that—the part about a march."

"Oh, the march. I'm going to the March on Washington. Dr. King is speaking, and I don't want to miss it."

Ralph's eyes lit up. "Wow!"

"You're not going, Francesco," Dad said firmly. "No way."

"Why not? You and Mom have always been for civil rights."

"This is different. There are much more constructive ways to support the Negro cause. When you're old enough—vote!"

Mom piped up. "There you go."

I pleaded, "I want to show my support now. Remember, Dad, when you told me why you became a doctor? It was to help people. Well, this is one way *I* want to help people."

"The paper said the turnout will be massive and that it could turn violent. Did you think of that?"

"I'm seventeen. I can handle it!"

"It's too risky."

"The march is about *nonviolence!*"

"I don't want to talk about it anymore. You're not going, and that's that."

Suddenly I wished I had never asked for permission. At the same time, I knew being sneaky was out of the question. Ever since I immersed myself in self-help books to build my confidence and character, dishonesty had become repulsive. Instead of going behind my parents' back, I would give my all to convince them to let me join the march.

"What do *you* think, Mom? This is *really* important to me."

She avoided my eyes and said, "Whatever your father says is what goes. He knows what's best, usually."

Dad gave her a look. "Usually?"

"Don't push it," she said, gathering dishes to take to the kitchen.

I called my buddy Jerry for sympathy and support, but he disappointed me. "I agree with your Dad. You put that many people together, and there's bound to be trouble."

A week later, I dejectedly watched the televised March on Washington. It took place only seven miles away from my family's home in Falls Church, Virginia, at the Lincoln Memorial. Over 250,000 people attended, armed with the courage to take nonviolent action against injustice. The music that day included Joan Baez singing "Oh Freedom" and "We Shall Overcome." She also joined Bob Dylan—her boyfriend at the time—in singing "When the Ship Comes In." Peter, Paul and Mary sang Dylan's "Blowin' in the Wind" and "If I Had a Hammer." And Odetta sang "I'm On My Way."

Activist John Lewis of the Student Nonviolent Coordinating Committee (SNCC) told the crowd to keep working and finish "the unfinished revolution of 1776." Lewis later became known worldwide as a leading civil rights activist for his Freedom Rides, frequent arrests (45 in all), and sit-ins at lunch counters. But few knew that he was also a conscientious objector—the first Black CO in Alabama.

Yet, when he passed away in 2020, not a single major publication mentioned it in his obituary.

When Dr. King took the microphone at the March On Washington, gospel singer Mahalia Jackson shouted, “Tell them about the dream, Martin!” King’s mesmerizing speech steadily rose with fervor: “I have a dream that my four little children will one day live in a nation where they will not be judged by the color of their skin but by the content of their character.”

At the White House, JFK watched Dr. King deliver his speech and exclaimed, “That guy is really good.”

As King’s moving words built into a cadence, I felt a wave of self-contempt. I had knuckled under and failed to act on what I *knew* was the right thing to do. I should have stood up to my parents and said, “I’m sorry you don’t want me to go, but this is too important to miss. If you want to punish me, fine.”

With resolute conviction, I made a pledge to myself: *Never again will I let anyone talk me out of standing up for what I deeply believe in.*

Shortly after the March on Washington, I moved to Staten Island, New York, and enrolled in the Pre-Med program at Wagner College. My major was preordained. There were five doctors in the family and I was expected to be Dr. Number Six. I wasn’t passionate about medicine but I figured that some plan was better than no plan.

My first year of college was a rude awakening. I had been raised in a mansion and served by maids. At college, I was confined to an off-campus rooming house and had no wheels. Dad was afraid a car would distract me from my studies. Each morning at dawn, I took two buses to get to college in frigid, windy weather. Frequently, gale-like winds brought the temperature down to zero degrees. I never could put on enough layers to counter it.

“(Love is Like a) Heat Wave” by Martha and the Vandellas was a big hit, but as a freshman, I found neither heat nor love. It was my first time living away from home, and though I felt relieved to be at a distance from my alcoholic family, I was lonely.

I began paying more attention to the news, not only as a distraction from my non-existent love life but because I felt inspired by President Kennedy’s idealism. In 1963, for example, he called for a nuclear test ban with the Soviet Union and the UK. The treaty prohibited nuclear testing in the atmosphere, in outer space, and underwater. I hoped that JFK would press for greater arms control throughout his administration.

Regardless of whether he would have done that, it seems very unlikely that he would have strongly escalated the war in Vietnam. According to Charles Kaiser, author of *1968 in America,* diplomat George Ball warned Kennedy a few months after his inauguration that defending Vietnam might require three hundred thousand

American troops. Kennedy laughed and replied, "Well, George, you're supposed to be one of the smartest guys in town but you're crazier than hell. That will never happen." And in the Fall of 1963, JFK was quoted as saying, "It is their [South Vietnam's] war. They have to win it or lose it." He said we should help South Vietnam but not do their fighting for them.

Inspired by Kennedy, I began following politics for the first time. It seemed America had a brilliant, diplomatic, and personable leader who would continue to motivate my generation to better their country over the next few years. But that hope was shattered on November 22nd in Dallas. After serving only a little more than one thousand days in office, President Kennedy was shot and killed.

Like millions of other Americans, I never forgot where I was that day.

Congressman John Lewis, an icon of the civil rights movement. (Photo: F. Da Vinci)

5

PRESIDENT KENNEDY IS KILLED

(November 22, 1963)

"Let us dedicate ourselves to what the Greeks wrote so many years ago: to tame the savageness of man and make gentle the life of this world."

—Robert F. Kennedy

On Friday, November 22nd, I dropped in at the campus cafeteria for lunch. To my surprise, there wasn't a single person in line. Everyone was clustered around tables, listening to radios. I tapped a guy on the shoulder. "What's going on?"

He turned, his face ashen. "Haven't you heard? President Kennedy was shot in Dallas!" I stared in disbelief. Then a news bulletin announced, "The president died at 1:00, a half-hour after he was shot." *President Kennedy died? It couldn't be true!*

In English class, the professor stood before us in silence. A commotion outside drew his attention to the window. As he stared out, the rest of us followed his gaze. On the front lawn, several students were lowering the flag to half-mast. Abruptly, the tearful professor turned on us and shouted, "Everyone out—*now*! Class dismissed!"

It wasn't until I was in the privacy of my off-campus apartment that I began to comprehend that the murder of the president was reality. Finally, I let everything out that I had been holding back and wept.

Secret Service whisked off Vice President Lyndon B. Johnson in an unmarked car to Love Field Airport in Dallas. The agents had Johnson, code-named Volunteer, stay below the car's window level as a precaution.

Once aboard Air Force One that carried the president's casket, LBJ took the oath of office.

He stood between Mrs. Johnson and Mrs. Kennedy. Jacqueline chose to remain in her blood-soaked clothes saying, "I want them to see what they've done to Jack."

After JFK was assassinated, columnist Mary McGrory told Labor Secretary assistant Daniel Patrick Moynihan that we'd never laugh again, to which Moynihan replied, "Heavens, Mary, we'll laugh again, but we'll never be young again."

The next day I called Jerry, who said, "Maybe it's not over yet. Maybe the sick bastard or bastards that killed Kennedy have a list."

"Who would do something like that?"

"Who knows what was behind it," Jerry said, "a pro-Castro assassin, a rogue C.I.A. agent, the Mafia, a secret international group. Maybe our spies tried to knock off somebody in a different country that rubbed the wrong people the wrong way. Maybe killing Kennedy was payback. But if the truth ever does come out, it probably won't happen in our lifetime."

I listened in utter shock.

Whether he was the fall guy or a lone killer, Lee Harvey Oswald, a 24-year-old former Marine, was charged with murdering the president using a rifle he had purchased by mail for $12.78. Adding to the wildfire of conspiracy theories was the fact that Oswald, a Marxist, had spent time in Russia and had even applied for Soviet citizenship. When his request for citizenship was denied, Oswald attempted suicide. He cut his wrist and was found unconscious in a bathtub.

Oswald's pro-Fidel Castro leafleting and talks attracted the attention of the FBI and the CIA. About three weeks before the assassination, Oswald learned that an FBI agent had stopped by his house and talked with his wife, Marina. Furious, Oswald went to the Dallas FBI office and, according to the receptionist, left a note that said, "Let this be a warning. I will blow up the FBI and the Dallas Police Department if you don't stop bothering my wife." FBI agent James Hosty received the letter and destroyed it two days after the assassination under orders from his superior. Senior officials at both the CIA and the FBI hid vital information from the Warren Commission's investigation of the murder, leading many to speculate that the agencies didn't want to give the impression that if they had acted more vigilantly they would have likely been able to prevent the assassination of the president.

After assassinating President Kennedy from a school depository building where he worked, Oswald was confronted on the street by policeman J.D. Tippit. Oswald killed the officer by shooting him with a revolver four times at point-blank range. Someone who had witnessed the shooting saw Oswald duck into a movie theater. The film running was *War is Hell.* After a struggle, Oswald was arrested at the theater. Two days later, live on NBC television from a Dallas jail garage, a nightclub operator—Jack Ruby—shot Oswald in the abdomen at close range as detectives were escorting him toward an armored car to be transferred to the county jail. Oswald was taken by ambulance to Parkland Memorial Hospital, where he died. Parkland was the same hospital where President Kennedy died two days earlier.

Some speculated that Ruby was acting on behalf of organized crime, that he had been instructed to silence Oswald forever so that Oswald could not confess and implicate others involved in the assassination.

Years later, Richard Goodwin, speechwriter and friend of Robert F. Kennedy, said that he only talked to Bobby once about his brother's assassination. Bobby said he didn't think it had anything to do with Cuba [or Russia], that it was more likely the work of organized crime.

About ten days after Kennedy's death, I took a train down to Washington, D.C., to pay my respects to the fallen president. At JFK's snow-covered gravesite at Arlington National Cemetery, I joined the long line of mourners. They were flanked on both sides by seemingly endless rows of white tombstones.

At the top of the incline, I photographed the president's flower-strewn grave and the Eternal Flame flickering in the breeze. I gazed back at the long serpentine procession of Americans paying their respects. In the distance were the Lincoln Memorial, the Washington Monument, and the Capitol. Grief-stricken, I recalled that only about three years ago, President Kennedy had waved to my buddy Jerry and me. The future had held so much promise. JFK had disillusioned cynics and imbued my generation with a renewed sense of altruistic purpose. Materialistic myopia had given way to an ethic of service to others.

As I stood before the gravesite, I ruminated on the young president's legacy—how proud he made us feel about ourselves and our country. How strongly we believed in our possibilities.

President Kennedy had inspired my generation, but our collective optimism plummeted out of the devastation of his death. No longer were seemingly impossible goals simply seen as challenges to make real. No longer were my generation's principled expectations on the sharp rise. Our former unshakeable sense that the best was yet to come evaporated.

Two weeks after JFK's death, I attended the candlelight service for President Kennedy at the Lincoln Memorial. There was shockingly little security, allowing me to film President Johnson from about nine or ten yards away. I regretted that my 8mm movie camera had no sound because what President Johnson said stuck with me: "We buried Abraham Lincoln and John Kennedy, but we did not bury their dreams . . ."

In the background, Abraham Lincoln's white marble statue, designed by Daniel Chester French, looked on somberly. The deep expressiveness etched on Lincoln's face seemed to convey the strain he was under trying to preserve the union.

I noted that the names of all the states were inscribed along the upper border of the Lincoln Memorial. But one state name, by coincidence, happened to be directly in the center over Lincoln's statue—JFK's home state of Massachusetts.

On Saturday, February 9th of 1964, Jerry traveled from the University of Virginia, and I sojourned from Wagner College in New York to meet at a bar in Washington, D.C. We didn't want to miss this day in music history—the appearance of a new import band from England called the Beatles.

Tickets to see John, Paul, Ringo, and George live on *The Ed Sullivan Show* were hard to come by. The Sullivan program received a record-setting 50,000 requests for tickets to the show, but only 728 lucky people got to see the performance live.

After the Fab Four played "I Saw Her Standing There," Jerry said, "Man, I don't know why the girls are going bonkers for those mop heads."

"I don't know either," I said, "but I'm thinking of letting my hair grow and learning guitar." We laughed, and I asked Jerry for an update on his plans for the future.

"I'm still in R.O.T.C. [Reserved Officers Training Corps]. In three years, I'll be on a destroyer. Hopefully, I'll see some action wherever the country needs us. It might be Vietnam. We're not at war with 'em now, but it looks like that's what's gonna go down."

"I read that we're sending *lots* of advisors there."

"Yeah, we've got about 16,000 there now," Jerry said.

I didn't know it at the time, but under the Geneva Accords, the US was only allowed to have 685 military advisors in southern Vietnam. Eisenhower secretly sent in several thousand, and Kennedy raised it from there. Some even took part in combat operations. "We need 'em for counter-insurgency," Jerry continued. "South Vietnam is gonna fall to the commies unless we get in there and kick some butt."

"Personally, I don't think we should be trying to police the world."

"If we don't do it, who will? I remember when we had bull sessions in high school about war. You always looked at things idealistically. That's fine and dandy in theory, but it doesn't stop tyrants in the real world."

"I still say we go to war way too easily. The US doesn't go to war because it has to; we go to war because we want to. The UN says, and I agree with it, there's no justification for war unless it's for *self-defense*. Just because we're a super power and *can* invade countries doesn't mean we *should*. How would we like it if another country tried to mess with our elections and change our system of government?"

"No offense, buddy, but it's not gonna be peaceniks that make the world safe for democracy. If you're drafted, you still thinking about being a CO?"

"I am."

"It's your call, but I don't think it's gonna sit well with our gung-ho Virginia draft board."

"That's down the road," I answered. "I'll deal with it when I have to."

"Have you even registered with the draft?"

"Not yet. I'm only a couple of months late."

"You gotta be kidding me!" Jerry exclaimed. "Man, you'd better get on that. If you haven't registered thirty days after turning eighteen, they can hit you with up to five years in jail, a $10,000 fine, or both."

I got on it!

Dad kindly offered to drive me to the draft board so I could register. It was rare that we did anything together, so I was grateful for his company.

I was in the kitchen stalling when Dad passed by without stopping. "I'll be in the garage."

Like most teenagers, I had a habit of leaning on the open fridge door and mulling over what to grab. Dad honked the horn from downstairs, and Mom urged, "Hurry!"

I grabbed a Pepsi and quipped, "If we leave now, we should be about three days early."

The moment I slid into the front seat of the car, Dad asked, "Where's your tie?"

"I want to be myself."

"You do what you want, but in my opinion, you're showing bad judgment."

As we pulled up in front of the Fairfax, Virginia draft board, I uneasily eyed the red brick, colonial building. Dad said, "I'll wait for you in the car."

I entered the modest interior of the draft office and walked past eight or so twentyish young men slouched in beat-up chairs, waiting to be called. The clerk looked up and said, "Your draft card, please."

"I don't have a card," I answered weakly. "I'm registering late." She gave me an aggravated look, took my name, and told me to take a seat. I asked, "What's your name?"

She looked up as if her head was heavy. "You don't need to know my name."

"I'd like to know it anyhow, if you don't mind."

She sighed. "Joyce. Take a seat."

"Thanks, Joyce."

An hour later, I reluctantly registered for the draft.

I headed for the exit and noticed the Virginia state flag in the corner. I had seen it many times before but never paid any attention to the circular emblem in the center. Up-close, I discovered it depicted two warriors in battle dress. The standing woman, representing Virginia and "Virtue," had her foot placed squarely on the chest of a dead leader representing "Tyranny." Around the image was the state motto in Latin: *"Sic Semper Tyrannis"*—Thus Ever to Tyrants.

"Is anything wrong?" said Joyce from behind her desk. The tone was accusing. I pointed to the flag emblem.

"A little hostile, don't you think?"

"Oh that," Joyce said, looking back down at her papers. "I'm not too crazy about it myself."

President Kennedy's gravesite about a week and a half after the assassination, December 1963. (Photos: F. Da Vinci)

My best friend Jerry, c. 1966.

The Virginia state flag.

6

CALLS TO CONSCIENCE
(1964)

"There comes a time when one must take a position that is neither safe, nor politic, nor popular, but he must take it because conscience tells him it is right."

—Martin Luther King, Jr.

On the long ride home from registering with the draft, I took advantage of one of the few times I could engage Dad in a father-son talk. "What do you think about war in general, Dad?"

He paused a moment to reflect, then launched into a thoughtful monologue. I wasn't expecting an exchange of ideas. Since he dutifully spent most of his days listening to patients, I figured this was *his* time to express himself.

"Love can defeat anything," Dad said, "even war, even racism. Love is what gives our life purpose. That's why I made our family motto, 'Work and Love Conquer Everything.' Hate and violence aren't the answer. History will tell you that. People will argue that we're born violent, but that's not true. We're born to love. I got that philosophy from my parents, mainly from my father. People who knew my dad would say they never met a kinder soul. In fact, Dad was so kind that when he died, I had President Lincoln's words engraved on his tombstone: 'With Malice Toward None.' That legacy of love lives on in me."

I stared down the road as the trees flicked by. "It'll live on in me too."

Throughout the following week, I thought back on how my parents and circumstances had influenced my beliefs.

Dad gave my brother and me a beautiful philosophy of life based on loving others, but he neglected to apply it at home. He was an absentee father and husband, completely focused on his career. As a boy, I never understood the apathy from my father or the hitting from my mother. I only knew I deeply detested both forms of violence.

Looking back on my early teen years, I was admittedly an incorrigible Rebel Without a Cause. Guidance counselors didn't know what to do with their number one mischief-maker. For my attention-getting pranks, I spent almost as much time in detention as I did in classes. One counselor suggested, "You know, Francesco, high school and college aren't meant for everyone. Maybe you should consider bricklaying. That's what my son does. It pays good."

I had no interest in bricks, but every day dropping out of high school looked better and better. Then, as I stood at the brink of despair, a totally unexpected offer from my folks turned my abysmal life around. Dad conferred with Ralph and me. "Boys, your mother and I are taking you out of school. We're going on a Mediterranean Cruise to three continents—Europe, the Soviet Union, and Africa."

We stared in shock. He had to be kidding!

"But if you take this cruise," Dad continued, "you'll need to miss three months of school. Do you need to think about it?" he asked with a sly grin.

Ralph and I looked at each other incredulously, and Ralph said, "Dad, if we have to think about it, we should be your patients."

Dad laughed and added, "We'll be gone during the election of the next president. Hopefully, it'll be Jack Kennedy."

On the day of our bon voyage from New York in October 1960, multi-colored streamers stretched and broke away from the *Caronia* as we slowly glided out of port. Every night, as we crossed the Atlantic, I would go out on deck and marvel at the spectacular beauty of the vibrant Moon and stars.

A month into the cruise, we received the results of the presidential election. Kennedy had barely defeated Nixon in the closest election since 1916. With over 68 million people voting, Kennedy won by only 112,000 plus votes!

The next morning a dozen veiled women emerged on an upper deck, draped in black. Somberly, they plodded by in a funeral procession, some dabbing tears.

"Who died?" I asked Dad.

"No one," he said. "They're Republicans."

I was my usual sullen self until the *Caronia* reached the Moroccan port of Tangier in northern Africa.

As the tour group walked along a narrow street, our guide pointed out historic sites. I lagged behind taking pictures when suddenly a gang of children in tattered rags mobbed me. They had serious skin diseases, with ribs protruding from their frail bodies. As they surrounded me and stared with piercing eyes, they cried out, "Hungry! No mother! No father!" When they weren't pulling at my clothes, they held out their hands for money. I felt pity, and due to my isolated, wealthy upbringing—disgust.

The tour was moving on, oblivious to my plight. "Hungry! Hungry!" came the cries, louder and more desperate. I stood frozen. From every direction, the children yanked fiercely at my clothes. The guide heard the commotion and hurried back to rescue me. From his pocket, he grabbed a handful of pink bubblegum pieces and tossed them out. The children fought ferociously for the gum as the guide pulled me free.

The tour continued, but all I saw in my mind were the forlorn faces of the starving children.

That evening, the ship's dazzling dining room was nearly empty. Apparently, the famine ashore had dampened many appetites. I stared at my full plate, still recalling the desperate faces. Abruptly, I left the table.

For the remainder of the cruise, I was a different person. The children of Tangier had shocked me out of my self-absorption. I brooded with anger that those children should be doomed to a life of cruel suffering and early death just because of their circumstances.

Upon my return to America, the daily scowl on my face had softened. I was a rebel *with* a cause, determined to one day do something to alleviate unnecessary suffering. I was changed in another way as well. For the first time, I felt a sense of gratitude for my privileged life.

My guidance counselors were stunned at the reversal in my attitude. Their dreaded delinquent had become civil. "Good morning, Mrs. Ferguson," I said to one of the guidance counselors in passing. She stared, suspiciously.

After my witness of starvation abroad, I was confronted with another call to conscience at home—the struggle for civil rights. Though I had been raised with a philosophical revulsion for racism, the realities of that social toxin were slow to sink in. I grew up in an all-white upper-class suburb of Falls Church, Virginia, where each mansion in the neighborhood was over two acres apart. A few families of senators and congressmen lived in the area: Senator Vance Hartke, Senator Herman Talmadge, and Representative John Jarman.

Oddly enough, what first awakened me to racial inequality was my Saturday afternoon ritual of going to the movies. In elementary school, my friends and I would go to the old State Theater to catch fantastical sci-fi movies: *Them, The Blob, Earth Vs. the Flying Saucers, Forbidden Planet, The Time Machine, The War of the Worlds, Invasion of the Body Snatchers* and *The Day the Earth Stood Still.* But the path to that fun escape contained a grim reality. Between my isolated neighborhood and the movie theater was a shockingly poor, all-Black shantytown that stretched for several blocks. Every Saturday, I took in the shocking sight of flimsy dwellings made from scrap materials. It was as if someone had opened a hidden door and revealed to me the world of have-nots.

In addition to an isolated upbringing in a segregated neighborhood, my errant education contributed to my ignorance of racism in America. My history books, for example, omitted that Columbus enslaved the hospitable Arawak Indians of the Bahama Islands. He wrote in his journal, "They would make fine servants . . . With fifty men we could subjugate them all and make them do whatever we want." Columbus's top priority was profit. He wrote in his log, "As soon as I arrived in the Indies, on the first Island which I found, I took some of the natives by force in order that they might learn and might give me information of whatever there is in these parts." Namely, gold. Whatever wealth Columbus brought back to Spain, the king and queen had promised him ten percent of the profits. To entice more support for another voyage, Columbus promised as much gold and as many slaves as they might need.

Growing up, my textbooks in elementary school and high school were abundant with misinformation. It wasn't until college, when I did my research, that I learned of my country's long history of slavery and invasions. I suppose every country, to some extent, is guilty of glorifying its history to infuse citizens with patriotism. Nevertheless, I felt betrayed.

Television turned out to be a wonderful source of education. It greatly helped raise my consciousness about civil rights. Amidst lighthearted sitcoms and comedies like the *Ozzie and Harriet Show*, *Beverly Hillbillies*, and *The Andy Griffith Show* came news broadcasts of hateful segregationists raining violence on nonviolent civil rights protesters. Intensely disillusioned, I asked myself, *How can this be happening in America, the country with a Constitution proclaiming justice for* all*?*

A key element that stirred my conscience was protest music with messages of social justice and peace through nonviolence. The inspiring lyrics not only prodded me toward activism but they also shamed me for my silence. The protest song that influenced me the most was Bob Dylan's 1963 anti-racism and anti-war anthem "Blowin' in the Wind."

Occasionally, I would sing along to a Dylan album, imitating that nasal tone that my parents found so peculiar. Dylan wailed about the revolution unfolding in America and told the older generation to make way for the new. His message for my generation—If you're not part of the solution, you're part of the problem. Don't be bystanders. Be activists!

Each call to conscience that I experienced planted a seed. Together those calls germinated and strengthened my sense of moral duty, the duty to serve others. I knew with certainty that I wanted to address suffering, better my country, and better the world. But I had no idea where to begin. Then the Vietnam War broke out.

A month before I was set to start college, President Johnson justified our invasion of Vietnam with the Gulf of Tonkin Resolution. At the time of the resolution in August 1964, I accepted everything President Johnson said without question. I wanted to believe my president and was naïve concerning the government's masterful art of deception. Through later revelations from the press and whistle-blowers, I learned the reality of how the war started.

On August 2, 1964, while on a spy mission off the coast of northern Vietnam, the destroyer USS *Maddox* fought three North Vietnamese Navy torpedo boats in the Gulf of Tonkin. Two days later, on the night of August 4, 1964, our jets fired in the area even though, as a pilot later testified, "there was nothing there." The very next morning, on August 5, LBJ ordered bombing raids on North Vietnamese military targets, which he said were in retaliation for the *alleged* incident of August 4. One of the attack pilots had been Commander James Bond Stockdale. Yes, 'James Bond' was really his name! Stockdale had responded to his order to attack in the Gulf, asking, "Retaliation for what?" Later he wrote, "I realized that this was a goddamned fiasco, and I was part of it."

Thus, in August of 1964, LBJ had used a bogus incident to gain authority from the U.S. Senate to take military action against North Vietnam—without a formal declaration of war. The vote for the Gulf of Tonkin Resolution was 88-2. Only Senators Ernest Gruening (Democrat-Alaska) and Wayne Morse (Democrat-Oregon) bravely dissented. It seemed a truism of all wars: In a time of battle, the public and politicians rally around the president, regardless of the merits of that conflict.

Regarding the manufactured reasons for the war, the public was skillfully kept in the dark. The mass media contributed greatly to fanning the flames of the conflict by spreading the administration's untruths about the "attack" by North Vietnam without corroboration. Defense Secretary McNamara had stated to the public that the *Maddox* was on "routine patrol" in the Gulf of Tonkin when, in fact, it was on a secret spy mission.

Seven years would pass before light was shed on the administration's machinations.

Finally, the orchestrated myth of 'military defense' in Vietnam was unequivocally shattered. In June 1971, *The New York Times*, via Pulitzer-winning reporter Neil Sheehan, published mind-boggling excerpts from the *Pentagon Papers*—7000 pages of top-secret documents released by Daniel Ellsberg, an aide at the Department of Defense, and his research colleague Anthony Russo. After the US government filed a court order restraining the *Times* from publishing further information, the *Washington Post* filed its own report.

The *Pentagon Papers* proved that the Johnson Administration, in particular, had systematically lied to the public and Congress. It turned out that the Tonkin Resolution had been drafted *before* the incident in the gulf occurred! The duplicity was further confirmed in 2003 when former Secretary of Defense Robert S. McNamara finally admitted that the August 4, 1964 attack in the Gulf of Tonkin never occurred.

But how did Sheehan obtain the *Pentagon Papers* from Ellsberg in the first place? It was not until 2015 when, at a reporter's request, Sheehan agreed to tell the real story of the classified documents on the condition that it not be published until his death. According to an article in the *New York Times* (published Jan. 7, 2021), Sheehan revealed that Ellsberg had told him that he could read the papers but not make copies. This restriction, Sheehan said, made him "quite angry." The popular belief was that Ellsberg simply gave the papers to Sheehan to publish. But in fact, Sheehan did what Ellsberg did while working for the Rand Corporation—he secretly smuggled the papers out. In this case, the papers were in an apartment in Cambridge, Massachusetts, where Ellsberg had stashed them. On the sly, Sheehan illegally copied the papers and took them to the *New York Times*. He asserts that Ellsberg [understandably so!] was conflicted between the desire to make the *Pentagon Papers* public and his fear of being sent to prison, possibly for the rest of his life. Near publication time, Sheehan told Ellsberg that he needed the documents, not just his own notes. Although Sheehan already had the documents, he felt he owed it to Ellsberg to get at least some kind of "tacit consent." When Sheehan once again asked for the documents, Ellsberg consented. The rest is history.

Fast forward nearly fifty years after the publication of the *Pentagon Papers*. Another revelation about the secret documents came to me personally when I attended a lecture by Ellsberg held at a Santa Monica art gallery. After Ellsberg's talk, the audience was invited to ask questions. I asked Ellsberg, "During the Vietnam War, how did you feel about conscientious objectors?" I never thought my question would have anything to do with the *Pentagon Papers*, but shockingly, it did. Ellsberg answered without pause, "I would never have done what I did, releasing the papers, if it wasn't for conscientious objectors. I heard a CO speak—Randy Kehler—and I heard him say without fear how he was willing to go to prison in opposition to the Vietnam War. I was so moved that I went to the men's room, sat on the floor, and cried. I knew then that I needed to act."

In the decades that followed, Ellsberg went on to continually protest nuclear weapons. In 2011, he was asked by CNN how many times he had been arrested. He answered casually, "Oh, about eighty times."

Less than one month after the Gulf of Tonkin Resolution was adopted, a neighbor in Virginia, who was a life-long Democrat, decided not to go to the National Convention in Atlantic City. "Francesco, forget everything you learned in your history classes," he said, handing me two passes. "This Thursday, you and a friend can witness history in the making! It's the last day of the convention, and it happens to be the 56th birthday of LBJ. It should be a blast."

When I invited Jerry to go to the convention with me, he said, "I'm Republican, you know."

"It doesn't matter," I encouraged. "You're to the right; I'm to the left. America is all about the mix. You'll be the loyal opposition."

On the *Caronia,* 1960. L-R: My mother; me; my brother, Ralph.

Daniel Ellsberg, 2017. (Photo: F. Da Vinci)

7

THE DEMOCRATIC NATIONAL CONVENTION—ATLANTIC CITY

(August 24–27, 1964)

"Do you want to know who you are? Don't ask. Act!
Action will delineate and define you."
—Thomas Jefferson

I felt pretty jazzed that as a 17-year old I was going to the 1964 Democratic National Convention.

On August 27th, under a crisp blue sky, Jerry and I headed on foot down a side road that led to the Convention Hall. We merged with a lively crowd of young volunteers decked out with straw hats and red, white, and blue banners. The picture-perfect weather seemed to symbolize that America, though still mourning JFK's assassination, was moving forward again.

Suddenly the girl beside me stood up on tiptoes and screamed, "Look! It's Bobby Kennedy!" The crowd of about two hundred mobbed Robert Kennedy's car. Bobby stepped out right in front of Jerry and me, brushed the hair off his forehead, and waved to the cheering volunteers.

"Speech! Speech!" someone called out. Kennedy, in a charcoal gray suit, was helped onto the roof of his chauffeur-driven car along with a man wearing a boat-shaped hat that read *LBJ/USA.* I took out my 35mm camera and 8mm movie camera—no sound—alternating them as Kennedy urged us to get involved in the presidential campaign and make a difference. "Your voice matters," Kennedy said.

As I photographed and filmed Bobby with Jerry looking on, I had a moment of déjà vu—just three years ago, Jerry and I heard President Kennedy urge our generation to ask what we could do for our country; now, Bobby challenged us. The crowd around me gave Bobby a rousing cheer mixed with a new chant that picked up: "Kennedy for President! . . . Kennedy for President! . . ."

Bobby smiled, amused, then retreated inside his car and headed toward the Convention Hall. I looked at Jerry ecstatically. "That was worth the whole trip right there. If Bobby would run, I'd work for him . . . stuff envelopes, whatever."

Jerry said, "I like Goldwater because he's tough on the commies, but I could see myself switching to Kennedy."

Just after Jerry and I arrived at the convention hall, a large contingent of press filed in. When a security guard saw my camera, he mistook me for a reporter and barked, "Stay to the right and follow the rest of the press." The photographers impatiently shoved me along.

I looked to Jerry helplessly, and he shrugged. "Go for it! I'll wait here."

The press was given the best spot in the house—dead center the podium. I was so thrilled I wanted to climb up on a chair and wave back to Jerry, but I refrained. Barely.

Even if it was only for a day, being a member of the working press was a thrill. A mistake, but a thrill. In a particularly patriotic mood, I thought, what a great country that could boast such unmitigated freedom of the press.

Years later, that illusion was jolted. I learned that at the behest of President Johnson, the FBI had orders to undermine groups like the Mississippi Freedom Democratic Party, which challenged the seating of the Mississippi Democrats and the disfranchisement of Black Americans at the convention. FBI agents even posed as NBC reporters with the support of the network, determined to weaken the support of the Mississippi Freedom contingent.

Surrounded by established members of the national press—almost all men in dark sport coats—I tried to blend in with my "colleagues." Mission impossible. First of all, I was the only one in a light beige sport coat. I stood out like a beacon at night. Second, I was by far the youngest photojournalist in the entire press corps. And the last dead giveaway that I didn't belong was my pathetic photo equipment. Everyone had high-end cameras with cool-sounding motor drives. A pro photojournalist looked at my 35mm relic sympathetically and said to his buddy, "He must be with one of the wires. They're *really* cheap."

I didn't care that much about the speech-making politicians, but when Barbara Streisand belted out "People" with perfect pitch, I snapped away. In fact, I was so enraptured by the rendition that I failed to notice the tall blonde standing next to me. My eyes widened when I saw that it was Mary Travers of Peter, Paul & Mary.

Mary put her hand on my shoulder and asked, "Mind?" Before I could recover from the shock that Mary Travers was talking to me, she used my shoulder to hop up onto one of the folding chairs for a better view of Barbara's performance. As the song ended, Mary applauded fervently and yelled, "Beautiful, Barbara! Beautiful!" Barbara smiled warmly. Then Mary scrambled onto the stage with Peter and Paul, and the trio roused the crowd with "If I Had a Hammer."

I spotted Senator Hubert Humphrey near the stage. Since he was most likely going to be America's next vice president, I figured I should take a shot. But as I was about to take his picture, he disappeared from view. He had stumbled face-first into the lap of a woman sitting in the first row! Beet-red, Humphrey apologized profusely, bowing a few times.

Jerry and I left early to catch our train back to D.C., not knowing Bobby Kennedy would address the convention. It turned out to be what many considered the highlight of the entire four-day event—when Bobby appeared on-stage to speak, the delegates spontaneously erupted with 22 minutes of uninterrupted applause! RFK nearly broke into tears at the ovation. Referring to his brother, he quoted from *Romeo and Juliet*: "When he shall die, take him and cut him out into the stars, and he shall make the face of heaven so fine that all the world will be in love with night and pay no worship to the garish sun."

As Jerry and I left the convention hall, we came upon a dozen protesters sitting cross-legged in a circle on the boardwalk. Their placards demanded new civil rights legislation. I stopped and asked a protester, who sported a full beard, "What's this about?" With the intense eyes of a Rasputin, he stared at me like I was clueless—*which I was*—and pointed to a placard that bore photos of three young men.

"Who are they?" I queried.

"Schwerner, Chaney, and Goodman. They were murdered working for civil rights."

"What happened?"

"A black church in Mississippi was bombed, and they were investigating it. The police pulled 'em over for speeding and took 'em to jail. They released 'em that night but nobody ever saw 'em after that. Then, less than a month ago, the F.B.I fished their station wagon out of a swamp. They found the bodies later. All three had been shot to death. Goodman and Schwerner were shot in the heart. Chaney, the black guy, was beaten to a pulp."

Jerry uneasily took out a cigarette and said, "I'll be over by that hot dog stand."

The protester continued. "When people ask me if I'm against the war, I ask 'em which one."

"What do you mean?" I asked.

"I mean, there's the war in Vietnam, and there's the war right here at home, black against white . . . and things are gonna get a helluva lot worse before they get better. The writing is on the wall, man."

"How's that?"

"Do you really give a damn?" he glared.

"Yeah, I do," I said indignantly.

"Then what are you *doin'* about it?"

I kept my answer to myself: *The usual—nothing.*

The Democratic National Convention, 1964. (Photo: F. Da Vinci)

The arrow is pointing to where Jerry and I are standing—about three yards from Bobby Kennedy. (Photo: UPI)

Bobby Kennedy giving a spontaneous talk outside the Democratic National Convention, Atlantic City, New Jersey, 1964. (Photo: F. Da Vinci)

Peter, Paul & Mary, 1964. (Photo: F. Da Vinci)

8

THE PHILOSOPHY OF NONVIOLENCE
(1965–1966)

"Peace cannot be achieved through violence,
it can only be attained through understanding."
—Ralph Waldo Emerson

After attending the Democratic Convention, my interest in politics was piqued. I preferred Bobby Kennedy as the Democratic nominee but had to settle for Lyndon Johnson.

In the general election, Johnson versus the Republican Barry Goldwater of Arizona, the key issue was Armageddon—which candidate would be less likely to blow up the world. In contrast to Johnson, Goldwater favored an "offensive" foreign policy and scared the daylights out of people when he announced he would willingly "drop a low-yield atomic bomb on the Chinese supply routes in North Vietnam . . ."

The battle lines were drawn: Goldwater was perceived as the trigger-happy pro-war candidate, who charged Johnson with being soft on communist aggression. LBJ, a very savvy politician, exploited Goldwater's war-like candor and portrayed himself as the more reasonable "peace candidate" with an ambitious domestic program. Concerning Vietnam, LBJ voiced restraint, even claiming he would not send "American boys nine or ten thousand miles from home to do what Asian boys ought to be doing for themselves."

Johnson and his advisors used voter fear to their advantage, painting Goldwater as a reckless warmonger. It was hardly a surprise that Goldwater received a crushing defeat with Johnson carrying 44 of the 50 states.

While I was enrolled at Wagner College in New York, sheltered by a student deferment, dissent across America steadily mounted. For example, Students for a

Democratic Society (SDS) organized the largest peace march in American history up to that point in time—April 17th, 1965. Between 20,000 and 25,000 supporters showed up, mostly college students. At the Washington Monument, Paul Potter of SDS addressed the demonstrators: "The President says that we are defending freedom in Vietnam. Whose freedom? Not the freedom of the Vietnamese. The first act of the first dictator, Diem, the United States installed in Vietnam, was to systematically begin the persecution of all political opposition, non-Communist as well as Communist."

With the SDS march and my best friend Jerry angling to be deployed to Vietnam, I studied the war in-depth.

Back in 1963, my senior year of high school, my American Government class required a term paper on a foreign country. When I couldn't decide on one, I asked my teacher, a retired army colonel, for suggestions. Colonel Kait said prophetically, "I've got a good one for you, Francesco—Vietnam."

I was embarrassed to ask, but I asked anyhow. "Where's Vietnam?"

"Southeast Asia.

"The French lost 25,000 men to their effort there, and now we ought to pick up where they left off *if* the president has the guts to stand up to the godless communists. Want Vietnam as your paper, Da Vinci?"

"Sure."

"Mark my words, it's going to be a hotspot."

So, I researched the country I had never heard of, clipping out newspaper articles that indicated an ever-increasing number of "advisors" in a "helicopter war." Though the conflict was supposedly being waged to halt the further spread of Communism, the majority of the South Vietnamese people were reported as not wanting us in their country in the first place. I knew the Colonel didn't want to hear that, and I knew I wanted to graduate, so I told him what he wanted to hear.

Two years later, in 1965, Vietnam was indeed a hotspot. There seemed no end to President Johnson's steady escalation of the war. After taking office in 1964, he issued a stream of dubious justifications for a bombing campaign that had no deadline. Close advisors to the president later reported that Johnson deceived not only the country, but himself. He came to believe his distortions and outright lies. Even in 1965, it became increasingly clear that the war was unwinnable, yet the president acted as if some mysterious external force was making him stay a course that he *knew* underneath could only result in further tragedy.

Richard Goodwin, a speechwriter for Johnson, relates that LBJ said at a White House staff meeting, "Vietnam is like being in a plane without a parachute when all the engines go out. If you jump, you'll probably be killed, and if you stay in, you'll crash and probably burn. That's what it is."

Meanwhile, at home, LBJ was also in a serious dilemma. Despite his commendable passage of progressive legislation on civil rights, there was a huge discrepancy between the new laws and the enforcement of those laws. Although the US had outlawed the separation of races in 1954, the carrying out of that legislation was pathetically weak or altogether absent. By 1965, studies showed that more than 75 percent of the school districts in the South remained segregated. And those that protested racial injustice were being met with brutality by law enforcement.

I thought *America is raining violence here at home on civil rights protestors and abroad on the Vietnamese.* In my eyes, the violence in both areas was not only immoral, but it was also ineffective. That's when I delved deeply into the philosophy of nonviolence—a powerful, inspiring method of social change that called on its followers to give up passivity and be active; to make means and ends harmonious; to fight for change in a spirit of reconciliation.

My role models became Gandhi, Einstein, Cesar Chavez, and Dr. King. Each said in effect, *Stop talking about the need to stop the killing. Get off your butt and be the change you want to see in the world!*

Despite my enthusiasm for the principles of nonviolence, I had some serious doubts. Did I have the ability to live up to that demanding philosophy in my daily life? What would I do if I was attacked? Or worse, what if I saw someone in my family being attacked? Could I stop the aggressor without becoming violent? It was relatively easy to proclaim nonviolence philosophically, but would I abandon nonviolence if I was thrust into a violent situation?

That issue was put to the test one evening in New York when I walked down a street with three buddies. Single-file, we strode across the white-striped crossing, similar to The Beatles crossing at Abbey Road. I filled the George Harrison position—last. As I reached the middle of the street, the driver of a speeding car blinked its high beams and angrily laid on the horn. My buddies scurried to the other side. Indignant that the driver was bearing down on us even though we clearly had the right of way, I continued across at a normal pace instead of running. The driver of the car slammed on the brakes and leaned out the window. "Okay, pal, you asked for it!"

He jumped out of the car, and my eyes widened as I took in his generous height and muscular build. Then his buddy, with only a slightly less powerful physique, exited the car from the other side. The driver got right up in my face and raised his fists. "Put 'em up!"

I had never been in this kind of situation before and had no idea what to do. Instinctively, I raised not my fists but my open palms. He stared at my hands, confused, then threw a hard right. I deflected the powerful jab with my palm. Further infuriated, he unleashed a series of blows to my head and stomach. I steered all his punches to the right or to the left, which intensified his frustration. In a befuddled rage, he yelled, "Stop that shit and fight!"

With a menacing sneer, he pulled back his fist and punched my palm with such force. It knocked me down on one knee. Out of pride, I came back up to my feet even though this was my golden chance to bow out of the fight gracefully. Once again, I raised my palms rather than my fists.

One of my buddies, fed up with watching the bullying, stepped in and angrily said to the vexed driver, "Okay, that's it! Now you're going to fight someone your own size." In a flash, my friend peeled off his green and white Wagner jacket and put up his fists.

"Bill," I began. Before I could add, 'it's not worth it,' he had decked the driver with two sharp blows: one to the stomach that doubled him over and the other to the back of the driver's neck. Wham, bam, my assailant was on the ground.

My other buddy said to the driver's friend. "Want some advice? Pick up your pal and get him the hell outta here before things get worse." The guy helped his dazed and wobbly friend to his feet, and they retreated to their car and drove off.

I wrote Jerry about the incident, and he replied, "I rest my case. When that bozo attacked you, and you stood your ground, it showed that nonviolence *can* delay violence. But ultimately, like in WWII, it's only the fist that can defeat the evil out there, not the open hand."

9

TO KNOW WAR
(1965–1966)

"We must not confuse dissent with disloyalty. When the loyal opposition dies, I think the soul of America dies with it."

- Edward R. Murrow

In 1965, I transferred from modest-sized Wagner College in New York to the mega-University of Maryland in College Park. Because I lost so many credits in the transfer, I went in as a sophomore instead of a junior. One thing I learned in short order at Maryland, besides the deflating fact that our sports mascot was a *turtle*—I finally realized I had zero desire to become a doctor. When I had enrolled in the pre-med program at Wagner College, it was only to please my parents. Registering at Maryland, I declared a major in a field more aligned to my real interests—sociology. The joke around campus was, 'If you have absolutely no clue what you want to do in the future, you major in sociology.'

With the move to a large university, I felt freer than ever. I had my own car and an off-campus apartment. Life in the shelter of college, courtesy of Mom and Dad's blank checks, was seductive. My previous goal of applying nonviolence in the service of others conveniently slipped to the back-burner.

Blissfully, I went about my ivory-tower routine, studying, going to football and basketball games, and checking out the girls I was too shy to ask out. Occasionally, watching the news, I suffered pangs of conscience: when Dr. King was assaulted in an all-white neighborhood . . . when the news glorified heavy bombing in Vietnam . . . when high body counts were touted as progress.

The coverage of the deepening racial war at home and the escalating war abroad reminded me of the protester I had met outside the Democratic Convention who had said in effect—*There are two wars in America, and both wars are going to get a helluva lot worse before they get better.*

The more I ignored those wars, the more complicit I felt with them due to my inaction.

Meanwhile, my best buddy Jerry was actively following his sense of duty and becoming a naval officer. Respectfully agreeing to disagree, Jerry and I regularly exchanged letters on war and peace. We had in common the wish to make America better, but we battled relentlessly over the means. Jerry wrote from the University of Virginia:

> Dear Francesco,
>
> I truly believe freedom must be fought for with violence and strength. All the United Nations talk in the world will not solve the problem of evil leadership. Those who shout, '*No more war*' should offer a solution. We *all* want peace. The bottom line is the price we're willing to pay for it.
>
> Evil exists and always will. Would you sacrifice your life in the face of tyrants just to let your nonviolent successors continue suffering in the spirit of Gandhi? You would be crushed. I personally value life too much, in spite of its frequent pain. Hitler, the leaders of North Vietnam, and other oppressors can't be reasoned with. There's only one answer left, and it's not the United Nations. Peace through a strong military is our only hope. Now that I've solved the problems of the world, I'm turning in.

In reply, I wrote,

> Dear Jerry,
>
> Gandhi was once asked, 'What do you think of western civilization?' and he answered, 'I think it would be a good idea.' How can we call ourselves 'civilized' and accept the Vietnam War? There's no 'Great Society' without a humane society. Ever notice how paradoxical we are about war? Did you read what President Johnson said in his State of the Union address about Vietnam? He was blunt and truthful about the nature of war:
>
> > 'War is always the same. It is young men dying in the fullness of their promise. It is trying to kill a man that you do not even know well enough to hate. Therefore, to know war is to know that there is still madness in the world.'
>
> What a *great* president LBJ could be if he wasn't blinded by Vietnam, if he kept his focus on his War on Poverty, and on building a Great Society here at home. Instead, he recognizes the madness of war and *still* chooses to escalate it. That's true madness. As for me, I recognize that I'm adding to the insanity—with my silence.

Conscientious objection appeals more and more strongly because it fits with my moral beliefs against war. At the same time, whenever I apply, I realize there will be a heavy price to pay. If the draft board doesn't approve my CO claim, I'll have to go to prison.

Whether you know it or not, you've been a big influence in my life. After high school, you took a stand for your beliefs. I admire that. All I've been doing is riding a student deferment. But that's going to change.

In peace,
Francesco

Jerry's next letter made me appreciate our friendship that much more:

Dear Francesco,

Even though we often disagree on war and peace, I strongly value our debates, especially since they've always been based on our respect for each other. Few would understand how two guys with diametrically opposite political views could be such close friends. Am I right?

As you know, I strongly differ with your anti-war and conscientious objection views, including—if it must be—your decision to eventually go to prison. But thus far I haven't made a point of telling you that I whole-heartedly respect those views. Dissent made America independent. It gave us our freedom. But with today's incredible divisiveness, that's forgotten. In an ideal world, I suppose we wouldn't need those few that sacrifice for the good of the many. But the world is far from ideal. So what I'm trying to say is that while we're on different sides, we're on the same side.

We've got the freedom to disagree and the freedom to fight for what we believe in. That's a great thing that the un-free part of the world can't say. I'm grateful for that, and for our friendship.

Peace your way, or peace my way, let's have peace.
Jerry

10

FALLING IN LOVE
(Spring 1967)

"Being deeply loved by someone gives you strength,
while loving someone deeply gives you courage."

- Lao Tzu

On a Saturday night, I was stood up. Unwilling to accept the evening alone, I went to St. Mary's Hall, one of the women's dorms on the University of Maryland campus. I told the girl at the front desk my predicament. She gave me a sympathetic look and said, "Okay, let me see what I can do. I think Jane is around."

Shortly afterward, a striking, petite, slim woman with shoulder-length blondish brown hair entered the lobby, wearing a form-fitting sweater and snug bell-bottom slacks. I ignored her, figuring there was no way someone so good-looking would be without a date on the weekend.

"Well?" she asked. "Are we going out?"

I looked behind me. "Uh . . . sure!"

Across from each other at a bright white coffee shop punctuated with red booths, I looked into Jane's eyes and said, "You're very cute."

She smiled and asked, "I'm sure by calling me 'cute,' you didn't mean to degrade me as a *thing* not worthy of your respect, did you?"

"Can I answer that?" I asked.

"Why spoil the evening?"

Suddenly we both burst out laughing. "You may not believe this, but I'm a feminist," I said.

Jane's face brightened and the walls seemed to crumble. She opened up, and we discovered our common interests—a passionate aversion to the Vietnam War and a mania for movies and photography. I opened my camera bag and asked, "Mind if I take a quick portrait of you?"

"Want to break your camera?"

"I think it'll survive. Turn your head to the window and look out. That's great!" *Click.* I lowered the camera and showed her the lens. "See, still intact."

"How long have you been taking pictures?" she asked.

"Since I was a kid."

We spent the rest of the evening café-hopping, at each stop revealing more of ourselves. Toward the end of the night, at our last café, the upbeat song "Baby I Need Your Lovin'" by Johnny Rivers played. I lightly tapped my fingers to the beat when Jane said, "I'm tone-deaf. If you don't mind, would you take my hand and move it to the music?"

I took her hand in mine and thought, *I don't want to let go.*

Then came the slow song "Can't Take My Eyes Off Of You" by Frankie Valli. Emboldened, I asked Jane to dance. I wrapped my arms around her waist as she put her arms around my shoulders. We closed our eyes and swayed to the song as if in a dream. When I got home around 4 A.M., I was thinking, *She might be the one.*

One date led to another, and Jane and I became a couple. With the current sixties era of Free Love, we were the repressed exceptions to the rule. At twenty-one, both of us were still virgins, a fact that might have qualified us for the Guinness Book of Records. Abstinence was driving us crazy, so Jane moved into my one-bedroom off-campus apartment, and we joyfully made up for the lost time.

Previously, my world had been dimmed by the draft, which loomed in the distance like an approaching storm cloud. Now that I was in love, everything changed. The sky brightened, classes seemed more interesting, friends seemed friendlier, and food tasted better—*even* from the Student Union.

Beyond our physical chemistry, I was enamored with Jane's exceptional intelligence. She could quickly master almost any new subject. The first time we went to a Maryland Terrapins basketball game in Cole Field House, she asked me to explain the rules. By the second game, she knew more about basketball than I did.

She also had a keen artistic eye. Since I always had a camera handy, she would pick it up and snap away while I was studying or making charcoal sketches. Her photo portraits were amazing. I no longer wondered what she could do; I only wondered if there was anything she couldn't do.

One of our routines was to sit near the jukebox in the Student Union and line up our favorite songs like "Dedicated to the One I Love" by The Mamas & the Papas.

As Jane would bury herself in textbooks, I would focus on the latest horrific news about the escalating conflict in Vietnam. Without fail, a gnawing voice of conscience asked, *Why aren't you doing anything to stop this insane bloodbath?*

Lovebirds, Jane and I lived by a double standard—looking at our nation's faults, we had eagle vision; looking at each other's faults, we were starry-eyed. Neither of us had ever seriously disagreed on anything. Then one day, after watching the news about the war, Jane said, "At least with your student deferment, we don't have to worry about you being drafted for the war."

"Well," I began uneasily, "I'm thinking of giving that up."

Jane looked at me speechless a moment. "Why would you do that?"

My heart seemed to stop. I had dreaded this day, knowing that sooner or later, I would need to reveal the fact that I would one day apply as a conscientious objector. I knew I would be vilified for that stand, but I also knew that not taking it would be intolerable.

Desperately, I wanted to put off this conversation, fearing it would be the end of our relationship. But my conscience countered: *Hell, there's never going to be a right time!*

Hesitantly, I made myself push out the words: "I'm going to apply as a conscientious objector. I don't know when, but I know I'm going to do it."

Jane stared at me, and after what seemed an eternity, said, "I admire that."

I let out such a heavy sigh that it made her laugh. With the break in tension, I asked, "Do you know the running joke about conscientious objectors?"

"What?"

"No one knows what COs are, but *everyone* knows they hate them."

Jane laughed and admitted she didn't know much about them either.

"Basically, it's someone who, for moral reasons, refuses to kill. The CO applies to his draft board in his home state. Mine is in Fairfax, Virginia. Then the draft board decides if they think the CO is on the level or if he's faking it."

"What if your draft board doesn't think you're sincere? You could go to jail, couldn't you?"

"Technically, I could, but there's no way that's going to happen. When they see that my parents are pacifists and that going into the military would be against everything I believe in, they're bound to recognize me as a CO."

"There's still the risk. Are you *sure* you want to give up your student deferment for this?"

"I've been sure for a long time, but I keep putting it off."

As the bloodshed in Vietnam mounted, I had no idea where to begin to oppose the war. I ached to find some way to make public my protest. Then one day, as Jane and I strolled across a sprawling campus lawn, a sign tied to a tree caught my attention. Immediately, the sign resonated deeply with me: HELP STOP THE WAR AND BRING THE TROOPS HOME! MARCH ON THE PENTAGON—OCTOBER 21st.

For the last two years, I had felt complicit with the war due to my passivity. At that moment, I knew unequivocally it was time to end my silence. "I've *got* to go to this march," I said.

"I want to go, too," Jane said, "but what if we get our picture in the paper and get kicked out of school?"

"It'll be worth it."

Jane and I move in together, c. 1967. (Photo: F. Da Vinci)

11

THE MARCH ON THE PENTAGON
(October 21, 1967)

"There is no greater importance in all the world like knowing
you are right and that the wave of the world is wrong,
yet the wave crashes upon you."

—Norman Mailer, *The Armies of the Night*

On a luminous Saturday, over 100,000 people from across America gathered at the Lincoln Memorial to make their abhorrence for the war public.

Jane and I stood near the front of the march, just behind the line of notables, such as novelist Norman Mailer and Dr. Benjamin Spock. Mailer had a premeditated plan to get arrested at the Pentagon to show the press that it was not simply America's youth against the Vietnam War.

A mixture of fear and bravery filled the air. The protesters feared violence from the police and soldiers; the police and soldiers feared violence from the protesters. Nevertheless, both sides were determined to follow their sense of duty.

Neither Jane nor I had ever participated in a march before. Apprehensively, we wondered, *Are we marching into battle? In protesting violence, will we have to endure violence?* Even if mayhem loomed ahead, I felt gratified that Jane and I had stopped being mere spectators to the war that was being waged in our name. We had reached a turning point in our lives. No longer were we *watching* history; we were *making* history.

As the endless battalion of marchers assembled on the Arlington Memorial Bridge, the monitors, wearing armbands, raised bullhorns and ordered us to sit down. I remained standing, focused my camera, and took a shot of the sea of protesters sitting on the bridge. That frozen moment told me that, as Bob Dylan put it, the times were definitely a-changin'. No longer were anti-war protesters just students. They represented a broad cross-section of America.

"Let's go!" a monitor shouted. En masse, the marchers stood and moved across the half-mile long bridge and into Arlington, Virginia, where the tomb-like Pentagon, with its 17.5 miles of corridors, came into view.

We walked onto the Pentagon lawn, and a march monitor called for our attention. "You need to know your rights," she said. "It's perfectly legal to stay here on the lawn, but the minute you go up the steps of the Pentagon, you're committing an act of civil disobedience and you can be arrested."

"Everything is so polarized," I complained to Jane. "The pro-war people are up there; the anti-war people are down here. I want to talk to the soldiers."

Jane motioned to the grim-faced guardsmen poised with bayoneted rifles. "Do they *look* like they want to be talked to?"

"I want to try anyhow."

"I don't think it's a good idea. You could get arrested."

"Well, if I'm not back in a half-hour, call a lawyer."

Jane nodded and stared at me with restrained alarm.

While she waited below at the base of the steps, I slipped my camera bag over my shoulder and ran up to where the soldiers stood. Already, dozens of protesters had preceded me, most of them cordial to those guarding the Pentagon.

Military police stood at ten-foot intervals. Within the circle of MPs, 300 Deputy Marshals were gathered. The Department of Defense had assembled legions of troops, police, National Guard, and U.S. Marshals. Just in case those weren't enough, thousands of Army troops armed with rifles and bayonets were hidden inside the Pentagon and other government buildings.

Slowly, I walked along a line of young stoic military police. I scanned the faces of the MPs, searching for a kind face and a willingness to listen. I stopped in front of an MP about my age—21. He stared straight ahead, his eyes framed by the brim of his helmet.

"I just want you to know that I'm not against you," I said. "I'm against the war."

He remained silent, yet I knew he was listening by the barely discernible nod of his head. Suddenly, a man in a dark suit lunged from behind the MP and shoved his camera in front of my face. I knew if I didn't turn away immediately, my photo would end up in a Pentagon file. As the government photographer kept snapping pictures of me, I turned and raised my hand to shield my face. Then, in a moment of clarity, I thought, *Why should I hide?* Although unnerved, I ordered myself to stand proud until the picture-taking stopped.

As I walked on, a disturbing sight brought me to an abrupt halt. A half dozen protesters pressed forward toward the soldiers, jeering ferociously. I wondered which of the agitators were real protesters and which were undercover government provocateurs determined to discredit our opposition to the war.

A protester (or provocateur) screamed, "Bloody fascists!" Another yelled, "Fucking pigs!" One waved a North Vietnamese flag, yelling: "Stop imperialist aggression against the Third World!" Spiteful protesters diluted the spirit of the nonviolent march with a mounting wave of hatred. The angriest and most outlandish demonstrators were the delight of press photographers who were hungry for dramatic shots. The crasser the protesters, the more the media flocked to them.

A stocky guy in a T-shirt and blue jeans screamed in the face of a soldier, "You robots are no better than the Nazis!"

The soldier stood motionless like a statue, but his face began to redden with hurt and anger. The protester didn't let up. I made my way to him and said, "Hey, man, take it easy. He's doing his thing, and you're doing your thing. This march is *supposed* to be about peace, right?"

He turned and shouted, "Whose side are you on anyhow!" He scoffed at the soldier in front of him, "They're not human. They're mindless killing machines."

Suddenly I found myself caught up in a swarm of demonstrators surging toward the wall of soldiers. We were pressed together so tight, I found myself hemmed in. Soldiers, holding their rifles diagonally, shoved back, using the butts of their guns to club protesters. Some of us fell. Some were bashed in the head. Trapped in the middle, I was hit in the ribs.

When I reconnected with Jane, she was irate that we had come to the march and that I had been injured. She wondered as I did—*What is the country coming to?*

Silence reigned on the drive from D.C. back to our off-campus College Park apartment. I figured Jane would never want to come to another march. But when we arrived home, she spoke with an iron-clad determination that I hadn't ever seen in her. "I decided that as long as you're going to marches, I'm going. I was wrong about 'em. They're our only hope to stop the war."

Author Norman Mailer, who had a premeditated plan to be arrested at the March on the Pentagon. (Photo: F. Da Vinci)

The March on the Pentagon started at the Lincoln Memorial, October 21, 1967. (Photo: F. Da Vinci)

100,000 protestors crossing Arlington Memorial Bridge en route to the Pentagon, October 21, 1967. (Photo: F. Da Vinci)

The March on the Pentagon. (Photo: F. Da Vinci)

Couple at the March on the Pentagon. (Photo: F. Da Vinci)

Protesters talking to the soldiers. The March on the Pentagon, 1967. (Photo: F. Da Vinci)

12

INSPIRED BY MARTIN LUTHER KING AND MUHAMMAD ALI

(1967)

"Service to others is the rent you pay for your room here on Earth."

—Muhammad Ali

Since 1964, it was not uncommon for newspapers and magazines to marginalize and slander demonstrators. Rarely did reporters acknowledge that protesters could be patriotic as the loyal opposition.

In a letter to Jerry, I quoted Mark Twain: "Patriotism is supporting your country all the time, and your government when it deserves it."

In Jerry's reply, he wrote: "To each their own, buddy. Guess what—I'm finally going to see action in Vietnam. I'll be on the USS *Boston,* a guided-missile heavy cruiser. We'll be on a combat tour with the 7th Fleet, firing the big guns. Can't wait."

Although I detested the war, I admired Jerry for fulfilling his mission in life—serving the country militarily. It was time I fulfilled my destiny—serving my country as a CO and nonviolent activist. Although Jerry and I were both serving our country in our own way, there was an enormous difference in the public's perception of our actions. Service in the military was seen as honorable, sometimes heroic. However, refusal of induction was generally viewed as cowardly and unpatriotic, even though the United Nations had defended conscientious objection as a worldwide right under their Human Rights Declaration of 1948.

The aspersions hurled at COs were even worse than those aimed at anti-war marchers: *draft-dodgers, commie sympathizers, subversives, saboteurs* of *our country's war effort.* Many regarded the act of applying as a conscientious objector in and of itself as treasonous. Almost nowhere in the media were COs being supported, and whatever was written about them was almost invariably distorted.

As President Johnson demeaned demonstrators and extolled strong "military leadership in Vietnam," I asked, *Where's the strengthening of our* moral *leadership?* It seemed long overdue that someone would take an unequivocal stand against the war and lift the shroud of hate and darkness that unjustly enveloped conscientious objection to war. Then, in a brave, moving speech at the Riverside Church in New York City, Dr. King came forward and voiced support for those who told their draft boards they would not kill.

> As we counsel young men concerning military service, we must clarify for them our nation's role in Vietnam and challenge them with the alternative of conscientious objection . . . Every man of humane conviction must decide on the protest that best suits his convictions, but we must *all* protest.

Jane and I felt heartened by the speech but were stunned by the reaction from the media. The same press that had lionized Dr. King for his nonviolent campaigns for civil rights now harshly criticized him, saying that he was "helping North Vietnam." Mean-spirited editorials painted Dr. King as a "traitor" who should either "love his country the way it is, or leave it!"

Out of frustration, I said to Jane, "It took guts for Dr. King to question the war and call for conscientious objection. He's not a traitor. If he didn't care about the country, he wouldn't be working so hard to better it."

The more Dr. King opposed the war, the more the FBI targeted him with a vengeance. They tapped his private phone conversations, documented his marital affairs, and even suggested that he commit suicide.

Then another fearless figure of moral authority came forward, inspiring me and conscientious objectors everywhere. Less than one month after Dr. King's powerful speech, Muhammad Ali, The Champ, stepped up for what, perhaps, was his greatest fight ever—declaring himself a conscientious objector.

In Houston, Texas, Ali refused induction, and as a result, was threatened with a five-year prison term. Unjustly stripped of his boxing license that day, Ali lost nearly four years of his prime time as an athlete. When Ali was arrested and found guilty on draft evasion charges, it was a time when almost 99% of the draft boards were all white.

Although the World Boxing Association took away Ali's heavyweight title, Ali retained the world's respect. His valor, along with Dr. King's, encouraged me as a CO in the making.

It took nearly four years for Ali's appeal to reach the Supreme Court. Meanwhile, Dr. King told people to "admire" Ali's courage and added, "He is giving up fame. He is giving up millions of dollars to do what his conscience tells him is right."

Eventually, on June 28, 1971, the Supreme Court declared Ali the winner in his long battle of principle by unanimous decision. Though technical legal reasons influenced the outcome, Ali's victory made him a world symbol for Black pride, civil rights, and conscientious objection to war.

While I felt renewed by Ali's and Dr. King's support of conscientious objection, Jane uneasily absorbed the hateful reactions they engendered. It was a poignant reminder that I would soon be jeopardizing our future by applying as a CO and risking prison. "I'm not sure being a CO is such a good idea after all," she said.

"I thought you admired it?"

"That was when we first started going out, and I saw you on a white horse. Now I see you behind bars."

Throughout 1967, televised reports from Vietnam hurled the horrors of the war into our living room in shocking and painful detail. For example, during one broadcast, Jane and I watched a report that showed images of an eleven-year-old Vietnamese girl who had lost her sight and her right leg in an explosion from one of our bombs. If we had read about her, it would have been one thing; seeing her image on TV was another.

The relentless violence shown on TV left Jane and me in anguish. There seemed little we could do to counter it other than join peace marches and vote at election time. Meanwhile, the tragedies in Vietnam surged. Despite endless talk of peace from the Johnson administration, U.S. battalions swept Cambodia's border, mined rivers in North Vietnam, and moved B-52 bombers to Thailand. I felt outraged that the president relentlessly escalated the bombing and saw fit to invade more Asian countries. Where were the checks and balances that were there on paper but not there in practice? Why wasn't Congress furiously opposing what amounted to the genocide of Asians?

It dawned on me that a large part of my anger was out of self-contempt. I knew in my heart that applying as a conscientious objector was the right thing to do. Finally, it seemed, I had built up enough moxie to take a stand as a CO. Then, unexpectedly, Dad took the wind out of my sails. In the summer of 1967, he called and asked, "What are you doing for the next three months?"

"Well . . ."

"Well, forget it and pack up! Your mother and I are taking you and Ralph on a cruise to Europe!"

Muhammad Ali.
(Photo: F. Da Vinci)

Conscientious objectors Francesco and Muhammad Ali.

13

EUROPEANS AGAINST THE WAR

(Late 1967)

"The real voyage of discovery consists not in seeking new landscapes, but in having new eyes."

—Marcel Proust

Part of me couldn't wait to see Europe for the first time. Another part worried that being apart from Jane for the next three months might hurt our relationship, especially since Jane had new misgivings about my decision to apply as a CO.

Jane and I talked about the separation and decided, maybe rationalized, that my family's cruise to Europe would be a good test—either the distance would bring us closer or it would reveal that we were not meant to be together.

I wrote Jane frequently from our family's home base in Europe, a charming, almost magical villa in Santa Margherita on the Italian Riviera. The main window offered a breathtaking view of the beach, a plethora of colorful boats, distant hillsides lined with Cypress trees, and breathtaking sunsets. Italy exuded romance, making me miss Jane that much more.

Our time apart greatly strengthened my appreciation of her. She meant more to me than I had realized. I missed everything about her—her sharp wit, sense of humor, ever-curious engaging eyes, and even the cute way she twitched her nose when she had allergies. A million silly little things, and I missed all of them.

Ralph and I decided to explore Europe by car and visit nearly every country on the continent. Memorable sights that stood out were standing eye-to-eye with the Mona Lisa at the Louvre in Paris; riding the glass elevator to the top of the Eiffel Tower; gazing in awe at the works of Leonardo and Michelangelo in Italy; playing with the wild monkeys on the Rock of Gibraltar; ascending the snow-covered Alps by cable car, and my favorite simple pastime—people-watching at an outdoor café on the Champs-Elysees and savoring warm croissants, cherry preserves, and rich coffee.

But the tranquility and joy of our travels were almost invariably diluted. We had figured that the war would be a relatively minor subject abroad. It turned out that *everywhere* we went, we were inundated by the topic. In Rome, college students asked about the war with barely restrained resentment. "Why are you Americans bombing Vietnam? Why not let the people of South Vietnam decide for themselves what kind of government they want?" The venting was similar in Venice, Paris, Vienna, Madrid, Hamburg, and London.

Finally, I didn't feel so alone in viewing the war as an illegal and immoral invasion. But I was too shy to express my opinion until I was in Zurich, Switzerland. At an outdoor table, anti-war students gathered signatures on a petition to present to the United Nations. I said to myself *Even if it's a small gesture, here's your chance to stand up for what you believe in.* As I signed the petition, an on-looking American shouted, "You're disgracing our country!"

Momentarily, I felt like a kid caught with his hand in the cookie jar. Then I thought, *It's* not *putting my name on the petition that would be the shame; the shame would be staying silent and doing nothing.* Though signing the petition was a relatively insignificant act, it was personally significant. I was saying to the world, *This is who I am. This is what I believe, and I'm not ashamed of it.*

Overwhelmingly, the majority of Europeans we met strongly favored an *immediate* withdrawal of U.S. forces from Vietnam. They told us that they had the bitter experience of fighting wars on their own soil, unlike Americans. A German taxi driver, for example, slowed and pointed out a bombed building that was left up as a reminder of the war's devastation. "You Americans think war is a John Wayne movie," he said. "You see a problem like Vietnam and you think you can just send in the cavalry and everyone will walk off into the sunset. The reality is that your young boys are coming home in coffins or without arms or legs. And that's not to mention the thousands and thousands of Asians you're killing. I ask you, for what?"

It wasn't until I returned to the US that I realized the impact anti-war Europeans had made on me. They helped me see the news at home as extremely sanitized and distorted regarding the horrors of the war in Southeast Asia.

By the time I returned to my studies at Maryland, I felt more determined than ever to stand up for my beliefs and speak out publicly against the war. That's what I had planned to do before the cruise, and now nothing was going to stop me from putting that plan into action.

14

SPEAKING OUT IN CLASSES
(1967)

"The most courageous act is still to think for yourself. Aloud."
—Coco Chanel

My first opportunity to advocate an immediate end to the war came in the sociology class I shared with Jane. The desks were arranged in long rows. As over one hundred students filed into the classroom, Jane and I took seats next to each other.

"I'm going to suggest we have a workshop on the war," I said, still uncertain that I could muster the nerve to do it.

Jane said, "You do that, and there goes your grade *and* mine for being associated with you."

My palms were sweaty, but I pushed myself not to back down. While the professor droned on about Margaret Mead's cultural studies, I half-raised my hand. Fear began to paralyze me. I had read that most people's number one fear in life was speaking in public, and I was no exception.

Knowing that few would like what I had to say, my heart pounded as I held my hand high.

The professor had a smile on his face, and I thought, *I'm going to ruin his mood.* I glanced at Jane. She shook her head no with a dire sense of urgency. "Don't!"

"Yes, Mr. Da Vinci?" the professor called out.

I stammered. "I'd . . . well . . . uh . . . I'd like to suggest that we have a workshop on the war."

The professor frowned. "I'm afraid that wouldn't be within the proper sphere of this course. As I was saying . . ."

"Excuse me," I said, pressing my luck.

The professor sighed heavily. "Yes, Mr. Da Vinci?"

I fought back the temptation to say, *Never mind.* "About the war . . . it affects *all* of us every day, so I don't see how we can study sociology in America *without* talking about it."

He paused. "You may have a point. Very well, everyone, close your books."

A student near the front kicked things off. "I feel the main reason that we're having so many problems in Vietnam is because the generals' hands are tied. We should bomb North Vietnam to the peace table. That's the only language they understand." A few students applauded.

Another student said, "I agree, but I'd take it a step further. We should nuke North Vietnam and show 'em we mean business. Why not get the war over with, like we did with Japan?"

I couldn't take it anymore. "This is nuclear war you're talking about!" I said with an intensity that surprised me. "That means the immediate death of thousands of men, women, and children. That's not counting the maiming and the slow deaths from radiation. I'm for immediate withdrawal in Vietnam. It's not our right to decide what the people of South Vietnam want. We need to worry more about saving lives than about saving face."

The professor grimaced. "Your dissent has been duly noted, Mr. Da Vinci. Why don't we take a vote and see how many favor your suggestion of immediate withdrawal from Vietnam."

Out of over one hundred students, my hand was the only one raised. Not even Jane supported my view.

She whispered, "I'm for withdrawal but not *immediate* withdrawal."

Someone muttered, "You ought to be ashamed of yourself, Da Vinci."

After class, Jane gave me a perfunctory kiss on the cheek and briskly walked off.

Upset with Jane and the whole ordeal, I accidentally dropped one of my textbooks. When I went to pick it up, all the other books in my arms fell to the floor. "Great," I muttered. "Just great." It was my worst day of college ever, but the next week it would seem like a good day.

The war became a heated debate in another class that Jane and I shared—Psychology.

In this workshop on the war, I again advocated immediate withdrawal from Vietnam and spoke of the cost of prolonging it. "Every day that goes by means more senseless death and maiming on both sides! Just because we don't see the slaughter doesn't mean we shouldn't stop it. This isn't a war of self-defense. We invaded Vietnam. This war is a crime against humanity—nothing less."

A student asked sarcastically, "When *you're* drafted, Da Vinci, what are you going to do? Serve in Canada?"

The class snickered.

"Yeah," another student said, "what *are* you going to do?"

"I'm going to apply as a conscientious objector," I answered. Hearing myself say it strengthened my conviction.

The large packed room held an unnerving hush.

"Really!" the professor said, folding his arms. Slowly, he walked down a long aisle towards my desk. My cheeks flushed with embarrassment for being singled out. Standing directly in front of me, the professor made a mock gun with his right hand and aimed it at my forehead. With theatrical flair, he said loudly, "If I had a gun right now, I'd do our country a favor and *gladly* shoot any CO I see." Then he pulled the mock trigger. "Class dismissed."

Shaken and humiliated, I figured Jane would be as indignant as I was over the professor's behavior. Instead, she said, "You antagonized him! It's one thing for you to want immediate withdrawal; it's another to throw your opinion in everyone's face! It was way too much!" She turned on her heel and stormed off.

Later that day, we went to our apartment for 'a talk.' Jane said, "I'm sorry. I shouldn't have walked out on you. That wasn't right."

"Thanks."

"But I want you to think about what happened. If you're getting heat now just from *talking* about being a CO, imagine when you become one. It'll be a hundred times worse. You do what you have to do, but maybe being a CO just isn't worth it. Think about it, okay?"

"I will."

On Jane's 21st birthday, I asked, "How do you want to celebrate?"

"Let's go see *Guess Who's Coming to Dinner.*"

"What's it about?" I asked.

"A white girl who brings her African American fiancé home to meet her folks. It's just like us, only I'll be bringing home a CO."

She gave a half-hearted chuckle, and I asked, "Was that more a jab or a joke?"

"A mix."

15

SENATOR EUGENE MCCARTHY: THE PEACE CANDIDATE

(1967)

"It isn't enough to talk about peace. One must believe in it. And it isn't enough to believe in it. One must work at it."

—Eleanor Roosevelt

At last, a breath of fresh air. On November 30th, 1967, fifty-one-year-old Senator Eugene McCarthy announced his candidacy for the presidency, unequivocally calling for an end to the bloodshed in Vietnam. Joyfully, I said to Jane, "We're not alone anymore."

In his statement, McCarthy said, "I am concerned that the Administration [Lyndon Johnson] seems to have set no limit to the price it is willing to pay for a military victory."

McCarthy cited the terrible cost of the war: so far, there were over 15,000 American combat dead and nearly 95,000 wounded. On the economic side, expenditures were running between $2 and $3 billion *monthly*. That's not to mention the damage to America's international reputation, with more and more countries viewing the U.S. as the world's leading perpetrator of violence.

Before McCarthy's candidacy, Jane and I were deeply disappointed that not one Democratic Presidential candidate had come forward to oppose LBJ and run as a peace candidate. With Johnson's incessant escalation of the war, we had hoped Bobby Kennedy or another peace-minded senator would set aside politically pragmatic concerns and run for president. Finally, McCarthy—a courageous politician and serious poet, decided he would not wait until it was expedient to run for president.

Previously, Senator McCarthy had approached Senator Robert Kennedy to see if he would run against Johnson. McCarthy knew that Kennedy stood a much better chance of defeating Johnson in the Democratic primaries, but Kennedy felt he would fare better in the election of 1972. Later, after McCarthy did so well in the New Hampshire primary, Kennedy saw that he had seriously underestimated the hunger for a change in the presidency. Four days after the primary results, he entered the race.

Since 1965, the vast majority of those openly opposing the war were students. And we paid the price: we were harassed, beaten, and arrested. That's not to mention that we endured the scorn of the majority of Americans. But now that a *U.S. Senator* embraced our generation's call to end the war and change America's priorities, it was no longer so easy to deride the nation's youth-led protest.

As I researched McCarthy's background, I learned that he had little fear of being unconventional. Over dinner, I told Jane that instead of the usual politician's background of business or law, McCarthy actually considered becoming a monk.

"Was he serious?" she asked.

"Serious enough that he spent nine months at the Monastery of St. John." McCarthy's bio stated that in 1958 he was elected to the U.S. Senate. In 1964 he was considered as LBJ's running mate, but Senator Humphrey was picked instead.

Years later, in the '90s, McCarthy and I became good friends even though I had ended up supporting Bobby Kennedy for president in 1968. In New York City, I arranged to have McCarthy speak at a Borders Bookstore. As I introduced him to the large audience, I said, "And now I give you Senator Eugene McCarthy, a man over-qualified for the presidency!" The sharp-witted McCarthy retorted, "Maybe for the vice-presidency!"

On one occasion, I visited the senator at his bucolic home in Woodville, Virginia. The house had an expansive lawn that gently sloped down to a large lake that the senator said "gives me a sense of peace."

McCarthy and I settled into his simple, old-fashioned all-wood living room and re-visited 1968. I told the senator, "Your candidacy for the presidency meant the world to me, and still does. You became an icon for peace."

He looked down and said, "I never wanted to be an icon."

"I have a question about your relationship with President Johnson. Some said it was a rocky one. If that's true, what's an example?"

McCarthy looked off a moment. "Well, Lyndon had a habit of taking U.S. Senators with him to hunt by car at his 300-acre ranch in Texas. It was a kind of loyalty test. He would pass out rifles to new Senators, and they would cruise in Lyndon's convertible looking for deer to kill."

Not a fan of hunting, I made a face.

"I agree," McCarthy said with a wry smile. "In a few books, there's a reputed story that Jack Kennedy was one of those given the test. They came across a deer, but Jack didn't like the idea of shooting it, so he missed twice on purpose. The third time he fired his rifle, the deer fell dead. Shocked, Jack turned to LBJ and said, 'But

I missed it.' LBJ said, 'Secret Service shot it for you.' It was Jack's first time hunting, and it was reported that he felt sick to his stomach. Later, I came down to the ranch for the obligatory hunting with Lyndon. We got into his convertible, and when we came to a deer, I refused to shoot it. Lyndon killed it, then offered me the head, telling me that I could mount it and put it on my wall. I said, 'No thank you.' Then Lyndon offered me sausages made from the deer, and again I said, 'No thank you.' But Lyndon kept on and suggested I give the sausages to friends.' I told him, 'I don't want to give them to my friends either.' I don't think that sat well with him."

McCarthy's alliance with LBJ seemed an uneasy one at best. Yet, McCarthy detested being labeled as part of the "Dump Johnson" movement. Time and time again, he said he was not out to dump Johnson or demonize him; he was out to offer alternative policies and new leadership. But on one occasion, LBJ got under his skin, and he remarked: "You know when I first thought I might have a chance? When I realized that you could go into any bar in the country and insult Lyndon Johnson, and nobody would punch you in the nose."

A conversation with McCarthy that stands out in memory was when I interviewed him at the Algonquin Hotel in New York City. We were talking about the senator's long career when he said, "Turn off the tape recorder. You can share this, but I don't want it on tape."

I hit the stop button.

McCarthy looked off silently as if he had something he wanted to get off his chest. "I made the biggest mistake of my career . . ."

I waited, wondering if he was changing his mind about sharing it. "What was the mistake?"

His eyes returned to mine. "The mistake was when Nixon asked me to be his Ambassador to the United Nations . . . I turned it down."

"Why?"

"The Democrats didn't want me to support a Republican president."

McCarthy looked off again, brooding with regret.

In December, Jane and I watched a television program that looked back on 1967 as "a year of crisis and divisiveness." Despite escalating national protest, the Johnson Administration seemed void of the wisdom of cutting our losses and ending the futile war in Vietnam. Proudly, the president pointed to civil rights legislation and higher standards of living, as if saying, "Why worry about the war?"

The Johnson Administration still blindly insisted that a U.S. victory in Vietnam was *inevitable!* By this time, Johnson's main motivation for persisting with the war and its bloody cost was reduced largely to a matter of stubborn pride.

On New Year's Eve, my 22nd birthday, Jane asked, "How do you want to celebrate?"

"A double-feature."

"Great. What did you have in mind?"

"First, *The Graduate.* It's the story of a guy who's seduced by an older woman. Then he falls in love with her daughter."

"Complicated!"

"The music is supposed to be great—Simon and Garfunkel."

"Second one?"

"Think you can handle a sci-fi movie?"

"For your birthday, I could. What's it about?"

"A homicidal computer."

"Now *that's* my kind of movie," she joked.

After *The Graduate* and *2001: A Space Odyssey,* we went home, popped a small bottle of champagne, and watched the ball slowly drop in Times Square. The background music was "All You Need Is Love" by the Beatles. "1968!" flashed on the screen, and Jane and I kissed. I held her in my arms, and Jane asked, "You optimistic about the new year?"

"Oh yeah. There's only one way to go—up!"

As dissent to the war mounted, the peace movement was unexpectedly given a big boost on February 27th, 1968. Trusted CBS anchor Walter Cronkite stunned Jane and me and millions of viewers when he editorialized on America's role in Vietnam, saying, "It seems now more certain than ever that the bloody experience of Vietnam is to end in a stalemate. To say that we are closer to victory today is to believe, in the face of the evidence, the optimists who have been wrong in the past." He essentially pronounced the war a deadlock and suggested we negotiate our way out and bring the troops home.

"This might help change the way the public sees the war," I said. Even though I felt grateful for Cronkite's assessment and knew it would invite many in the older generation to reevaluate their support of the war, I couldn't help but regard it as a case of The Establishment catching up to the youth. Idealistic students had been marching and speaking to the futility and immorality of the war for years prior. Even so, LBJ continued to scapegoat anti-war students, calling them "nervous nellies" and adding that they would not succeed in dividing the war effort. I asked Jane, "Why can't he see that it's the *war* that's dividing the country, not the people trying to stop it?"

Youthful citizen protests resounded around the world, from Paris to Prague and beyond. It knew no boundaries. The young everywhere were rising up as if connected in spirit. No one could explain it. There seemed a worldwide declaration: *We choose civil rights over racism, the nonviolent resolution of conflict over war, and love over hate.* There were many authority figures who suspected that this 'linked happening' was evidence of a worldwide communist conspiracy among demonstrators. But no evidence was ever found to support such a theory.

In a similar paranoid vein, during the Chicago 7 Trial, Abbie Hoffman was asked if all seven defendants had conspired to incite violence during the Democratic National Convention. Hoffman laughed and said, "An agreement? We couldn't agree on lunch!"

President Kennedy and Senator Eugene McCarthy, c. 1961. (Photo courtesy Senator Eugene McCarthy)

Portrait of Senator Eugene McCarthy. (Photo: F. Da Vinci)

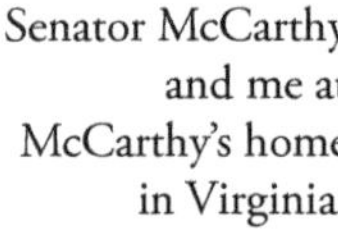

Senator McCarthy and me at McCarthy's home in Virginia.

Newsman Walter Cronkite. (Photo: F. Da Vinci)

16

BOBBY KENNEDY FOR PRESIDENT
(1968)

"Only those who dare to fail greatly can ever achieve greatly."
—Robert F. Kennedy

Although I still hoped Robert Kennedy would enter the race for president and thought he had the best chance of unseating President Johnson, I greatly admired Senator Eugene McCarthy for having the courage to declare his candidacy and address the "deepening moral crisis in America." Unless Bobby decided to enter the race, I would work for McCarthy to support his civil rights and peace platform.

Across the nation, "McCarthy" and "peace" became synonymous. Initially, Jane and I completely dismissed McCarthy's chances for president. We supported him, not for any practical reasons, but simply because we felt it was the right thing to do. Even the pundits expected McCarthy to get clobbered at the polls. Gene McCarthy was relatively unknown, and his New Hampshire campaign started with a paltry $400 in the bank.

The McCarthy organization—what there was of it—faced a daunting challenge. But things picked up big time when actor Paul Newman joined the campaign in New Hampshire. Newman drew crowds and the media. At one campaign stop, Newman said, "I didn't come here to help Gene McCarthy. I need McCarthy's help." However, it *was* Newman that made McCarthy a national figure, especially in the early days.

In *The Power and the Glitter* by Ronald Brownstein, campaign worker Tony Podesta described the way the campaign effectively used Newman in their strategy: "Once we figured out what was going on here, we began to advance him harder than we advanced the candidate . . ."

Antiwar Paul Newman campaigned for McCarthy so well that it earned him the 19th ranking on President Nixon's "enemies list," which Newman said was "the highest single honor I've ever received."

Then came the national shocker—the results of the New Hampshire primary—March 12, 1968. McCarthy received a whopping 42.2% of the vote! Newman didn't win that for McCarthy, but he had certainly helped, significantly raising McCarthy's name recognition.

Usually, in elections, I ended up supporting the lesser of two evils. Now, with two peace candidates running for president in '68, I wholeheartedly supported both Gene McCarthy *and* Bobby Kennedy.

On the day that Kennedy declared his candidacy, I brought Jane to my home in Virginia to share the special moment. We gathered around the living room TV, joined by my parents, Ralph, and my dear boxer, Rex. It was a rare gathering with everyone in the immediate family in one place at one time.

As we waited anxiously for Robert Kennedy to throw his hat in the ring, Jane asked my parents, "Did Francesco tell you how he literally bumped into Bobby Kennedy?" Dad and Mom looked at each other and shook their heads no.

"For real?" asked Ralph.

Jane turned to me. "Tell them about it."

"Well, it happened about a month ago," I began. "Jane and I went to a benefit at Constitution Hall in D.C. to hear Kennedy speak. The place was packed. After Bobby spoke, Sammy Davis, Jr. sang and danced. Jane and I had to leave early to study for a sociology test, so right before intermission we slipped out of the show and rushed down a side corridor. I pushed open a door and—*Bam*—I ran smack into someone, chest to chest. I said, 'Excuse me,' and he said, 'Excuse *me*.' I was too embarrassed to look him in the eye, but I saw Jane staring with her hand over her mouth. She said, 'Oh . . . my . . . *God*! Bobby Kennedy!"

Mom, Dad, and Ralph looked to Jane, and she nodded that it was true. "Francesco tried to get his act together, but he stuttered." She imitated me mercilessly. "'I . . . uh . . . I'd like to say something, Senator . . . if you don't mind?' Bobby said, 'Please.' Most politicians in that situation would give a fake smile and look everywhere except at who's talking to them. But Bobby gave Francesco all his attention. He listened in a way that made me feel that whatever Francesco had to say, it was important to him."

"What did you say to him, Francesco?" Ralph asked.

"I said, 'Senator, the country needs you as president. You're the *only* one who can bring us back together again.' And Bobby said, 'I appreciate that. I really do.'"

Jane added, "The moment we were outside, we burst out laughing. I said to Francesco, 'Can you believe it! You practically decked the guy who might be our next president!'"

I glanced at Dad, who beamed a smile that seemed to say, *My son met Bobby Kennedy!*

Moments later, everyone turned back to the television as Robert Francis Kennedy entered the same Senate Caucus room where his brother, John Fitzgerald

Kennedy, had announced his candidacy for the presidency in January of 1960. Near Bobby stood his wife Ethel and nine of their ten children. As soon as Kennedy walked up to the microphone, a chant began, "Now! Now! Now!"

I looked at Ralph and gave him a thumbs-up. He smiled in amusement. Ralph did not share my passion for politics, but he knew how deeply I wanted Kennedy to run.

The 42-year-old Kennedy spoke to the nation: "I am announcing today my candidacy for the Presidency of the United States."

Jane and I applauded and exchanged wide smiles. We sat on the edge of our chairs holding hands as the Senator continued, "I do not run for the presidency merely to oppose any man, but to propose new policies . . . to end the bloodshed in Vietnam and in our cities . . . to close the gaps between black and white, rich and poor, young and old, in this country and around the world."

I turned to my family. "If Bobby becomes president, he's going to push for civil rights and an end to the war."

"That'd be great," Jane said, "but don't get your hopes up because Johnson isn't going to give up without a fight."

McCarthy, being the first to run against Johnson, had made dissent to the war respectable; Kennedy, with a broader base of support, had made dissent practical.

Part of me felt sorry for Senator McCarthy and his dedicated volunteers. They had been the first to challenge the President and to adopt a strong peace platform. Theodore White would later write, quoting one of McCarthy's student volunteers: 'We woke up after the New Hampshire primary like it was Christmas Day. And when we went down to the tree, we found Bobby Kennedy had stolen our Christmas presents.'

In late March, Jane said, "I like McCarthy more than Kennedy. Even though he doesn't have much of a chance, I'm going to volunteer for him."

I retorted, "Well, I like Kennedy more than McCarthy, and I'm going to volunteer for him."

Jane playfully grabbed my shirt in both her fists. "This means war."

Paul Newman, who actively campaigned for McCarthy in New Hampshire. (Photo: F. Da Vinci)

Shortly before Jane and I met Bobby Kennedy at Constitution Hall, 1968.

17

MARTIN LUTHER KING IS KILLED

(April 4, 1968)

"There are only two forces in the world, the sword and the spirit. In the long run, the sword will always be conquered by the spirit."

—Napoleon Bonaparte

On March 31st, 1968, Jane and I were unhappily glued to the TV, figuring that President Johnson was about to justify another escalation of the war in Vietnam. Instead, LBJ announced a partial bombing halt then dropped a bomb of his own: "I shall not seek, and I will not accept the nomination of my party for another term as your president."

We turned to each other with wild-eyed excitement, and Jane asked incredulously, "Did he say what I think he said?"

Now, with the likely election of Bobby Kennedy as president, peace in Vietnam and peace at home seemed only a matter of time.

"We can't let up now," I said. I paused a moment to proudly reflect on the extraordinary accomplishment of our generation over the last three years, which had not been given its due in the media. The early, lonely, and persistent call for peace in Vietnam by the youth of America helped change the tide of history. Increasingly, the dissent to the war that the majority had despised so vehemently was not only accepted now but it was also viewed as pragmatic and patriotic. And yet, even though the significant numbers of people were moving toward an anti-war position, I realized we likely still had a long way to go before the war would be officially ended.

With President Johnson's resignation, combined with Kennedy's and McCarthy's candidacies and Dr. King's call for racial equality, Jane and I excitedly looked forward to a new era, to a more humanistic America.

But on April 4, 1968, only four days after LBJ's stunning resignation, a news bulletin interrupted TV programming: "Thirty-nine-year-old Martin Luther King,

Jr. has been assassinated this evening in Memphis, Tennessee." Jane and I were numb in disbelief. Like the murder of President Kennedy, it was another hammer to the heart.

The night before his assassination, Dr. King had traveled to Memphis to call for economic equality and social justice for striking sanitation workers.

I thought back to the days when Dr. King helped organize the Montgomery bus boycott, to his "I Have a Dream" speech, to the March On Selma, to his speeches against the Vietnam War, and to his call to draft-age young men like me to become conscientious objectors . . .

On the day of King's murder, Bobby Kennedy had just arrived in Indianapolis to campaign. He received word that King had been killed and decided to speak to the assembled crowd spontaneously. The speech he gave is one that many have said was the best of his career, words that poured straight from the heart:

> For those of you who are black . . . you can be filled with bitterness, with hatred, and a desire for revenge. We can move in that direction as a country, in great polarization—black people amongst black, white people amongst white, filled with hatred toward one another. Or we can make an effort, as Martin Luther King did, to understand and to comprehend, and to replace that violence, that stain of bloodshed that has spread across our land, with an effort to understand compassion and love. For those of you who are black and are tempted to fill with hatred and mistrust of the injustice of such an act, against all white people, I would only say that I can also feel in my own heart the same kind of feeling. I had a member of my family killed, but he was killed by a white man.
>
> . . . let's dedicate ourselves to what the Greeks wrote so many years ago: to tame the savageness of man and make gentle the life of this world.

That evening, Jane and I drove toward a popular off-campus diner in College Park. Grief-stricken, we felt the need to get out of the apartment despite the warnings of possible violence on the streets in reaction to King's assassination. Along the way to the diner, we saw stores closing early. Police sirens screamed in the distance, cutting through the air that was thick with rage.

At the café, Jane and I took a window table and saw a gathering of Black students on a corner across the street. They were yelling at every white driver that passed by. Several of the students came inside the diner and leaned in on our table. A tall, lanky guy glared as if ready to fight. I said to him, "Don't take it out on us. We hate it too."

The guy stared at me a few moments as if judging whether I was sincere, then nodded and led his friends away.

That evening on the news, we saw Stokely Carmichael of the Student Nonviolent Coordinating Committee (SNCC—pronounced "snick") urge a crowd to grab their guns. Many seemed to have forgotten the many positive, dramatic changes that resulted from applying the power of nonviolence. For example, after Rosa Parks refused to give her bus seat to a white man on December 1st, 1955, Dr. King led the bus boycott in Montgomery, Alabama. Because of Parks' stand, she was fired from her job as a seamstress and received a stream of death threats. Nevertheless, her nonviolent action ended up as a call for social justice that reverberated throughout the entire nation.

Another example of nonviolent action that sparked a movement across the South was the following: On February 1st, 1960, SNCC's nonviolent campaign of "sit-ins" had college students refuse to leave a Woolworth's lunch counter in North Carolina where they had been denied service.

SNCC played an important role in the civil rights movement. It was created on the campus of Shaw University in Raleigh, North Carolina, and later became a leading organization in the fight for social justice, coordinating sit-ins and organizing voter registration drives throughout the South. In the rapidly changing political climate of the mid-1960s, SNCC struggled to define its philosophy. A major shift occurred—the former call for nonviolence was muffled by the call for "black power," a phrase coined by Stokely Carmichael.

In 1966, Huey Newton and Bobby Seale founded the Black Panther Party in Oakland, California. The initial focus was an armed patrol of Black neighborhoods to protect residents from police brutality. FBI Director J. Edgar Hoover developed a counterintelligence program that included surveillance, infiltration, and assassination in response. The killings and arrests resulted in increased support among Black Americans for the Black Panther Party.

By 1968, many in the civil rights movement felt the increased calls to violence were a slap in the face to Dr. King's legacy of nonviolence and reconciliation. Those pushing for Black militancy pointed to the brutal repression by the FBI and public figures such as Chicago Mayor Daley. When asked how to handle the rioting in 1968, Daley responded, "I said to him [the police superintendent] very emphatically and very definitely that an order be issued by him immediately to shoot to kill any arsonist or anyone with a Molotov cocktail in his hand . . ."

Divisiveness was the order of the day, and Dr. King's dream seemed to be going up in smoke as cities across the nation burned.

When I spoke with Dad on the phone, he said, "Your mother and I have lived here near D.C. for almost 30 years, and I never thought I'd see something like this. So many new laws have been passed for civil rights. I just don't understand these riots."

"Just because the laws are on the books doesn't mean they're put into action, Dad."

As over 7,000 fires raged in the nation's capital, 46 people were killed. I thought, if only the words of Dr. King, America's champion of nonviolence, were put into practice: "Hate cannot drive out hate; only love can do that."

King's family had endured hatred and suffering for so long, yet more tragedy struck even after Dr. King's death. Six years after Dr. King's assassination, King's mother was also murdered. As 69-year-old Alberta King played the organ at a Sunday service at Ebenezer Baptist Church, a deranged man rose from the front pew and fired two pistols. King's mother was killed at the very site where her son had preached nonviolence.

An obituary of Dr. King's life mentioned that he had traveled to India in 1959 to study Gandhi's techniques of nonviolent social change. The article quoted the radio address that Dr. King had made on his last day of the visit: ". . . since being in India, I am more convinced than ever before that the method of nonviolent resistance is the most potent weapon available to oppressed people in their struggle for justice and human dignity."

Though praised and scorned in the extreme during his lifetime, I knew that Martin Luther King's legacy would endure and inspire. Dr. King went to jail 29 times in order to win freedom for others. He put his life on the line, preaching nonviolence and leading the civil rights movement to victories across America.

As I reflected on Dr. King's legacy, I recalled how he had inspired me as a conscientious objector and how he had demonstrated to the entire world the potential for fundamental change through nonviolence. In meditation one evening, I said, *Thanks, Dr. King, for your life of service. Today I pledge that throughout my life, I'll ask myself the question that you urged every American to ask: What am I doing for others?*

Rosa Parks, who became an international icon for civil rights.
(Photo: F. Da Vinci)

18

APPLYING AS A CONSCIENTIOUS OBJECTOR
(1968)

"The time to take control of your fears is before you make an important battle decision. That's the time to listen to every fear you can imagine! When you have collected all the facts and fears and made your decision, turn off all your fears and go ahead!"

—General George S. Patton, Jr.

I found myself standing at the edge of a moral abyss, struggling with a clear choice—take the leap and apply as a conscientious objector, or back off and ride out my student deferment as long as possible.

One evening, as I watched the evening news about the war, a sign came on warning viewers that they might find the following images "graphic and disturbing." I had already endured the latest body counts, so I stayed with the broadcast and witnessed images of Asian children horribly maimed by our napalm drops. I said to myself, *Enough.* Without giving myself time to equivocate, I picked up the phone, called Joyce, the clerk at my Fairfax, Virginia, draft board, and requested a CO form.

When Jane came home that evening, and I broke the news that I had requested the form, she said, "I thought I'd be ready for this. I'm not."

"I've got to do this, Jane. I've been putting it off so long I can't stand to look at myself in the mirror."

"If this is something you have to do, I support it. I don't like it, but I support it."

The following week, I visited my folks and began, "I need to talk to you about something important."

Mom said, "This doesn't sound good."

Dad, Mom, and I gathered around the dining room table, and I announced, "You know how Jerry is serving in Vietnam? He's doing something about what he believes. It's time I did what I think is right. I'm going to apply as a conscientious objector."

My parents glanced at each other anxiously, then Dad said, "Just because you don't believe in the war doesn't mean you have to be a martyr. You realize, of course, that if you go ahead with this, you'll end up in prison?"

"It's possible."

"This is Virginia. It's not possible; it's almost guaranteed. I want you to think about another way to deal with the draft. I'm getting your brother out of it through a lawyer friend, and I can get you out too."

"Thanks, Dad, but . . ."

"Hear me out. Here's all it'll take—you visit a psychiatrist I know. See him a couple of times, and he'll write a letter about some kind of debilitating stress you're experiencing in college."

"The debilitating stress is from *home*."

"I'll ignore that. Did you ever stop to consider Jane?"

"Of course. But it's my life, and I don't want a fake deferment. I'm going to refuse induction to make a statement. The more people that stand up to wars . . ."

"Well, one of them doesn't have to be you! You're complicating this when you don't have to!" Dad said, his voice rising.

"Everyone else is complicating it. I'm trying to keep it simple by being what I am—a CO." I looked to Mom.

"Oh, no," she said. "Leave me out of this."

When it became apparent that nothing Dad said would convince me otherwise, he muttered, "You're too stubborn for your own good. This is going to have grave consequences for your future. You'll be a *felon*."

"It's my decision to make and the only way I'll be able to sleep at night."

"Fine. You sleep good," he said sarcastically, "and to hell with the rest of the family." Dad stood from the table and walked off.

The CO application form arrived from my Virginia draft board, and I read Jane their definition of a conscientious objector:

> I am, by reason of my religious training and belief, conscientiously opposed to participation in war in any form, and I am further conscientiously opposed to participation in noncombatant training and service in the Armed Forces.
>
> —Selective Service Form 150

As I studied the form in depth, particularly the part that required that I describe my beliefs and family influences, I began to see just how much my father's views had influenced me. As an altruistic agnostic, he studied the world's major religions and found a common tenet—Love as life's main purpose.

Dad regarded love as the saving grace of humanity. He abhorred what he felt was love's opposite—violence. As a compassionate psychiatrist, he saw hunting as barbaric, capital punishment as legal murder, and war as insanity in the name of patriotism.

Although my Mom had an abusive side, she had another altruistic side. Countless times I saw her brighten people's day with witty, humorous banter that turned someone's frown into a smile or laugh. And her whole life, she kept in touch with a circle of friends without families.

Another part of the CO form asked for "religious" influences. Most conscientious objectors could state that the light of traditional organized religion guided them. In my case, I was guided by a non-religious but spiritual philosophy—a set of ethics that countered violence and racial injustice with nonviolent action.

I suspected my individualistic religion of "nonviolent activism" would undoubtedly put my CO case in jeopardy. Nevertheless, I was determined to be truthful and direct with the draft board rather than pretend I belonged to a church.

As I summarized my beliefs on the form, I found the introspective process liberating. The act of putting my philosophy down on paper affirmed who I really was at heart. In essence, my application as a CO became my personal Declaration of Independence.

Where the form asked for my role models, I knew my conservative, pro-war draft board would probably prefer the likes of Robert E. Lee, J.E.B. Stuart, and Jefferson Davis. Instead, I gave them Gandhi, Albert Einstein, Cesar Chavez, and Dr. King.

Upon completing my CO form, I thought it prudent to show a rough copy to a draft lawyer at an on-campus "Draft Coffee" organized by dedicated attorneys and ministers.

Instantly, I felt a special bond with the twenty-plus COs that attended. In a way, they were extended family. Each of us knew full well the stigma attached to taking a stand as one who refuses to kill.

A draft attorney in a turtleneck and sport coat asked to look over my CO statement. He pointed to the absurd question on the form: *Do you believe in God, yes or no?* "That's Selective Service for you," he said. "They only see things in black and white. No middle or gray. Where's your draft board, Da Vinci?"

"Fairfax, Virginia."

"That's a tough one. You've clearly stated your beliefs on the form. Now I'd suggest you gather letters of support that attest to the sincerity of your beliefs. Anybody come to mind?"

"There's a congressman from Oklahoma that lives across the street from my parents. He's known me my whole life."

"Is he conservative or liberal?"

"Conservative and pro-war."

"Perfect," the attorney said, surprising me. "A letter from him will carry weight. Draft boards tend to be more impressed with letters that say, 'He may be a nut, but he's a sincere nut.'"

"That would be me."

19

GATHERING LETTERS OF SUPPORT (1968)

"My dear friend, clear your mind of can't."
—Samuel Johnson

My eyes lifted to the bronze Statue of Freedom placed atop the U.S. Capitol building in 1863. I thought, *This is what I'm fighting for—freedom—the freedom to follow my conscience and refuse to kill.*

From the foyer of the congressional office, the receptionist led me back to the inner sanctum. The congressman greeted me with an extended hand and said, "Your folks told me that you need a letter of recommendation. I'm only too glad to help. What's it for?"

"It's for my draft board. I'm applying as a conscientious objector and I need a letter of support that says . . ."

"Whoa! *That* I can't help you with."

"You don't have to agree with me," I said. "The draft board just needs to know that I'm sincere."

"That doesn't matter, son. Let me clue you in on the political realities here. It's less than a year before my election, and if it got back to my home state that I in *any* way supported a CO, it would have devastating repercussions for my campaign."

"But . . ."

The congressman held up his hand like a STOP sign. "Guess what the key issue will be against my main opponent?" I shrugged. "It's the fact that *he* was a CO! So, obviously, I can't get involved in helping you avoid the draft."

I bristled. There was that buzzword that annoyed the heck out of me—"avoid." I took a breath. "With all due respect, I'm not *avoiding* the draft. I'm facing it as a CO. In fact, if you write a letter to my draft board, you can tell them how much you *hate* what I'm doing. They only want to know that I'm sincere."

"Being your neighbor and all, I'd like to help. But politics being what it is . . . well . . . I'm sure you understand. Give my regards to your folks, will you."

The phone rang mercilessly, and I groggily one-eyed the clock. It was 5 A.M. "Hello?"

"I talked over your situation with your cousin," Dad said, "and he doesn't think you have a *chance* of winning as a CO, especially on the grounds of a personal religion. Not a chance!"

I had never heard my father so panicked. Normally his psychiatric voice was tranquil and void of emotion. "Dad, it's five in the morning!"

"I couldn't sleep."

"Look, I know it's an uphill battle . . ."

"It's not uphill; it's hopeless!" Dad exclaimed. "I also talked with a lawyer, and he said the only way you can get out of this is to beat them at their own game. He suggested you temporarily adopt a religion so you can say that you belong to a church. Since we're Italian, he suggested you tell your draft board you're Catholic."

"Did you ever think how ironic it would be for me to lie about religion? I'm prepared to go to prison if I have to."

"That's exactly the point, Francesco—you *don't* have to! Now listen to reason. I've got a high-level lawyer friend who says he'll be glad to counsel you on your rights. Call him tomorrow and make an appointment. Will you at least do that?"

Sleepy and ticked off, I felt tempted to lie and tell Dad that I'd make the call even though I had no intention of it. Instead, I forced myself to compromise for Dad's sake and in the hope that the lawyer would write a letter of support for my claim. "Okay, I'll meet with him as long as it's clear that I'm not going to fake my way out of the draft."

"Good. I'm starting to wonder if you *want* to go to prison. I think you have a self-destructive impulse that you're not dealing with."

That did it. "You know what, Dad, you're always behind the couch judging me. How about taking a good look in the mirror and thinking about how much you drink? You *know* you drink way too much. *That's* what's self-destructive."

He hung up on me. I regretted that I had turned things around on him and counter-attacked. At least, for a change, he was showing that he cared about me. With a long history of almost total neglect, it was strange to see Dad in a totally new role—concerned parent.

Two days later, in the middle of the night, the phone rang. It had to be Dad. I debated on whether to answer but begrudgingly picked up.

Without even saying hello, Dad said, "I still think you're using *very* bad judgment by compulsively insisting on this CO thing. Are you still meeting with my lawyer-friend tomorrow?"

"Yes."

"Don should be able to counsel you on your rights and at least give you a terrific letter of support. He's got connections all the way up to The White House."

As I waited for Dad's lawyer-friend in the reception area of an opulent office in Washington, D.C., I perused the latest issue of *Newsweek* and winced at its graphic images of the war.

Don emerged from his office with a grin. "Hi there, Francesco. What brings you here?"

"This," I said, holding open the *Newsweek* war photos. He nodded uneasily.

"C'mon back." He turned to his secretary. "Peggy, if the curtain man calls, put him right through."

"Of course."

From behind his desk, Don made small talk like a nervous father about to lecture his son about sex for the first time. "Okay, now about this CO deal, what's the pitch you're working on?"

I looked at him, stunned. "No pitch. I'm a CO."

He studied me curiously and lit up a big Havana. "I don't know much about COs. Tell me your position."

"It's simple. The military organizes people for violence. I want to serve my country nonviolently, doing something like community service work. But if the draft board rejects my CO application . . ."

The phone rang. Don took the call, rolled his eyes as if he couldn't wait to get off, and hung up. "Where were we?"

"I was telling you why I'm a CO. I was saying that if . . ."

The intercom buzzed. "It's *him,*" the receptionist said. Don sat up in his chair. "Good! Put him on." Don leaned in close to the intercom. "Hey, Henry, can you stop by and take a look at the curtain disaster in my office? I've got a big-shot in Johnson's Cabinet coming over next week, for God's sake. The Cuban Missile Crisis was at DEFCON 2. My office is DEFCON 1! Get the picture? You're in the neighborhood *now*? Just down the street! Fantastic! Hold on a sec'." He leaned away from the intercom. "Francesco, mind if Henry comes in while we're talking? It's an emergency."

"Fine." *I mean, what could be a bigger emergency than how the damn curtains hang!*

Don hung up and looked back at me. "I want to get rid of this curtain guy, but I don't want to get rid of you. Tell me, are you against this war or all wars?"

"All wars."

Don took another call, and then Henry shuffled in wearing overalls and holding his grey cap in his hand.

"Henry, you're harder to get a hold of than an honest politician!" They laughed, and Don pointed at his curtains. "See, they hang like hell."

I stood. "Maybe I should come back another time."

"*Hell* no," Don insisted. "Sit down! I'll be with you in a jiffy." He turned back to Henry, who was taking measurements. "Is this going to cost me a bundle?" Henry made an estimate. "That's a little more than I wanted to pay," Don said. The curtain man came down in price, and Don grabbed his hand and shook it. "Deal!" Don grinned at me. "If only they could settle things like this in Vietnam!"

Henry started toward the door. "Well, I'll get out of your way. I'll take care of those curtains first thing tomorrow morning."

Don shifted his attention to me. "You know what I'm thinking? Anybody would have to be an *idiot* to like this war. But don't you think it's important to serve?"

"Sure, but there are lots of ways to serve the country outside the military . . . hospital work, community work . . . Forcing guys to be trained to kill is just plain wrong. It goes against everything America is supposed to stand for, like individual freedom. Would you agree?"

Don nodded. "Let's call the curtain guy back in and see what *he* thinks! I'm *kidding*! Listen, I'll be glad to write a letter as long as I don't have to agree with you."

"Even better."

20

THE MINISTER'S LETTER
(1968)

"The essence of all religions is one.
Only their approaches are different."
—Mahatma Gandhi

In my quest to gather another letter of support for my CO claim, I met with the young University of Maryland campus minister. Fortunately, there were no curtains in his office that were in a state of Defcon 1.

The setting for our talk was a room soothingly stark and simple as if only truth and spirituality were of importance. I started the conversation with, "Will it be a problem that I'm not Christian?"

"What are you?" the minister asked.

"A spiritual agnostic with a religion of love. I follow the principles of Gandhian nonviolence."

He raised an eyebrow. "Tell me more about that."

"Well, I accept all religions and non-religions. I don't like to judge others and say that my way is better than someone else's. It's what's right for me."

The minister stared solemnly for a few moments. I wondered if I had offended him and if he was about to show me the door.

"No, it won't be a problem that you're not Christian," he said. "I appreciate your candor. Before we begin, let's agree that we'll accept each other's differences."

"Agreed," I said, relieved. We shook on it and dived into an hour-long moral discourse on war and peace. It included a skim of the heavy history of warfare and the rise of the military-industrial complex.

We also discussed means and ends. I cited how Jerry and I respectfully differed in perspective on that. "We both want peace," I said, "but Jerry's way is by military might, and mine is by the force of nonviolent action."

I even brought evolution and the rarity of life in the solar system into the picture. "Maybe if we—human beings that evolved over a course of about four *billion* years—learned to appreciate how incredibly precious life is, war might be less likely."

"It's truly a gift," the minister said, putting his hands together in a prayer-like fashion. He lowered his head in thought. "Was there ever a time when you participated in violence?"

"No." Then I thought back. "Well, actually, there were a few times when I was a junior and senior in high school. I played boys club football."

I explained that our tough coach told us to tackle as hard as we could. Since I was smaller than most guys on the team, I felt I had something to prove. The coach would say that he wanted every one of us to be a hitman, to hit so hard that the guy we slammed wouldn't know which way to go back to the huddle.

I was on defense when their quarterback handed the ball off to their hefty fullback. As he mowed down a few guys, I circled in, picking up speed. He didn't see me coming, then WHAM! I threw all my weight in a dive and hit him chest high. We crashed to the ground so hard that his helmet came flying off. I stayed on top of him because I wanted him to know that the small guy was the guy that brought him down. Then I saw something I'd never forget. His eyes were as wide as fifty-cent pieces with pure unadulterated fear. I hate to admit it, but it made me smile. The ref had to pull me off of him. When the guy tried to get up, he groaned in pain, holding his knee, and limped off the field. Back on the sidelines, the coach patted me on the back and shouted at the team, "I want *all* you guys to hit like that!" I sat down on the bench and asked myself, *What the hell are you turning into?*

"We've all taken wrong turns along the way," the minister said. "The important thing is that you learned from it."

Just when I thought all was said and done, the minister said, "For me to feel comfortable writing a thoughtful letter of support for your CO claim, I'd like to have you come back for one more extensive interview. I don't know if I've ever heard such a unique set of beliefs, or as you put it, *a religion of all religions . . . and non-religions.* I need to make sure I fully understand your nonviolent philosophy, which is a bit . . ."

"Mutant?"

He laughed. "Maybe *unconventional* is a better word."

In our next session, the minister asked, "What if you had to define your religion in one or two sentences?"

"Well, I think I can give that to you in two words—active love."

Periodically, the minister would nod and scribble notes. On the first day's interview, out of respect for his religious convictions, I held back about my beliefs that I knew ran counter to his. I talked about my personal religion, but I didn't elaborate on it as much as I would have liked. This second interview gave me the opportunity and confidence to open up more. In effect, I was saying, *I know my religious/philosophical views are those held by a minority of a minority. But so what. They're my sincere views from the heart; they're my truth.*

I felt pleased that the minister showed respect for my 'unconventional' ethical views. Like Jerry, he had no problem accepting our differences because he made tolerance and empathy his top priority.

At the end of our second talk, the minister walked me outside. "Before we part company," he said, "I'd like to review a few key points you made. First, you stated that your objection to war comes out of your non-traditional religious training and belief. If I understand you correctly, the closest you come to accepting a Supreme Being is in terms of love in the form of nonviolent action. "

"Yes, that's it."

"Second, you object to all wars, not a particular war."

"True."

"Are there times when you go against your personal religion?"

"Every day. White lies. Not helping someone I could have helped. Impatience. Being abrupt. It's a long list."

"For what it's worth, I appreciate your stand and your candor. You seem to be direct even when it's not in your own interest. But . . ."

"What?"

"I'm afraid your Virginia draft board . . . well, with your unorthodox spiritual views . . . I don't mean to be negative, but in the event that they come down hard on you, are you prepared for prison?"

"Yes, but what I'm doing is *nothing* compared to the COs before me that gave up their freedom . . . sometimes their lives."

The minister nodded solemnly. "It's chilling to think how many in the past made the ultimate sacrifice because of their religious and spiritual convictions. Have you heard about Maximilianus?"

"No," I answered.

"In the year 295, the first recorded CO that I know of was Maximilianus. He was conscripted into the Roman army, but he told the consul that because of his scruples, he could not serve in the military. He was executed and was eventually canonized as Saint Maximilian."

I added, "I read about COs that were sent to Alcatraz in WWI. Their hands were chained to the bars of their cells so that their toes barely touched the floor. They'd also put COs in solitary confinement in a filthy cell they called 'the hole' for long periods of time. They had to survive on just bread and water. And there were COs in WWII in Nazi Germany. They were executed. So you see, what I'm doing is minor compared to their sacrifice."

A week after my meeting with the college campus minister, I received his letter of support concerning the sincerity of my conscientious objection claim. At the living room table, Jane read the minister's letter aloud:

To the Chairman of the Local Draft board:

> Sir:
>
> I had two extensive, in-depth conversations with Mr. Francesco Da Vinci regarding his religious reasons for conscientious objection to serving in the Armed Forces. I believe in his sincerity, and I believe that his beliefs are well-grounded in his personal faith, even though I do not entirely share his beliefs.
>
> Mr. Da Vinci says he believes in a force, a loving force, which is larger than human life. He says he believes hate is as natural as love but that our loving force can be used to overcome hatred. Mr. Da Vinci does not believe in killing other human beings, and his reverence for animal life is only slightly less than his reverence for human life.
>
> I truly believe Mr. Da Vinci is a man of courage and sincerity who has the best interest of our country at heart. Eagerly he would engage in humanitarian work in a civilian capacity. He believes that people are not 'naturally' killers of each other and that war is not inevitable.
>
> Though Mr. Da Vinci is unwilling to be part of our Armed Forces, I believe he is a man of such deep moral conviction that he would willingly die for what he believes. In conclusion, I think it would not be in the best interest of our country to draft a man who has such a strong religious aversion to war. Mr. Da Vinci strikes me as a scrupulously truthful conscientious objector, and I, therefore, recommend permitting him to work where his heart and mind work together—for the civilian betterment of America.

Jane lowered the letter, walked over to me, and gave me a long hug. "This letter is amazing," she said. "With this statement, how can your draft board *not* know you're sincere? If your religion of nonviolence could move a minister like this, then who knows, maybe there *is* a chance the draft board will get it."

My Boys Club football days, 1963.

21

PRE-INDUCTION ORDER ONE—FORT HOLABIRD, MARYLAND (1968)

"A little sincerity is a dangerous thing, and a great deal of it is absolutely fatal."
—Oscar Wilde

In early May, a month after Dr. King's assassination, Jerry wrote from Vietnam and said, "Here's a copy of the Letter of Support for your CO claim that I mailed off to your draft board. I wanted them to understand that you're not a 'draft-dodger.' I know how they think. They figure COs are chickens, and if I didn't know you, that's how I'd see it too."

I showed Jerry's letter to Jane when she came home from work.

To the Members of the Draft Board:

For five years I have sworn my allegiance to the President and to my country as a Midshipman USNR. I will serve my country proudly, both militarily and in any other capacity the President may call upon me to perform. I begin this letter in this way so you might know that I would never consider conscientious objection for myself, and may more objectively evaluate the disposition of Francesco Da Vinci, my closest friend since our teen years. Though I do not personally ascribe to Francesco's outlook on war, violence, pacifism, and the universality of love, I know well his philosophy and the intense strength of his convictions.

Since we were juniors in high school, I have known Francesco to be the kind of person who would not 'harm a fly.' I know that he is sincerely idealistic, but sometimes not pragmatic in how international conflicts can be effectively resolved. For example, under no circumstances would he consider any war justified.

In this respect, we are much different. But I know these are his most sincere convictions because we have been the closest and very best of friends growing up together. I am certain, beyond any doubt whatsoever, that he will gladly serve his country, but only by nonviolent means in a civilian capacity.

Respectfully,
Jerry Ingerski

"That *should* help a lot," Jane said. "It's coming from their own military perspective."

Uneasily, I watched her face brighten with optimism. Truthfully, my fear of being rejected by my draft board was equal to my fear of seeing Jane's hopes dashed.

Less than a month before Jane and I graduated from Maryland in the Class of 1968, I received a notice from Selective Service. Uneasily, I opened the letter. Apparently, the letters of support I had submitted from the campus minister, my family's lawyer-friend, and Jerry had absolutely no influence on my draft board. My CO claim was rejected by a vote of four to nothing.

Jane said bitterly, "I don't think it would matter how many letters of support you sent them. They're supposed to judge you on whether you're sincere. But obviously, they don't give a damn about that. They hate what you stand for, and now they're set on sending you to jail."

Shortly afterward, I received an order to report for a pre-induction physical at Ft. Holabird, Maryland. A draft attorney advised me to take the physical and explain that I'm appealing the rejection of my CO stand.

The day before my physical at Fort Holabird, Jane kindly asked if she could come along and wait in the car. "It'll probably take a long time," I said. "At least an hour or two."

"I'll study," she insisted.

"Okay. I'd like the company." I smiled, touched by her support, and kissed her on the cheek.

The outside of Ft. Holabird was nondescript other than a tall steel fence crowned with large curls of barbed wire. I hugged Jane, and she held on unusually tight.

As I neared the base, I converged with hundreds of sleepy, disgruntled draftees. Clearly, very few wanted to be there. The moment I entered the building, one of the officers welcomed us with, "SHUT UP AND LISTEN UP! Fall in line and follow the tape on the floor."

At the hearing test, an officer instructed, "Push the button whenever you hear a beep." I heard the first "beep," pressed the button, and it jammed. I heard the second beep, the third beep, and the fourth, all the while struggling to get the button unstuck. When I stepped out of the booth to explain the problem, the officer handed me a graph. "You passed. Move on."

"That can't be right," I said. "The machine was broken."

"Move on!" he snapped.

"But the button was stuck."

"And I said MOVE ON!"

At the end of the Kafkaesque process, I stated in writing why I was a conscientious objector to war and explained, "I'm appealing my draft board's rejection of my CO claim."

I couldn't wait to leave the building and rejoin Jane, who was waiting outside in my car. All the draftees dressed and assembled in a cavernous, barren room. We sat on long benches waiting for our release. Once again, we were greeted with the salutation: "SHUT UP AND LISTEN UP!" The room quieted. "Da Vinci, Francesco! Where are you? Raise your hand."

A sickening knot formed in my stomach. "Here," I said, raising my hand.

"Da Vinci, you're to remain here. Everyone else can go!" The draftees stampeded out of the room like children released on the last day of school. Alone, I waited glumly for about ten or fifteen minutes, and then an officer escorted me to a small room.

"Why am I being kept here?" I asked.

"Just take a seat and wait." Another officer joined him and said, "You need to be interviewed, Da Vinci."

"Why?"

He shrugged. "Don't know."

"Then who does?" I saw the color change on his face.

"Look, either you cooperate, or we'll keep you here overnight. What's it going to be?" He stared with menace.

At the age of 22, I did not know my legal rights. I just knew that I wanted to get the heck out of the place. "Don't I have a right to know *why* I'm being kept here?"

"Last time I'm asking. Either the interview, or you stay overnight. It doesn't make any difference to me."

Fearful of spending the night in a military jail, exhausted from the whole ordeal, and conscious that Jane was outside waiting in the car, I caved in. "Okay, let's get it over with."

A short, chubby, balding man in coat and tie approached and dismissed the two officers guarding me. "We need you to answer a few questions." He spoke with a foreign accent that I couldn't pinpoint.

Waves of anger and confusion swept over me. I asked, "Don't I have *any* rights here? I want to know what's going on!"

"This won't take long. Follow me. Like you, Mr. Da Vinci, I want to get this over with as soon as possible."

He led me outside along a wall of high barbed wire fence. I didn't know where I was going, and I didn't know *what* would happen once I got there. We entered a large busy office lined with countless rotary file cabinets. The place resembled an ant farm as workers crossed each other's path, filing and retrieving folders.

My escort motioned toward a small, windowless room furnished with only two chairs and a table. "In here."

I staved off panic and asked, "Am I being interrogated?" No answer. Again, I asked, "Why am I here? And who are you anyhow—military intelligence, FBI, CIA, NSA?"

He shrugged. "Please don't make this any more difficult than it has to be. Let's finish this up, and you'll be on your way."

I sighed, pulling up a chair. "I've got nothing to hide, but I want to know, can I leave immediately after this? Can you give me your word on that?"

"Of course. Before we begin, Mr. Da Vinci, do you swear to God that what you tell me will be the truth?"

"Yes, but there must be some reason why I'm being questioned."

"No particular reason."

I looked him in the eye. "Right now, do *you* swear to God that *you're* telling the truth?"

"Just . . . just . . . answer the questions!" he stammered angrily.

I couldn't help but smile, thinking that at least he cared about his word under oath. My thoughts went to Jane. I knew she would be plenty worried by now. I wanted to tell the interrogator that my girlfriend was out in the car waiting for me. Then I figured he might want to interrogate *her*, so I kept silent.

The interrogator probed my views: *How do you feel about the draft?—What about the war?—Why are you applying as a CO?* . . . About twenty-plus minutes went by, and then I was asked, "Do you want to make a final statement?"

I hesitated before answering, searching for some common ground. "I do. I'm sure that we both, in our own way, want to make the country better. We just disagree on how to do that. You believe the best way is by military means; I believe the best way is by nonviolent means. That's my final statement."

There was no reply. Just a twisted smile. "You can go now."

Another officer approached and whispered something to my interrogator. The interrogator turned to me and said, "I'm afraid we can't release you just yet."

"What do you mean? You said I could go."

"I answer to higher-ups, and they need your fingerprints."

"This is outrageous."

"I'm afraid it's absolutely necessary. Then you can go."

One by one, my fingers were rolled in black ink as if I was a criminal. I washed off my hands, and an officer led me outside the fort. One glorious word came to mind, and I muttered it aloud—"Freedom!" It was terrific to stand on civilian territory again. I jogged over to my car, and Jane quickly opened the door. She looked sick with worry. "What happened? I was so scared!"

"I think they were too."

Several years later, Fort Holabird made national news for its secret spying on American citizens. The *New York Times* revealed that 1,000 Army agents were keeping records on individuals that they deemed "suspects." The military, under its program, dubbed "Continental U.S. Intelligence," was furtively compiling dossiers on *25 million* American civilians. In the U.S. Senate investigation of Fort Holabird, the report stated that Army Intelligence "operated on the assumption that *all* forms of political dissent were within its jurisdiction to monitor."

22

THE POOR PEOPLE'S CAMPAIGN
(1968)

"I saw courage both in the Vietnam War and in the struggle to stop it. I learned that patriotism includes protest, not just military service."

—John F. Kerry

On May 12th, 1968, Ethel Kennedy joined Coretta King at the opening of the Poor People's Campaign in the nation's capital. A few days later, Jane and I visited the encampment of 3,000 makeshift tents known as Resurrection City.

We hoped that the nonviolent campaign would serve as a wake-up call and motivate President Johnson to reassess his priorities—end the war and address poverty at home. Shockingly, the 1960 labor statistics estimated that anywhere from 40 to 60 million Americans (22 to 33 percent) lived below the poverty line. Particularly Blacks and women suffered from racism and sexism that greatly exacerbated their burden of impoverishment.

While Jane and I toured the camp, I couldn't help but ruminate on the assassination of Dr. King, who had organized the march. How I missed his inspiring and eloquent calls to better ourselves and America with empathy and altruistic acts.

In a photo that Jane took at the camp, I'm standing near a poster of Dr. King. I felt burned out and demoralized. My face mirrored the deep melancholy that enveloped Jane and me due to the assassination of Dr. King only a month before. Approaching mid-1968, our dreams for a new America hinged on one last hope—Bobby Kennedy's campaign for the presidency.

It felt as if Dr. King's spirit was present at the Poor People's Campaign, reminding me of a fact that I kept pushing to the back of my mind—the fact that he was gone along with his bold, moral leadership. As we roamed the camp and talked with the residents that had come from all corners of the country, I couldn't quite give my full attention to where I was. I felt partly in a trance, wondering, *"If only JFK had lived . . . if only Martin were still here fighting for all of us and encouraging us to do our part . . ."* But both American heroes were gone, and I asked myself the unthinkable—what if Bobby is next?

Two weeks later, Sirhan Sirhan, a 24-year-old Palestinian-American, wrote in his journal: "R.F.K. must die . . . My determination to eliminate R.F.K. is becoming more and more of an unshakable obsession . . ."

To sweeten our disturbing after-dinner topic—the draft—I surprised Jane by ordering Chinese takeout. Immediately after Chow Mein and dumplings, Jane opened her fortune cookie with a smile. But when she read it, her face fell.

Bad timing, I thought. *We're about to talk about the draft and the threat of prison, and* this *time she gets a fortune that spells doom.*

"What did it say?" I asked. "It can't be that bad."

"You don't care about fortunes, but I do. How come you always get the good ones," she said, miffed. "I really wanted a good one tonight."

I couldn't believe that she was near tears over this damn fortune cookie. Nevertheless, I wanted to respect her feelings. I held her and encouraged her to share the fortune: "No matter what it says, Jane, we're going to get through this."

Jane read her fortune aloud, "'When hungry, order more Chinese food!'"

"*That's* what you were so upset about!"

Jane wiped away a tear, nodded, and chuckled at herself. "See what the draft is doing to my brain?"

We had a good laugh over it, then got down to talking about the un-American system of involuntary servitude—the draft that lived with us 24-7 and clouded our future. I rummaged through my desk and pulled out my brief chronology of conscientious objection in America.

"I read up a little on COs that went to prison for refusing induction," I said. "I'll read you my notes. They made me realize that I'm not so alone in this."

"You mean there are more of you?"

"Funny, Jane. Did you know that COs have been around in the US since the time of George Washington?"

"Really?"

"Yeah. Here's an overview of the so-called 'misfits' that refused the draft. I'll start with the Quakers. They're the ones that came up with the phrase 'conscientious objection.' In colonial times, the Quakers—also called the Society of Friends—opposed all war. For not killing native Americans, they faced prison terms, public beatings, and whippings. By 1658, four Quakers had been executed just for refusing to kill.

"During the American Revolution at Valley Forge, George Washington's troops tried to force Quakers to kill the British. But Washington ordered that the Quakers be set free and sent home.

"In the Civil War, the Confederacy allowed CO exemptions for some *religious sects*. The Union, however, stood against conscientious objection and adopted a mercenary policy. A CO could buy his way out of the war or find a substitute. It was called a 'commutation fee,' and it was sometimes a whole year's pay.

"Opposition to COs was serious during WWI. The Hutterites, a religious sect dating back to 1524, suffered incredible persecution. Many of them had to flee to Canada for their safety. Others lost their freedom. Two brothers, for example, were sent to Alcatraz. Once there, Joseph and Michael refused to wear the military clothing that they were ordered to wear. Officials beat them and hosed them down in freezing weather 'til both brothers caught pneumonia and died. Their bodies were returned home. When Joseph's coffin was opened, he was wearing the military uniform he had refused to put on.

"COs who wouldn't drill or do noncombatant service were court-martialed and sentenced to two of the worst prisons in the country—Alcatraz and Ft. Leavenworth. Some COs were manacled and put in solitary confinement.

"Ben Salmon, a Catholic conscientious objector during WWI, wrote a letter to President Wilson in 1917, stating, 'Conscience, my infallible guide, impels me to tell you that prison, death, or both, are infinitely preferable to joining any branch of the Army.' In 1918, Salmon was arrested for refusing to report for induction. He was locked in a guardhouse for refusing to wear a uniform and forced to work in the yard. Despite never having been inducted, he was court-martialed and charged with desertion and spreading propaganda. The sentence he received—death. Later he was re-sentenced to 25 years of hard labor and sent to Leavenworth prison, where he began a hunger strike. Salmon received force-feedings, and beatings that permanently damaged his health. The government claimed that Salmon's fast was due to mental illness and sent him to a ward for the criminally insane. The American Civil Liberties Union defended Salmon in court and secured a pardon for him. Salmon was issued a 'dishonorable discharge' from the military service, which he had never joined!

"In WWII, 72,354 Americans applied for conscientious objector status. About 37,000 were recognized as COs. The COs who volunteered to work in hospitals for the mentally ill exposed inhumane conditions and helped change the way barbaric hospitals were run.

"In Germany, the Nazis executed 271 conscientious objectors who were Jehovah Witnesses. The first execution took place in a concentration camp before all the prisoners, including 400 Jehovah Witness inmates. A German officer threatened more of the same killing, but none of the 400 witnesses renounced their CO position.

"In the Korean War, from 1952 to 1955, nearly 10,000 men were granted status as COs in a civilian capacity. Only about 25 men left their assigned job without authorization.

"Now, with maybe our most unpopular war—Vietnam—thousands and thousands of guys are saying the war has no claim on them. And it's not just draftees. Guys already in the military are saying no, too. And let's not forget that Vietnam is a war that was never officially declared by the U.S." Jane raised her hand, and I pointed to her. "Yes, the lovely lady in the front row."

"Why isn't all this in our history books?" she asked.

"Excellent question."

At the Poor People's Campaign, 1968. (Photo: Jane)

The Poor People's Campaign, June 1968. (Photo: F. Da Vinci)

The call for jobs and social justice, June 1968. (Photo: F. Da Vinci)

23

BOBBY KENNEDY IS KILLED

(June 5, 1968)

"Some men see things as they are and say, 'Why?'
I dream of things that never were, and say, 'Why not.'"
—Senator Edward Kennedy, quoting his brother Bobby

As the call for peace in Vietnam increased dramatically, Jane and I felt tremendously heartened. In February 1968, a Gallup poll showed that opposition to the war had risen from a minority position to fifty percent. Adding to the growing anti-war perspective was the unforgettable sight of Vietnam Veterans on television throwing away the medals they had earned during the war.

With hopeful anticipation, I looked to the near future for a dramatic change in the country's direction. If Bobby Kennedy won the California Primary and became president, I felt confident that he would end the war in Vietnam and support legislation that reflected Dr. King's vision of equal justice and racial harmony.

On the morning of the California Primary, June 4, 1968, Dad invited Jane and me to join him at the Shoreham Hotel in Washington, D.C., for the American Booksellers Convention. Dad's latest self-help book would be at one of the exhibits.

The moment we entered the lobby, it seemed we were witnessing a Norman Rockwell painting come to life. There was 6'2" Joe DiMaggio, former center fielder for the Yankees, leaning down and signing a baseball for an awe-struck Little Leaguer. I didn't need a camera to remember that Americana image forever.

The featured speaker in the hotel dining room was folksinger and nonviolent activist Joan Baez. Joan's pitch-black hair framed her riveting, soulful eyes. I felt captivated by the passion resonating in her voice as she warned, "Violence, in one form or another, permeates our society. We've become numb and shock-resistant to it."

Later I read that during Joan's early childhood, her family converted to Quakerism. Joan mirrored that commitment to pacifism and social justice throughout her life. In 1967, she was arrested twice for blocking the entrance of the Armed

Forces Induction Center in Oakland, California. In an interview, she said, "I went to jail . . . for disturbing the peace; I was trying to disturb the war."

Moved by Joan's eloquent speech at the book convention, Jane and I went up to her afterward, and I asked, "Do you still work with the Institute for the Study of Non-Violence in Carmel?"

Her eyes lit up at the mention of it. "Yes," she answered.

I introduced Jane and said, "We might move to California this summer, and if we do, we'd like to visit."

"I'll write down the address and phone number for you," Joan said. "Come by."

After Jane and I came home from the book convention, we stayed up late to watch the California Primary returns. When it became apparent that Kennedy had won, Jane and I hugged with joy and renewed hope.

Around 3 A.M., Bobby gave his victory speech from the Ambassador Hotel in Los Angeles. With characteristic humor, he noted that Dodger pitcher, Don Drysdale, had pitched his sixth straight shutout that evening and added that he hoped to do as well in the primaries. Then he thanked everyone for their support and closed with, "My thanks to all of you, and on to Chicago, and let's win there."

Many in the jubilant crowd joined in singing the Woody Guthrie classic "This Land is Your Land," a song I preferred as our national anthem for its nonviolent celebration of America.

Overjoyed with Kennedy's victory, I clicked off the TV, and Jane said with a big smile, "I think he's going to be our next president."

"Where's the cynicism?" I teased.

Meanwhile, back at the Ambassador, Senator Kennedy was led toward the hotel kitchen area to exit. Following behind him was his wife, Ethel. She was in her third month of pregnancy with Rory Kennedy.

Early the next morning, the persistent ring of the phone awakened us. I answered, figuring it was Dad with a new avoid-the-draft scheme. Instead, it was one of Jane's girlfriends. "Did you hear the news? Senator Kennedy was shot last night!"

I woke Jane and flipped on the TV. Over and over, stations replayed the tragedy. It seemed beyond belief. The shooting happened just after we had turned off Kennedy's victory speech. A news tape that had recorded the mayhem showed the indelible image of Senator Kennedy sprawled on the floor in a pool of blood, his head cradled by a 17-year-old kitchen worker who was shaking Kennedy's hand when Sirhan Sirhan fired the shots. The report listed Senator Kennedy's condition as "critical" and stated that he had shown "definite life signs."

We clung to hope. I looked at Jane, torn with anguish and anger. "Only two months ago, Martin Luther King was shot, and now Bobby. What the hell is happening!"

"Let's get out of here and take a long drive," Jane suggested.

"Where?" I asked.

"Anywhere."

We ended up at a park in Annapolis and laid down in the grass amidst clusters of yellow flowers. The still lake in front of us was lined with weeping willow trees. Even Nature seemed to be in mourning.

On the drive home, we listened to the news for updates on Bobby's condition. He was in the operating room at Good Samaritan Hospital. Things looked grim. Early the next morning, Robert F. Kennedy was pronounced dead. Journalist and political advisor Frank Mankiewicz, whose father Herman J. Mankiewicz, wrote *Citizen Kane,* announced, "Senator Robert Francis Kennedy died at 1:44 A.M. today, June 6, 1968."

Grief-stricken, I called the President of the University of Maryland, Dr. Wilson H. Elkins. I asked that we honor Senator Kennedy at the graduation ceremony since it fell on the same day as Kennedy's burial service at Arlington National Cemetery. The president's secretary explained that President Elkins was too busy to come on the line. Hurt and bitter, I insisted on speaking with him. "It'll only take a minute," I insisted.

"Again, I can't do that, but I'll be happy to relay any message you have."

"I'd like to request that we honor Senator Kennedy at graduation with a moment of silence. It's the least we can do."

"I'll pass on your message and get back to you." Less than an hour later, she called back. "I'm sorry, Mr. Da Vinci, but the president said the ceremony could not be politicized with a reference to Senator Kennedy. He feels it would be improper."

I sighed. "Please tell the president that I feel his decision is what's improper. Thanks."

I hung up, and Jane looked at me uneasily.

"I can see the wheels turning," she said. "What's up?"

"I'm not going to our graduation; I'm going to Bobby's funeral."

"There's going to be a helluva lot of security. How would you get in?"

"I'll wait until everyone leaves."

"I'm sad about Bobby, too, but our graduation is something that only happens once in our life."

"Bobby's funeral is more important to me . . . much more."

"Why can't you do both, go to graduation first and then the funeral that night?"

"In the afternoon, there's a train coming down from New York with Bobby's casket on it. I want to stand at the tracks as it goes by."

Jane shook her head bitterly. "Well, I'm definitely going to graduation."

"You do what you have to do, and I'll do what I have to do."

"Do you know how cold you sound now? I know you're upset, but you don't have to take it out on me."

"Sorry."

"Sorry, but you're going to ignore everything I say anyhow. If you care about my feelings, then go with me to graduation."

"I'm going to the funeral."

"Fine, then I'll go to graduation myself. I *thought* that this was something special that we'd share and never forget. But I guess that's not important to you." She grabbed her purse and turned at the door. "I'll be at my parents'."

From my off-campus apartment in College Park, Maryland, I drove to the railroad tracks that would soon bear Kennedy's funeral train. From Manhattan to the nation's capital, two million well-wishers lined the tracks. I stood near the rails between several Little Leaguers in uniform and a family of four holding hands. Then came the sound of the funeral train approaching in its journey to Union Station just as President Lincoln's body had been carried 103 years before.

People stood quietly. Many saluted or, like myself, held their hand over their heart. As the slow-moving train roared up, I saw the flag-draped casket through a large glass window. The car carrying the coffin was at the very end of the train. It had been raised on red velvet chairs to be seen by the thousands of bystanders. As the train passed, I said, "We'll miss you, Bobby."

Meanwhile, at the University of Maryland's Cole Field House, Jane's parents proudly watched their daughter receive her diploma. President Johnson had sent a letter on his White House stationery: "To The 1968 Graduating Class University of Maryland—Few moments equal the joy, the satisfaction, and the fulfillment of graduation. It is a personal and permanent victory, an honor to last a lifetime. To each of you, I extend my sincere congratulations."

Late that afternoon, while I was at my off-campus apartment, Jane happened to call. "I'm not mad at you anymore. When I thought about how important it is for you to do what you're doing, I figured it wasn't right for me to take that away from you. I'm sorry."

"I'm sorry too. I had my mind made up, and I shut you out."

"Thanks. If you're not too upset, I'd like to come with you to the cemetery."

"I'd like that," I said.

"I just went through royal *hell* with my parents. I'll tell you about it when I see you."

When I opened the door, Jane looked torn between tears and anger. We hugged, then sat at the dining room table. "What happened?" I asked.

"My parents told me I should dump you."

"What did they say?"

"I'll tell you, but don't say anything. Just listen. I need to get it out."

"Sure."

"After I got my diploma, the three of us walked outside. All the families around us were taking pictures and hugging. But not my parents. My father said, 'I'm sorry, but this Francesco guy has nothing going for him." I asked him why he said that, and he said, 'Where is he today? He's a no-show. He has no religion, no steady job, and no intention of serving.'" My mom backed him up. Then Dad said, 'You've got your whole life in front of you. Don't waste it on this damn draft-dodger." I told him that you weren't a draft-dodger, that you're facing the draft. I said you're even willing to go to prison for your beliefs. Dad just said, 'And that would make your precious boyfriend a felon! Some common sense, Jane. Dump him!'"

I took Jane's hand.

"No matter what my parents say, they're not going to poison me about you and what we have."

As the sky began to darken, we drove to Arlington National Cemetery.

It was the first time in the history of the cemetery that a funeral was held at night. As Jane and I started up a hill that cut through several hundred thousand white tombstones, a guard stopped us. "Sorry, but the funeral site isn't open to the public." We started back down the hill when suddenly I stopped walking. "We've got to go back," I said.

Jane eyed me with a mix of alarm and weary resignation. "I don't think it's a good idea . . . but okay."

We waited until every last visitor had left, then started up the hill that led to the gravesite. A soldier coming the other way stopped us. "We're all closed up now," he said. "You can come back in the morning. There's nothing to see, and I'd appreciate it if you took the shortest route back." He pointed down the hill. I remained motionless. Jane tugged at my arm, and slowly I started back with her.

The soldier walked off, and I said, "He's gone."

Jane gave me her "Oh no" look.

"I'm not leaving," I said. "I have to do this. If you want, I'll meet you later down at the car."

She shook her head and said, "I came this far. I'm staying." I squeezed her hand, and we hurried back up the hill towards the gravesite only about thirty yards from JFK's grave. Jane stopped and said, "I don't want to go any further. This is your time. You should have it alone. I'll stay here and stand guard."

I looked into her eyes, thinking, *That's my Jane.*

Not one person was around as I approached the gravesite. I stood there under a gibbous Moon that had an eerie reddish halo surrounding it and bowed my head. Thinking of Bobby's legacy, a quote from his speech to South Africans came to mind: "Each time a man stands up for an ideal . . . he sends a tiny ripple of hope . . ."

In meditation, I reflected that, like his brother, JFK, Bobby motivated me to become an active citizen . . . to work that much harder for social justice and peace. *Thanks, Bobby.*

Then the tears broke.

Joan Baez. (Photo: F. Da Vinci)

Jane. (Photo: F. Da Vinci)

Years later, I revisited Bobby Kennedy's gravesite at Arlington National Cemetery.

24

CALIFORNIA DREAMIN'
(1968)

"Twenty years from now, you will be more disappointed by the things you didn't do than by the ones you did do. So throw off the bowlines, sail away from the safe harbor. Catch the trade winds in your sails. Explore. Dream. Discover."

—Mark Twain

After graduating in the historic Class of 1968, Jane and I decided to move to the mecca of the counterculture—California. A big inspiration was the Mamas and the Papas song "California Dreamin'." It beckoned us, as Tennyson put it, to 'seek a newer world.' It was also an opportunity to distance ourselves from our dysfunctional and disapproving families.

Our itinerary—drive across the country along the Southern route, cross Texas, then head north to San Francisco, "The City of Love." After two months in the Bay Area, we planned to move down to San Diego, a tropical paradise 120 miles south of Los Angeles. Jane had a job lined up there as a social worker. I planned to go for my Master's degree at U.S. International University, San Diego (now Alliant University), majoring in Social Psychology.

The day before embarking on our cross-country trek, we visited my good buddy Jerry, who was on leave to visit his folks in northern Virginia. We pulled up into the driveway of Jerry's parents' home, and there was Jerry with an ever-present cigarette in hand, leaning against his light brown Nash. As soon as he saw us, he took a long last drag on the nub of his cigarette, then crushed it on the asphalt. We hugged, then went to a café for coffee and pie. As usual, the conversation turned to the draft.

"Draftees here have it good compared to guys who get drafted in South Vietnam," Jerry said. "Here we take 'em from 18 to 25. President Thieu takes 'em from 16 to 50."

"I hope that one day America and the whole world will abolish the draft," I commented.

"Not likely anytime soon," Jerry said. "By the way, when are you two gonna tie the knot?"

Jane and I looked at each other uneasily and shrugged. "Everything is up in the air 'cause of his CO case," Jane said.

"Good luck with it, Francesco," Jerry said. "If the government ends up putting you in prison, then in my eyes, they'd be committing a crime."

"Thanks, buddy," I said. "And good luck in Vietnam."

Jane said, "I don't know how you guys stay friends when politically you're on *totally* different roads."

Jerry smiled and added, "I'd say Francesco is definitely on the less traveled one!"

"*See,*" Jane exclaimed. "*He* knows what I'm putting up with!"

When we were back at Jerry's, and it was time to part, Jerry said hesitantly, "Well . . . goodbye."

"Don't say goodbye," Jane said adamantly. "Just say, 'See you later.'"

"Okay," Jerry said with a half-smile. "See you later."

In the light of resplendent dawn, Jane and I packed up my Chevy convertible and set out on our trek across America.

We grinned at each other with excitement. The top of the Chevy was down, the wind blew through our hair, and the radio was cranked up with "Hey Jude"—the song Paul McCartney wrote to comfort John Lennon's five-year old son Julian during his parents' divorce.

From state to state, we gained a new appreciation for America's awe-inspiring, diverse beauty. After a long flat drive across west Texas, Jane said, "I'm famished. Let's pull over and grab a bite to eat."

The gravel fretted beneath my Chevy as I pulled into the parking lot of a long, low diner. We slid into a blue booth that had matching color gaffer tape here and there to cover the rips and tears. Immediately, Jane buried her face in the menu. Slowly it dawned on me that *everything* in the coffee shop had come to a grinding halt. A half-dozen rough-looking cowboys at the counter glared at us along with the waitresses and a dozen customers. I heard someone mutter, "Hippies."

I recalled the words of one of my sociology professors: "Your generation may think it's cool wearing your hair long and dressing hippie-style, but when the older generation looks at it, it screams, '*Fuck you!*'"

I glanced out the window and winced. Three cowboys, checking out my car, paused at the rear bumper and looked down disapprovingly. I knew they were reading my two peace stickers: WAR IS NOT HEALTHY FOR CHILDREN AND OTHER LIVING THINGS and SUPPORT OUR TROOPS—BRING THEM HOME! Jerry had suggested I take them off and switch to LOVE IT OR LEAVE IT to make it less likely that the police would pull us over.

Dead silence filled the diner except for one voice—Jane's. "I can't decide whether to have the cheeseburger or the tuna."

"Don't turn around," I said to her quietly but firmly. "We're not ordering."

"Why not? I'm starved!" she said loudly.

"Notice how no one is talking in here except us?"

Only her eyes moved.

"Trust me; we gotta leave. Put down the menu and walk in front of me."

Jane remained motionless.

"You can do this." I put my hand on hers, and she smiled back weakly.

"Good. Now we're gonna walk to the door. Don't look back, and don't run. Here, take the keys. If I don't make it out, take the car and go for help." There was panic in her eyes, and I knew the sooner we got moving, the better. "Let's go."

I let her pass in front of me, and we stepped outside. One of the three cowboys had planted himself directly in front of the driver's door. Jane slipped in on the passenger side and waited for me. The cowboy stared for a few eternal moments.

"Going somewhere, hippie?" he asked.

"Yeah, we're headin' to California."

"College boy?"

Before I could answer, another cowboy added, "A *peacenik* college boy."

"Yeah," I nodded, trying to break the tension with a smile. I stepped up my slight Virginia accent. "But we're all proud to be livin' in the same country, don't you think? You're doin' your thing; we're doin' ours. But we're all Americans, right?"

The cowboy glared a moment or two, then nodded and slowly moved aside. I backed the Chevy out nice and easy and turned the car around. Jane excessively nodded goodbye to the cowboys with a smile so fake that I was surprised it didn't break into a thousand pieces and fall on the floor.

On the road again, neither of us said a word. A bit later, we came upon another diner. In unison, we looked at each other and firmly shook our heads no.

"Question," Jane said, breaking the stillness. "Back there, were you scared?"

I nodded. "Oh yeah, I was scared plenty."

When we finally reached the Bay Area, we were overwhelmed by a simple yet exhilarating experience that more than made up for our incident in Texas. Just as we started to drive across the majestic Golden Gate Bridge, Scott McKenzie's *Flowers in Your Hair* miraculously came on the radio. I cranked it up.

It was one of those unforgettable moments—you connect a special song with a special place, and you know the memory will stay forever.

In San Francisco, Jane and I found a modest apartment to sublet for our 2-month stay before moving down to San Diego. It quickly became apparent that we had arrived in San Francisco a year too late. The Haight-Ashbury '67 Summer of Love was long gone. Last year, San Francisco was a haven for the counterculture:

music, protests, and love-ins. The city by the bay was the undisputed world capital of Flower Power. But by the summer of '68, Jane and I discovered to our dismay that the community had become heavily commercialized, driving many of the idealistic youth out of the neighborhood. Still, we hoped for a lingering remnant of the magic.

As we walked along the streets of Haight-Ashbury, we passed young people shooting up in the shadowed spaces between buildings. Streets and public sidewalks were littered with discarded syringes. Our counterculture's would-be paradise had morphed into hell.

The sixties were a decade of extremes. Juxtaposed were excesses of sex and drugs with one of the most idealistic, enlightening decades in American history. The amazing positive aspects of the sixties included the fact that the civil rights movement was expanding, virtually all the minorities were empowered, the voting age was being lowered to 18, an environmental campaign was underway to establish an "Earth Day," gay rights and women's rights were championed, and a powerful anti-war movement emerged, the likes of which America had never seen.

During our stay in the Bay area, Jane and I adopted a favorite hangout—the Japanese Tea Gardens in Golden State Park. With acres of natural beauty and scores of brilliantly colored butterflies, it became our Shangri-La. Whenever we needed to talk something out or take a break from dealing with the draft, we'd pack up a picnic basket and a Frisbee.

Our short stay in San Francisco renewed and strengthened our love. With no school or work distractions, Jane and I had the free time to appreciate each other and talk things out more than ever before.

When it was time to move down to San Diego, we took Route 1, a breathtaking winding drive that bordered the Pacific Ocean. Eventually, we arrived at a scenic coastal area of northern San Diego called La Jolla. Fittingly, La Jolla translates to "the gem." As easterners unaccustomed to walks along the ocean, we felt a moral obligation to head straight to the beach.

As the sun neared the horizon, I pulled over at a panoramic vista called Windansea. Jane and I walked along the shore to feast on the view of the ocean that glowed golden in the fading light. It seemed we had landed on another planet. Surfers rode the waves, pelicans flew by, and leaning in on us overhead were towering palm trees. We stopped to toss pieces of bread in the air for the seagulls, then shed our socks and shoes and walked along the water's edge.

Along the way, I pointed out a beautiful elliptical reef close to shore. With the reef accessible in low tide, Jane and I rolled up our bell-bottom jeans and climbed up on the cratered surface. The sun, our life-giving star, slipped below the Pacific, and I said, "Let's come back to this reef. I can't explain it, but I feel connected to it. It gives me peace."

Jane smiled. "I feel it too."

California Dreamin' becomes real, 1968. (Photo: Jane)

Jane and I move to California, 1968. I'm holding one of my oil paintings. (Photo: Jane)

The reef in La Jolla that became my meditation retreat for three years. (Photo: F. Da Vinci)

25

DEMOCRATIC NATIONAL CONVENTION—CHICAGO

(August 26–29, 1968)

"There's a lot of things that need to change.
One specifically? Police brutality."
—Colin Kaepernick

Once Jane and I settled into our new apartment in Pacific Beach, we turned our attention to the upcoming presidential election. Bleakly. Since our political heroes—President Kennedy, Dr. King, and Bobby Kennedy had been assassinated, the candidacy of Senator Eugene McCarthy seemed our last and best hope for progressive policies.

Humphrey was almost a lock-in for the nomination at the upcoming Democratic National Convention in Chicago, especially since he would undoubtedly have the support of Mayor Daley as well as the behind-the-scenes help of President Johnson. Ignoring that political reality, Jane and I decided to work for McCarthy purely on principle. So what if it seemed we were charging windmills. Anything seemed better than simply giving up.

Around our studies, Jane and I worked for Senator McCarthy at a lower than low level by handing out brochures at grocery stores and shopping malls.

The more I talked with San Diegans, the more pessimistic I became concerning the upcoming Democratic Convention and the mood of the country. The top priority of most voters had little or nothing to do with civil rights or peace in Vietnam. Instead, the predominant sentiment of the public seemed to be the need to get back to the status quo. They had had it with the last four years of civil rights and anti-war protests. Right-wing politicos exploited that backlash and developed a strategic platform of "law and order."

As the Democratic National Convention in Chicago approached, most of those on the front lines of the civil rights and peace movement viewed the selection of the nominee with a jaundiced eye. Even if Humphrey became the presidential candidate and defeated Nixon, so what? It seemed inevitable that Humphrey would continue Johnson's escalation of the war in Vietnam at the expense of social programs at home. The same could be said if Nixon won.

In mid-August, shortly before the Democratic Convention, I flew from San Diego to Virginia to visit Mom and Dad at their house in Falls Church. My father had just seen a young patient in our home library. "Francesco, this is Chip," Dad said. "Chip said he belongs to the Youth International Party, whatever that is, and that he's going to the Democratic Convention in Chicago."

"Yeah, I'm a Yippie," Chip interjected. "Yippies are kind of an off-shoot of the free speech and anti-war movements."

Dad said, "Chip wondered if next week you'd like to go to the Democratic Convention with him and his friends."

Chip nodded. "Yeah, a group of us are drivin' up."

I looked at Dad in shock. Was this the same Dad that had turned down my request to go to the March on Washington because it might be too dangerous? I figured he was utterly clueless that the Chicago Convention was bound to be a far more perilous setting than Dr. King's '63 March On Washington, which he had forbidden me to attend.

"What do the Yippies stand for?" Dad asked.

"We don't have a formal structure, Doc. We're a real loose group. If we stand for anything, it's freedom. We're creative, and we get our ideas across with stuff like street theatre. You can't really peg a Yippie. We're unpredictable."

Dad stared at him blankly, and I tried to pick up the slack. "What do you plan to do in Chicago, Chip?"

Chip's eyes lit up. "For our first order of business, Abbie Hoffman is gonna levitate the Pentagon all the way from Chicago!" Dad chuckled, but I saw that Chip was earnest. As he outlined a wide array of creatively disruptive actions that included "making love, not war," "partying all night," and "tripping in Lincoln Park," Dad looked at me quizzically.

"He's serious," I said.

"Oh yeah," Chip concurred, "I'm dead serious. Like Timothy Leary said, we're gonna turn on, tune in, and drop out!"

"Any political plans that might be more pragmatic?" I asked gently.

"Oh, yeah. We're gonna take a live pig and nominate it for president."

"Of the Yippies?"

"No. Of America."

I glanced at Dad, who was looking on open-mouthed.

"You gonna come with us, Francesco?" asked Chip.

"Thanks, but I'll stay here and work to support McCarthy's campaign."

"You're pretty mainstream, huh? Far out." I thought of how relative politics was. I was "mainstream" to Chip, but to traditional Democrats, I was "left" beyond the solar system. To conservative Republicans, I was in another galaxy, perhaps in another universe!

Upon returning to San Diego from my visit with Mom and Dad, Jane and I watched the convention on television on August 28th, the same day of my parents' anniversary, and the same day that Dr. King had delivered his historic *I Have a Dream* speech in 1963.

Outside the convention hall in Chicago, as the crowd thickened, musician Phil Ochs sang, "I Ain't Marchin' Anymore"—*It's always the old who lead us to war, always the young to fall.* As Ochs performed, scores of young men burned their draft cards.

Meanwhile, over 10,000 anti-war demonstrators coalesced. They were met by 23,000 police and National Guardsmen. The Chicago police clashed with protesters that were, for the most part, nonviolent and respectful. Some protesters, however, taunted police verbally and threw bags of urine.

Chicago became a nightmarish battlefield. The police rioted and savagely beat young unarmed students. Reporters and photographers were not spared. They also tear-gassed the crowd and sprayed demonstrators and bystanders indiscriminately with mace. True, some protesters provoked the police, but none of their actions warranted the senseless spilling of blood by law enforcement officials. I felt sickened and infuriated seeing the police use billy clubs to beat the protesters to the ground. As the police escalated their brutality, protesters continued to chant *The whole world is watching!*

Inside the convention hall, Chicago police roughed up newsmen Mike Wallace and Dan Rather. When Rather was slugged to the floor by a policeman, news anchor Walter Cronkite uncharacteristically lost his cool and called the police "thugs."

A full-blown battle between the liberal and conservative elements of the Democratic party erupted. When Senator Ribicoff of Connecticut gave his nominating speech for Senator George McGovern, he said, "With George McGovern, we wouldn't have Gestapo tactics on the streets of Chicago." On live television, Mayor Daley responded to Ribicoff by flipping him the finger.

The violence from the police outside the convention escalated. Jane and I watched from our living room in horror. America seemed to be in the midst of a second civil war.

It was revealed that the authorities had overreacted to their imagined threat of the protesters to such an unreasonable extent that the National Guard was issued flamethrowers and bazookas! Regarding the police, many of Chicago's officers had removed their badges to beat demonstrators without accountability. Often, protesters who were ordered to hold their hands above their heads to be arrested were struck hard in the genitals with clubs.

Though 90 million Americans watched the televised "police riot," a shocking number of viewers, according to polls, said the protesters got their just due. Jane's parents echoed that sentiment. Letters of praise were sent to the Mayor, applauding the police brutality. Many said that, if anything, the Mayor's police were "too lenient" and that the demonstrations were probably the result of a Jewish or communist conspiracy.

Later in the week, Jane and I were still talking about the public's indifference to the police violence in Chicago. I felt outraged and a sense of inspirational dissatisfaction—the need to work that much harder for change. Jane, however, looked demoralized. "Face it," she said, "the country doesn't want real change. All they care about is what you heard when you leafleted for McCarthy at shopping centers—law and order. What's left? Nothing! McCarthy just got knocked out of the race by Humphrey. Everything we were working for—it's over."

"It's *not* over unless we give up," I argued. "We've gotta come back from this. If we don't, the war is gonna keep dragging on and we'll be stuck with another president that cares more about saving face than bringing the troops home."

26

FACING PRISON

(1969)

"While there is a lower class, I am in it, while there is a criminal element, I am of it, and while there is a soul in prison, I am not free."

—Eugene V. Debs

When I applied as a conscientious objector, I knew I would inevitably be vilified. What I had not counted on was that the hateful scorn that my stand engendered would spill over to my family. I thought my fight for recognition as a CO would be my battle and my battle alone. But that myth was shattered one night when Dad called me at 1 A.M. His voice quaked with hurt and anger.

"Your mother and I were at a cocktail party having a drink when a couple we didn't know walked over and confronted us about you being a CO. The husband shouted at us and said, 'We heard your son is applying as a conscientious objector.' I told him it was true, and he said, 'In our book, that makes your boy nothing less than a coward and a traitor who's aiding the enemy.' Then the man's wife said, '*Our* son is serving in Vietnam.' Everyone at the party was looking at us, and her husband said, 'Your boy should go where he *really* belongs—North Vietnam.' People applauded! Your mother, who you know rarely gets upset, ran off in tears."

An awkward silence followed as I absorbed the pain that my parents endured. "I'm so sorry you and Mom had to go through that, Dad."

"*Sorry* isn't good enough! If you were really sorry, you'd stop being so selfish and drop this CO thing once and for all!" *Click!*

One evening, the never-ending pressure of the draft got to Jane and me. It seemed unbearable. Spontaneously, we almost spoke at the same time and said, "Let's go to the ocean."

As usual, on our strolls along the beach, we stopped to visit our favorite reef near the shore that had become my sanctuary for meditation. Snuggled tight, we watched the rose-colored sun sink over the horizon, then returned home with a sense of renewal. Our joy, however, was obliterated the next day. A new draft card arrived in the mail. I was registered "1-A," meaning ready for war. The draft board was stepping things up.

I called my latest draft attorney, who informed me that I had the right to appeal the draft board's rejection of my CO stand and request a personal interview in Virginia. When I hung up, Jane said, "What's wrong with your draft board? If ever anybody was a CO, it's you."

I replied, "They're turning down what they don't understand. I've got the right to meet with them face-to-face."

"I don't think it'll make a difference, but we might as well try."

An item in the paper said that Bill Sands, an ex-convict and the author of *My Shadow Ran Fast,* was going to give a college lecture on prison life. With the never-ending threat of the draft and prison, I wanted to attend in the hope that I would be a bit more educated on the realities of life incarcerated.

At the lecture, I learned that Bill had served time on three convictions for armed robbery before he was 21. Sands began his talk by telling us how the prisons themselves are crimes against humanity and added, "Right here in San Diego, as in many cities, there are caged-up men and women who will likely come out much worse than when they went into prison." Sands estimated that nationally about 80% of released convicts return to prison.

My dad, who would occasionally testify in criminal cases, argued that nothing is ever going to change about recidivism until our prisons are turned into treatment centers.

"Every day a young man enters jail for the first time," Sands continued, "he's tossed into a cell with a hardened criminal, and he's raped," Sands said. "If he doesn't submit, a bunch of prisoners gang up on him. It's time we face the fact that prison conditions in America are primitive and brutal." He added that in Cincinnati, Ohio, prisoners were being held in "coffin-like" cells with no toilets, and in Louisiana, there was whipping. When Sands was in prison himself, he had talked back to the guards, and they punished him by breaking 33 bones in his body. Holding his hands down, they broke every finger one at a time.

The lecture had given me a new and disturbing awareness of prison conditions in America. I felt grateful to Sands for sharing his ordeal and shedding light on "state-approved violence," including the legal murder we call capital punishment. It's hard for the public to be morally outraged by our brutal "corrections" system when it's largely invisible.

On the drive home from the Sands talk on prison life, I felt deep resentment of America's draft laws unjustly making felons out of those who refused to participate in violence.

When I arrived home and walked in the door, Jane looked up from Michael Harrington's book, *The Other America: Poverty in the United States.* There was a somber look in her eyes. "What's up?" I asked.

"We need to talk. I was thinking about your draft situation. I think if you *really* wanted us to stay together, you'd either accept a fake deferment or go to Canada with me. At least then we'd have a life together."

"You know those aren't options for me. I want us to stay together, Jane."

"You say that, but . . ." Her face tightened. "I'm beginning to think *you're* crazy and that *I'm* crazy for putting up with this."

I countered, "I don't like this situation any more than you do." She didn't seem convinced. "Stay with me on this," I said. "In only a few weeks, I'll be appealing my case with a personal appearance before my draft board. I should have a much better chance this time. It's one thing for them to read what I believe in as a CO on paper; it's another for them to hear and see me in person, don't you think?"

Jane didn't answer directly, but her eyes said, *It's hopeless.*

The night before I was to fly to Virginia for the interview with my draft board, I felt compelled to visit my favorite reef at Windansea.

I stepped up onto the reef now illuminated by the Moon and took a deep breath. In meditation, I decided I would make a point of apologizing to Jane and my parents for putting them through the hellish ordeal of my CO stand. And in spirit, I honored all the COs in history who had refused to kill, no matter the cost.

Afterward, I broke into a run along the ocean, then jogged atop a long stretch of smooth sandstone rocks. Suddenly I came to a sizable gap between one rock and another. In the dimness, I couldn't quite judge the distance of the gap. Giving it my all, I took an impetuous leap. Just as I jumped, a large wave roared in fast, broke against the base of the rocks below, and showered me as I barely made it to the next flat rock. Happily out of breath, I felt renewed and ready to face my draft board.

The next day, at my own expense, I flew 3,000 miles cross-country to my Fairfax, Virginia draft board. The pressure was on. I knew this interview might very well make or break my CO case. This was my big chance to turn around the injustice of the draft board's previous rejection.

Dad kindly picked me up at Dulles Airport and drove me to the draft board. As we pulled up to the colonial-style red brick building, my heart started to pound. A lot was on the line.

"Don't wait for me, Dad. This might take a while. I'll cab home."

"Do you want my advice about the interview?"

"Sure."

"Before you talk with them, you should be aware of a liability you have."

"What's that?"

"You have a *big* problem with authority. My point is this—it's not going to help your case to go to war with them."

"I agree. Thanks, Dad."

Anxiously, I entered the draft board office. The reception area contained a dozen or so listless draftees waiting to be called.

I was surprised to see that Joyce, the clerk I had met when I first registered for the draft about three years ago, still worked there. "You probably don't remember me."

"Everybody here is familiar with your case," she said, smiling. "I don't suppose you have your draft card with you?"

"Sorry." I was set for disdain or a lecture, but she simply shrugged.

"Okay. Take a seat, Francesco."

Over an hour passed before Joyce said, "You can go in now. Good luck."

27

FACE-TO-FACE WITH MY DRAFT BOARD

(1969)

"I'm not concerned with your liking or disliking me . . .
All I ask is that you respect me as a human being."

—Jackie Robinson

As I entered the inner sanctum of my Fairfax, Virginia draft board, I froze. My eyes lifted to a huge floor-to-ceiling American flag bordered with gold tassels that covered the entire back wall, dwarfing the three elderly draft board members below it.

"One of our colleagues couldn't make it," a member explained, breaking my stare. I took a seat as the member opened my file and flipped through it. "Let's begin with this question on the CO form: *Under what circumstances, if any, do you believe in the use of force?*

"Well, I believe in the use of force if the force is nonviolent," I began. "I believe in the power of love for social change." Immediately I thought, *How naïve and trite that must sound.* "What I mean is, I see love as a creative force that builds, and violence as a negative force that destroys."

My jitters were making it difficult for me to think and speak coherently. I had imagined myself concisely explaining my personal religion, but now that I was actually before the draft board, I struggled for the right words. *Don't blow this. Calm down.*

"In your application, you mentioned you were against the concept of 'enemy,'" a member noted. "Why is that?"

"I know there are people in this world who do horrible, evil things," I replied, "but in my opinion, the label of 'enemy' doesn't help. It dehumanizes people and makes it too easy to go to war. If you show me a photo of someone and you tell me about his or her family, I'm going to react differently than if you show me the photo and simply say, 'This is the 'enemy.'"

A board member smirked. "Tell that to the Viet Cong!"

"Or Hitler," another chimed in.

I responded, "I'm not saying we should look the other way at atrocities. We need to fight back. But there are different ways to fight. In Denmark, the Danes fought Hitler by letting him occupy their country, then smuggling over 7,000 Jews out of Denmark and into Sweden. Because they *didn't* use guns, something like 99% of Denmark's Jews survived the Holocaust."

Another member asked, "Do you attend church?"

"I attend churches," I said. Immediately I chided myself: *You're here to relate to them, not to be a smart-ass.* "I like the diversity of different religions, and I like being independent. I try to find my own truth instead of letting others decide that for me."

"So you don't believe in God?"

"I agree with Einstein, who said, 'I'm a deeply religious non-believer.' I feel I'm spiritual, just not in a traditional way. For example, when I study the cosmos, I'm filled with reverence. But I don't feel I have to know the answers to appreciate it."

The wrinkled expression on the member's face was one of naked antipathy. "*That's* your belief?" he asked incredulously. "Non-belief?"

"It's not non-belief. It's a personal spiritual religion based on nonviolence. It allows for doubt, for not knowing the mysteries of the universe." I started to add, *or maybe many universes,* but stopped myself. "Just because I don't belong to a church doesn't mean I'm not spiritual. My dad taught me that being religious means showing love here and now. Basically, life is my church, and being kind and altruistic is my way of being religious."

"Who are your role models?"

"Gandhi, Einstein, Cesar Chavez, and Dr. King." I thought, *In their eyes, I just gave them an Asian, a Jew, a Chicano, and an African American—four humanistic rebels they no doubt find suspect at best.*

A member asked, "What about the teachings of Jesus Christ?"

I thought silently, *What about the teachings of Islam, Hinduism, Buddhism, or Judaism?* "The teachings of Jesus on love are important to me, but I don't believe in the super-natural acts described in the Bible." *Don't talk about what you're against. Focus on what you're for.* "I try to look for the positive in religions. Buddha taught that hatred fuels more hatred. The Dalai Lama spoke to that too and said that whatever we win through hatred won't be lasting. I believe that the most effective and moral counter to hate is nonviolent action."

"How often do you attend church?" the member continued.

"Not often, maybe once or twice a year, if that. It depends on how I feel. More important than going to church, in my opinion, is the way I live my life. My dad told me that when his father was asked, what's your religion, he would just point to his heart."

I knew religion was a touchy subject, but I had hoped my draft board would have the open approach of my campus minister who 'agreed to disagree' in a spirit of mutual respect. Instead, the disgruntled expressions on the faces of the draft board members told me I was losing them, or worse, that the interview was over from the start.

"So *no* religion?" a member asked.

"Yes . . . I mean no. Like I said before, I have a personal religion based on nonviolence, on active love."

"What do you think about those who *dodge* the draft?" The tone was accusing.

I thought, *Here we go again with the stereotype myth.* I took a calming breath. "I'm not *dodging* the draft," I began. "The fact that I've applied as a CO and that I'm here talking with you today shows that I'm *facing* the draft. COs, in general, want to serve their country as much as anyone else, but not with a gun."

"What do you think about nonviolent students who become violent?"

"I don't believe in violence whether it's used by students or by the military. Gandhi said that we should make the way we do something just as important as what we want. Violence doesn't solve problems. That's why I'm against the death penalty. Answering one murder with another just adds to the violence."

"You said in your CO application that you don't believe in hunting?"

"That's right. I look at animals as friends. I feel connected to them."

Another member broke in. "Do you feel *any* obligation to serve your country?"

"Yes . . . nonviolently. If people feel they want to join the military and accept being trained to kill, that should be their choice. A true democracy doesn't force people to do that through a draft. And I agree with the United Nations that said every person in every country should have the right not to kill."

"Be honest, Mr. Da Vinci. Aren't you and all the others who say they're COs just taking the *easy* way out?"

My eyes focused on his sneer. I wanted to stay calm, but I could feel resentment rising. Maybe he was baiting me, and if he was, it was working. I felt my sense of peace weakening.

Maybe he wanted to see if I would be a hypocrite to my beliefs. The adrenaline was flowing, and I felt a knee-jerk reaction to deliver a verbal punch. Or better yet . . .

I eyed the member's Styrofoam cup of hot coffee and imagined throwing it on his shirt.

Then the daydream evaporated. "No, I'm not taking the *easy* way out, and neither have COs throughout history. They've made great sacrifices to take their stand."

A member asked, "Did you ever think that COs might be betraying our country?

Countless men have died for the liberties you enjoy, Mr. Da Vinci. It could be argued that COs are greatly undermining and weakening America. What's your response to that?"

"COs question war, and I think that's healthy. If we lose the freedom to question war, I think we're in danger of losing *all* our freedoms."

"In closing, Mr. Da Vinci, is there anything else you wish to add?" a member asked. I could almost hear him thinking, *God, I hope not.*

"Yes. I want each of you to know that I'm not trying to play any games here. I know that by taking my stand, I'm risking prison, but this is who I really am—a conscientious objector. And I can tell you this right now—you may be able to take away my freedom and throw me in jail if you want, but you can *never* take away my right to say, 'I refuse to kill.'"

"I think we've heard quite enough, thank you."

Another member added, "We'll notify you of our decision at our earliest convenience."

I studied six eyes of stone. I didn't expect the draft board members to agree with me. I had only hoped they would make more of an effort to understand my position. After all, their duty today was to determine if I was genuine in my beliefs. Instead, as Jane had suspected, it seemed they were out to punish me for even applying as a CO.

I left the building with a tear in my eye, knowing with almost certainty that injustice would rule.

On my flight back to San Diego, I recalled my draft board interview as best I could and put it down in my journal while my memory was still fresh.

Maddeningly, I played and replayed the interview in my mind, then finally fell asleep against the plane window. It was not a respite, however, because the torture continued in my dreams.

28

RALPH'S MASTER PLAN
(1969)

"It is sometimes an appropriate response to reality to go insane."
—Philip K. Dick

"It's your favorite brother," Ralph said over the phone.

"You're my only brother."

"That's what I mean. I dropped out of college [the University of Tennessee] a while to take a road trip to California. I thought I'd start with San Diego, visit you a day or two, and work my way up the coast, maybe take in a concert or two. How's next weekend?"

"Perfect."

"Any news from Uncle Sam? I don't think he likes you very much."

"I guess you're right. I interviewed with the draft board last week. It didn't go so good."

"Sorry about that," said Ralph.

"What's your draft situation?" I asked.

"I've got it all under control. When I finish talking with the draft board, I'm gonna come out of it smellin' like a rose. I'll tell you about it when I see you."

When Ralph arrived, I took him to one of my favorite Mexican restaurants, El Indio. As soon as we picked up the menus, Ralph asked, "Why are you still hanging onto this CO thing? You don't have a prayer with the draft board."

"I'm not giving up, even if they turn me down again."

"If?"

"Okay, they'll probably turn me down."

"Forget 'probably.'"

"I've still got the right to update my CO claim and reapply."

"You just don't get it. It's no use."

Ralph lit up a cigarette as our waitress came to our table. "What'll it be, guys?"

We ordered burritos, then Ralph said to the waitress, "One other thing. Did you believe in love at first sight, or was it just after you saw me?" With a smirk, the waitress turned and disappeared. "Gee, that was a *great* line," Ralph said, "but I don't think she appreciated it. Guess I'll have to let my looks do the talking." He took a drag on his cigarette and exhaled to the side. "Listen, I've been thinking about your draft situation, and I've got it all figured out. Here are your options as I see 'em, okay? Ready for the master plan?"

"Lay it on me."

"Option one, go to Canada."

"Less than no interest," I said.

"But they do have great health care, and we have none."

"Ironic that we're talkin' about health, and you're dragging on those cancer sticks."

"Don't lecture me, or I'll just end up beggin' for a strait jacket."

"Got it."

"Okay, here's the second option: put yourself in jail and throw away the key. In other words, keep doing what you're doing as a CO."

"Thanks for being totally objective."

"No problem."

The waitress served our burritos, and we dug in. "Okay," Ralph continued. "Here's another option: do the smart thing and get out on a medical deferment."

"What's that mean?"

"The medical way, you injure yourself, temporarily. Of course, don't do anything extreme, like shoot your toes off."

"No thanks."

"Okay, forget that one. Here's the better way—psychiatric. You act wacko. That's what I'm gonna do."

"You're kidding?"

"I kid you not. Right before I go to the draft board, I put a little dish detergent in my left eye. That oughta start it twitchin'."

"You're not gonna ruin your eyes for this, are ya?"

"I hope not, but anything is better than Vietnam. Then every few minutes, I walk in circles. I'll show ya." Ralph stood out in the aisle between tables, leaned to one side a bit, acted jittery, and turned in a circle. "Last," Ralph said, "there's *the look*."

"The look?"

"Yeah, I look at 'em wide-eyed the whole time, with the left one twitching. It won't be over the top. Just enough to let 'em know I'm not dealin' with a full deck." Ralph demonstrated 'the look' while turning in circles. The waitress came by to warm up our coffees and stared at Ralph with alarm. "Am I scarin' you?" he asked.

She stood frozen and nodded.

"That's good!" Ralph exclaimed. "Real good." Happily, he rejoined me in the booth. "So, big brother, you gonna be smart or stupid?"

"I'm gonna be what I am," I said, "a CO."

"You know what you just did? You pulled the Monopoly card—GO DIRECTLY TO JAIL."

Richard Nixon won the presidential campaign of 1968 by one of the closest margins in US history, beating Humphrey by less than 500,000 votes. Nixon campaigned on a "law and order" platform designed to rile the working class and "silent majority." Throughout his campaign, he promised to "bring us together again." Neither Jane nor I ever bought the notion that Nixon would unify the country while continuing the war. And every time I heard Nixon utter that promise of bringing us together again, I thought back to the time I bumped into Bobby Kennedy and said to him, "You're the only one who can bring us back together again." Bobby, I believed, had that potential. It was more than likely that he would have ended the madness in Vietnam, saving thousands of American lives and several million Asian lives. In addition, he would have seriously addressed our social ills at home.

Instead of learning from Johnson's mistakes and implementing a foreign policy of reconciliation, Nixon intensified the already massive bombing of Vietnam, claiming it would lead to "peace with honor." The result was further divisiveness at home and a mounting death toll on both sides of the war.

After a televised broadcast of B-52 bombings that resulted in the deaths of several hundred men, women, and children, I wrote Jerry, who was stationed off the coast of Vietnam aboard the USS *Boston*.

> Dear Jerry,
>
> For years the government has been saying there's light at the end of the tunnel. How long is this tunnel? Every year we're told that the end of the war is in sight, and yet it's dragged on for about four and a half years now. How many more American and Asian deaths will it take until we stop the slaughter?
>
> Please take a hard look at the glaring contradiction between what President Nixon says and what he does. He promised peace, but instead he's escalated the war with massive B-52 bombings, and by April [1969] he brought the total U.S. troop level in South Vietnam up to a record high of 543,000!
>
> Please don't mimic the 'Good German' syndrome and look the other way in the face of our violence in Vietnam. As I've deeply considered

your viewpoint, please consider mine. This war is a tragic mistake, so let's end it and save lives, not face.

peace and friendship,
Francesco

Jerry wrote back about a month later. Every previous letter from my naval officer best buddy had mirrored staunch pro-war sentiment: "Our Commander-in-Chief knows best;" "It's kill or be killed;" "Nonviolence is naïve and for the weak." But this letter expressed deep soul-searching in words that hit me like seismic waves.

Dear Francesco,

Your views for peace and your concern for humanity have had more effect on me than you probably realize. I remain emotionally guarded in this conservative military context, but the good that was done in our talks will not ebb away. Currently I am 5200 yards off the DMZ in my stateroom. Soon I will stand a four-hour watch in the Main Engine Control, which involves making certain our steam plant is correctly turning the turbines. When in battle I am the Officer in Charge of Secondary Damage Control Central, the defensive arm of the ship. At least I am not pulling any triggers but as a repair officer I must admit I am indeed contributing. I do not agree with everything we are doing here but of course that is another subject we will undoubtedly talk about when we see each other again.

When the guns fire it is deafening. At night, add blinding. Flares and bombs burst on the land and we are certainly close enough to see everything. We try to stay off the main deck because people fire at us. No doubt about it—we are armed and trained to kill. My defenses, psychologically, will not allow me to become depressed, not often anyhow. Others do not fare so well. One of my close buddies, who fired the guns, finally could not take it anymore. One night in the middle of his shift, he snapped and said to an officer, "Stick it! I won't kill anymore!" He was taken away, but his conscience is clearer. It struck me that he was *immediately* replaced. That's why nonviolence will never work—because there will *always* be someone to pull the trigger.

Admittedly, though, I'm having serious second thoughts about the wisdom of this war and my participation in it.

I have to run, buddy. I have the watch.

Jerry

Ralph, Pre-Fake Psychosis, 1965. (Photo: F. Da Vinci)

Jerry's ship, the USS *Boston*.

29

PEOPLE'S PARK—BLOODY THURSDAY

(May 1969)

"Let A Thousand Parks Bloom"

—AIRPLANE BANNER OVER PEOPLE'S PARK

"If it takes a bloodbath, let's get it over with. No more appeasement."

—GOVERNOR RONALD REAGAN

Upon returning from my draft board interview in Virginia, I wrote the members to protest the hearing. I noted that they did not seem concerned about the sincerity of my views as much as they did with expressing their disapproval of my beliefs. I also mentioned that undue emphasis had been placed on Christianity and "church attendance."

After I read the letter to Jane, she said, "I'm sure you were overly direct with the draft board. Did you quote Einstein on religion?"

I winced.

"Of course you did," she said.

"I wanted to be straightforward with them so they'd see I'm sincere."

Jane went to the window and looked off.

"Do you want to talk about this?" I asked.

"Not really . . . not now."

After a few moments, I said, "Look, Jane, we're all talked out, and we're driving each other nuts. It's going to be a while before the draft board rejects or accepts my CO application, so let's take a break and maybe drive up the coast."

I could see the indecision in her eyes. Then she smiled slightly as if purging doubts.

"A getaway does sound good. Where would we go?"

"How about San Francisco for a few days." I put my arms around her.

"I guess the romance could use a little spark."

"Screw the draft," I said. "Just you, me, and one whole week of peace."

We checked into a modest yet charming hotel in Berkeley. Jane sat on the edge of the bed perusing a travel booklet, "Great Cheap Eats in San Francisco." I sat down next to her, and she asked, "Are you in the mood for pasta or Chinese?"

I took the book out of her hand and tossed it over my shoulder. Jane looked at me with surprise. We kissed passionately and fell back on the bed.

As the room brightened the next morning, Jane and I snuggled up in bed, half-watching TV, when a news bulletin appeared. The newswoman said that a serious battle had broken out between police and students. Yesterday's clash, she said, was referred to as 'Bloody Thursday' because the police had shot and gassed student protesters. Later, Jane and I picked up a few newspapers and read what led to the violence.

Neighborhood residents had invested their money, time, and energy into improving People's Park in Berkeley, a university-owned parcel, adding things like turf, swings for children, and picnic tables. But the chancellor of the Berkeley campus stated he would reclaim the park and convert it to a parking lot.

About 6,000 students and community members were rallying to protest the university administration takeover. Governor Reagan had intensified the polarization by characterizing the Berkeley student demonstrators as "communist sympathizers" and "sex deviants." Berkeley police, aided by state troopers, Alameda County sheriffs, and eventually the National Guard, confronted the demonstrators. Only exacerbating tensions, thoughtless students threw rocks and bottles at the police.

Even as the protesters retreated, sheriff's deputies chased them down Telegraph Avenue firing tear gas canisters. (In 1993, the International Chemical Weapons Convention, with the agreement of the U.S., would ban the use of tear gas in warfare. But countries like the U.S. insisted on the right to use it against its own people for "riot control," despite warnings from health agencies that tear gas was excessive and could inflict serious injuries, even death to people with pre-existing conditions). In addition to the tear gas, a helicopter sprayed the University of California campus with pepper gas. School children as far as two miles away became sick.

As the protestors fled, deputies fired birdshot into their backs. Some deputies used buckshot (larger lead pellets). James Rector, a 26-year old laborer, was shot to death, and Alan Blanchard, a carpenter and father of a three-month-old boy, was blinded. Blanchard and a friend he worked with had been standing on the roof of a two-story building when they saw a red-haired young man holding a rock in each hand. They yelled at him to stop, but the rocks were launched, landing without hitting anyone. Several deputies spun around and fired their shotguns toward the roofs. Birdshot struck both of Blanchard's eyes, and he was permanently blinded. At least 128 Berkeley residents were admitted to local hospitals.

Incensed by the unnecessary shooting, I told Jane, "I want to go to the rally today and give 'em my support. I want to show 'em we're not afraid."

"Great," Jane said. "Let's go and save the park."

"I meant I'm going alone. I'll meet you here later. It has to be that way. It's too risky for both of us to go."

"How about if *you* wait here, and *I* go to the march."

"Look, I'm serious about this. Yesterday they *killed* someone and blinded another, not to mention everyone they sent to the hospital."

"You can't *tell* me not to go to the park!" Jane said angrily. "I thought you believed in equal rights?" She looked at me hard and raised an eyebrow.

"Fine, but I don't like it, not a bit. If you change your mind . . ."

"I'm not changing my mind."

I studied her eyes, hoping to see a sliver of doubt. I only saw determination.

At the march, Jane and I merged with the crowd and headed toward People's Park. In San Diego, the over-thirty generation looked at us as 'hippies.' But here in San Francisco, we were conservative-looking.

At the beginning of the march, the mood was surprisingly friendly and upbeat. I had expected the air to be filled with tension. Instead, police officers leaned back against their patrol cars, smiling at the protesters, who smiled back. After yesterday's brutality, the word must have gone out to cool things down. Along the way, I spotted a strikingly angelic boy, maybe four years old, who had a red peace sign painted on his forehead. He looked so iconic for the sixties that I simply *had* to take a photo of him.

Shortly afterward, we came upon a police officer who was offered a flower by a student. The officer hesitated at first, then accepted the flower and fastened it to his shirt. All the on-lookers, including Jane and I, cheered him.

At one point, a half dozen topless women, wearing only jeans or bikini bottoms, danced past us. A few rode on the shoulders of their boyfriends. Their bodies were painted in swirling psychedelic patterns. Once we reached People's Park, however, the calm, even joyful, mood changed dramatically.

On the front line of the protest, we faced a legion of grim National Guard troops. We were divided from the troops only by a forbidding chain-link fence that protesters decorated with daisies in memory of James Rector, killed in yesterday's shooting. For a few moments, I closed my eyes in meditation for him.

My picture-taking drew the attention of a few of the troops, who stared cautiously, brandishing their bayoneted rifles. When I felt I had enough shots, Jane tapped me on the shoulder. "Okay, we showed our support, and we showed 'em we're not afraid," she said. "Ready to go back home?"

"Yeah, I guess so." But I couldn't quite shake the images surrounding us: the barbed wire fences and swarms of armed troops. As Assemblyman John Burton put it, Governor Reagan had turned Berkeley into "his own Vietnam."

Unfortunately, Governor Reagan never did express any regret for the death of James Rector, never addressed the fact that Sheriff Madigan had lied about issuing lethal buckshot to his deputies, and never condemned the excessive police force and shootings.

Only years later did I learn that Reagan was spying for the FBI. That revelation came in Seth Rosenfeld's 2013 book, *Subversives: The FBI's War on Student Radicals, and Reagan's Rise to Power.* Hoover and Reagan were friends, and as an informer, Reagan would gather information on people he suspected to be Communists or have Communist leanings. Pretending to be a member of a politically liberal organization, for example, he took the minutes from the meeting and handed them over to the FBI. In turn, the FBI secretly helped Reagan with his political career. Once again, I found myself asking, *The checks and balances are there in our Constitution, but where are they in practice?*

People's Park March. (Photo: F. Da Vinci)

Policeman & flower, People's Park March, May 1969. (Photo: F. Da Vinci)

People's Park, May 1969. (Photo: F. Da Vinci)

30

FIRST HUMAN ON THE MOON
(July 20, 1969)

"We came in peace for all mankind."

—Plaque on the lunar landing vehicle

Only five months remained in one of the most turbulent and progressive decades in American history. I reflected that the 1960s era was nothing less than a cultural and political revolution. And with so many jam-packed major changes in only a decade, one wondered if history's drama had reached its zenith.

But in a time when the norm was synonymous with the extraordinary, another epic event was on the cusp of unfolding. This one, however, was neither in terms of U.S. history nor even world history. It was in terms of the whole history of humanity!

As a bona fide space nerd, I slept erratically the night before the scheduled launch of Apollo 11. Eight years ago, on May 25, 1961, President Kennedy had set an ambitious goal of putting an American on the Moon before the end of the decade.

About 6 A.M., on Wednesday, July 16, 1969, I guided Jane in her sleepy traipse to the TV to watch the historic liftoff. The courageous crew consisted of astronauts Michael Collins, Buzz Aldrin, and Neil Armstrong. I had been following their careers for so long that I even knew their birthdays: Michael—Halloween; Buzz—Inauguration Day; and Neil—August 5th. Coincidentally, all three were born in 1930.

Jane gazed at the Cape Kennedy broadcast through half-open eyes. "Why are we doing this? I don't remember."

I looked at her incredulously. "It's the launch to put humans on the Moon! C'mon, Jane, imagine you get to watch the Wright Brothers launch the first airplane flight at Kitty Hawk!"

"It's a dream come true," Jane said wryly.

"Okay, look at it this way. Think about how it took life on Earth about 4 *billion* years of evolution to get to this day!"

"Goosebumps."

"You're hopeless."

I didn't know it at the time, but Armstrong was paying tribute to the historic Kitty Hawk flight by packing in his "personal preference kit" fragments of the 1903 Wright Flyer plane—a shard of wood from the left propeller and a piece of fabric from the upper left wing. I also wasn't privy to the fact that Charles Lindbergh, the first human to fly solo across the Atlantic Ocean, met privately with the Apollo 11 crew before their flight.

The 6:32 A.M. launch (PST) went flawlessly, and the Apollo 11 Saturn V rocket reached the speed necessary to escape Earth's gravity—seven miles per second. Finally, I was able to exhale. Jane, however, yawned through the launch, then went to her social work job.

On the drive to my grad school, I recalled the indelible *Earthrise* photo taken by astronaut Bill Anders in 1968. The first astronauts to orbit the Moon watched the Earth rise above the rocky, cratered rim. Anders exclaimed, "Oh my god! Look at that picture over there! There's the Earth coming up. Wow, that's pretty."

In rebellion of strict NASA protocol, Borman joked, "Hey, don't take that; it's not scheduled."

The iconic photo that Anders took (1/250th of a second at f/11) revealed an image that many said sparked the environmental movement—a moonscape pulverized by meteors stood in sharp contrast with our 'blue marble' planet. Over the rim of the barren Moon rose a world boasting life. Suddenly the wonder the astronauts felt viewing the Moon was shifted back home. Astronaut Frank Borman later said, "All the love songs that have been written about the Moon should have been written about the Earth."

Watching the images on television, I studied the contrasting worlds and wondered, Might our lunar neighbor serve as a warning, offering a preview of Earth as a wasteland destroyed by warring nations convinced they were acting on the highest notions of patriotism?

Modern humans had been around for 200,000 years, locked into a cycle of grisly wars. I wondered, *Will we someday stop rationalizing our violence and evolve enough to end our glorification of war? Or, will we stay on the path of ever-increasing technology misdirected for war, culminating in Armageddon?*

I felt saddened that we were venturing to the Moon when we still had not learned how to live on Earth. We lived on a planet where humans, the 'advanced' species, threatened each other with nuclear war, on a planet where two-thirds of the people lived in the narrow margin between poverty and starvation. In the realm of our solar system, only Earth was teeming with life. Perhaps, I hoped, space exploration would awaken humanity to the dire need for change among the super powers—a major redistribution of wealth coupled with a reduction of their excessive military budgets. Without the conversion of war economies to peace economies and without corporations paying their fair share, the gap between the haves and the have-nots would continue to widen. The result—a needless cycle of global suffering and death.

But, one step at a time. I figured I'd do whatever I could within my microcosm -becoming recognized as a conscientious objector while taking action to help stop the war in Vietnam.

When I returned home from grad school that day, I hurriedly checked the mail before going upstairs, excited to re-watch the launch of Apollo 11 on television. But when I opened the mailbox, my excitement crash-landed. Slowly I withdrew the brown envelope from Selective Service, knowing it contained the verdict of my Virginia draft board.

Considering that my face-to-face interview had been so strongly biased, I expected rejection of my CO claim. Yet, against all reason, I hoped for justice. It was in vain. My CO claim was not only rejected by a majority; it was rejected once again by a vote of four to nothing.

I skimmed the rest of the letter. In thirteen days I was to report to the Los Angeles Induction Center for a second pre-induction physical.

When Jane returned from work that evening, I told her about the turndown of my CO claim. Already cranky from lack of sleep, she shook her head bitterly. I took her in my arms in a silence that seemed deafening.

Before I took my second pre-induction physical, I hoped to find a draft lawyer to represent my CO case and give me counsel. But I was having a heck of a time finding one.

It was nothing new. Over the last four years, seven draft attorneys had passed me off like a hot potato. Each one confessed that they saw my case as hopeless, especially since, in their view, I wasn't willing to "compromise" and avoid the draft with a fake deferment. Out of genuine concern for my welfare, draft lawyers urged me to be "sensible" and, in their eyes, give up my chosen path of "self-sabotage."

Thankfully, I found a new attorney at the last minute who accepted my commitment to face the draft honestly. Carol articulately, and in clear language rather than legalese, advised that I declare my conscientious objection immediately after taking my pre-induction physical. "After that," she explained, "your local draft board in Virginia will decide whether or not to honor your appeal."

With my pre-induction physical only nine days away, the big day for Neil Armstrong's walk on the Moon arrived—Sunday, July 20th, 1969. It was a welcome distraction from the draft and war that raged in Vietnam.

Glued to our TV, Jane and I watched epic history in the making along with 500 million others around the world. In grainy black and white, the TV screen image was captioned: LIVE FROM THE SURFACE OF THE MOON. *Wow*, I thought, *we've left the cradle of spaceship Earth and are about to take our first baby steps into the Cosmos!*

Walter Cronkite commentated for CBS with guest-host astronaut Wally Schirra. When Armstrong descended to the last rung of the ladder, he would have to hop 3.5 feet to the Moon's surface. I wondered why NASA had not added another rung to make it easier for Neil to set foot on the Moon. Actually, I later learned, there *were* enough rungs. But Neil had set the Eagle down so skillfully and gently, the shock absorbers did not compress as expected.

At 7:56 P.M. (PST), Neil Alden Armstrong, an Ohio native, but today more an ambassador of Earth, planted his left foot, size 9-B, into about an inch of moondust. "That's one small step for a man, one giant leap for mankind." What a timeless moment! Even Walter Cronkite choked up, blurting to his co-host, "Wally, say something . . . I'm speechless!"

Unfortunately for the Russian people, their party leaders decided not to show live coverage of the Moon landing, which cosmonaut Alexey Leonov described in his journal as "a most stupid and short-sighted political decision, stemming from both pride and envy."

Nineteen minutes after Armstrong set foot on the Moon, Astronaut Buzz Aldrin descended the ladder. Unfortunately, as Buzz took the large leap from the bottom rung of the module ladder onto the Moon, his urine collection device broke. Buzz's left boot filled up with urine, and every step he took was sloshy.

Aldrin handed Neil a TV camera, and Neil aimed it at a small plaque affixed to the leg of the lunar landing vehicle. The plaque read: "Here men from planet Earth first set foot upon the Moon. July 1969 A.D. We came in peace for all mankind."

As super-thrilled as I was with the landing, and as super-proud of our three astronauts and the 400,000 NASA employees who made the journey possible, I had two reservations. First, while we came "in peace" to the Moon, back home, the war in Vietnam continued to maim and kill without an end in sight. Also, I wished the plaque didn't use male-dominated language. It could have read, Here *humans* from planet Earth first set foot upon the Moon. We came in peace for all *humanity.*

Journalist I.F. Stone had a different version in mind: "Here men first set foot outside the Earth on their way to the far stars. They speak of peace, but wherever they go, they bring war."

Jane surprised me when she said, "I had no idea how touched I'd be by the moonwalk."

I smiled. "I don't know if there's ever been a day like this. Today everyone on Earth is one family."

Little did I realize what the future would hold—that my hero Neil Armstrong would become one of my very best friends for over 20 years. It came about serendipitously. In the 1980s, I became Bob Hope's main photographer for his TV specials. During Bob's NASA show, featuring Armstrong as the honored guest, Neil and I met and later became best buddies. We corresponded regularly by email for two decades, right up until his death in 2012 due to heart problems.

Our last email exchange took place three weeks before Neil died:

> Hi Neil,
>
> You were about 20 years old when you were at the Naval Air Station North Island on Coronado [1950]. What was that stage of your life like? When I was about that age I had no idea what I would do for a career. After college, I majored in social psychology and went to grad school in San Diego around 1969. It was a brand new school called U.S. International University and it was right next to Miramar Naval Air Station ("Top Gun"). I had a convertible, and when I drove to classes I'd glimpse the jets flying overhead.
>
> Francesco

Neil replied:

> Hello Francesco,
>
> As a young jet pilot in those early days of the jets, I was completely immersed in trying to learn all I could about jets, aerial warfare, and tactics.
>
> Miramar was not open at the time, but had opened by the time we returned to the U.S. in mid-1952 [during the Korean War].
>
> neil

Over 20 years, Neil always signed his emails 'neil' in small letters or 'n.a.' What a wonderful role model he was for me and countless others. Always a mentor, Neil encouraged students to dare greatly and further space exploration: "There are places to go beyond belief. Those challenges are yours—in many fields, not the least of which is space, because there lies human destiny."

How I cherished our friendship! On one occasion, I met up with Neil and his wife, Carol, in New York. After brunch at Sarabeth's Restaurant on the upper eastside, I wanted to hug Neil goodbye, but I hesitated. I knew full well that he wasn't the demonstrative type. Yet something told me it was important to express my gratitude for our long-lasting friendship. When I hugged him, it was a bit awkward, but I was glad I did it. It turned out to be the last time I saw Neil before he died. On the evening of Neil's moonwalk, my brother Ralph called at 3:30 A.M. In a slightly slurred voice, he said, "I called 'cause I knew you'd be super psyched about Armstrong's moonwalk."

I had a mixed reaction hearing my brother's voice. It was always great to hear from him, but as was often the case, his tone was off due to downers or alcohol. "Yeah, I'm *very* psyched," I said. "In fact, I wish I was up there with Neil and Buzz, kicking up moondust. Where are you calling from?"

"I'm in San Francisco with a few buddies. We just came back from an Iron Butterfly concert, you know, the group that started a couple of years ago in San Diego."

"They did 'In-A-Gadda-Da-Vida,' right?"

"One of the best songs *ever!* Okay, picture this: Country Joe and the Fish are playing, and on a huge screen behind them, they show Armstrong walking on the Moon! What a combo! I'll never forget it." Ralph paused in reflection. "On second thought, I probably will. I'm kinda loaded. But hey, I remember it now, and I called to share it with you! Later." *Click.*

On July 24th, the three Apollo 11 astronauts returned from the Moon safely and splashed down in the Pacific just before dawn. They spent 21 days in quarantine for fear that they might bring back harmful pathogens from the lunar surface and unleash a modern plague on Earth. Many downplayed the risk of a worldwide pandemic—a situation we became all too familiar with in 2020 with COVID-19. Carl Sagan was a strong advocate on the side of scrupulous precautions—a better-safe-than-sorry logic. But to Sagan's dismay, there were numerous breaches in protocol. For example, when the space command module hit the water and divers opened the door, moondust got into the sea. Theoretically, there was the potential of contaminating our entire ocean biosphere. Other shaky procedures included the astronauts sharing a helicopter ride with navy pilots and the walk of the astronauts across the deck of the USS *Hornet* before entering the quarantine facility. Also, even after the astronauts were placed in the quarantine trailer in Houston, Buzz Aldrin reported that ants somehow found their way into the facility capsule.

The same day of the Apollo 11 splashdown, I met with my eighth draft attorney, Carol, at her San Diego office. She, like many dedicated draft attorneys, kindly donated her services out of moral opposition to the draft and the war.

As Carol looked over my CO file, I studied her features. She had dark shoulder-length hair, wore glasses, and had the pale, delicate face of a librarian who doesn't get out much. Extremely bright, she knew the draft laws inside and out. "Sorry that you have to go through a second pre-induction physical, Francesco, especially after that illegal detainment at Ft. Holabird, but it's a necessary step for becoming a CO."

"What if they try and detain me like they did before?"

"It's *very* unlikely that they would do that. I wouldn't worry about it." She handed me her card. "After the physical, declare that you're a CO, then call me. It should go smooth as silk."

Apollo 11 Crew, 20-year Reunion. L-R: Buzz Aldrin, Michael Collins, and Neil Armstrong. (Photo: F. Da Vinci)

Neil Armstrong and me on the set of a Bob Hope television special.

Portrait of Neil Armstrong, 1989. (Photo: F. Da Vinci)

31

PRE-INDUCTION ORDER TWO—LOS ANGELES

(1969)

"I honestly do not know if civil disobedience has any effect on the government. I can promise you it has a great effect on the person who chooses to do it."

—Martin Sheen

In the soft light of the dawn, I walked uneasily toward the entrance of the downtown Los Angeles induction center. A voice that pierced the air belonged to a petite young woman in a yellow dress who stood on a wooden platform. With restrained emotion, she called out the names and ages of those killed in the Vietnam war: "Dustin Leoni, 18 . . . Keith Simon, 21 . . . Jim Martinez, 20 . . ." The woman's steady call embodied a mixed tone of anguish and spiritual resolve. "The average age of an American soldier's death in Vietnam is 23," she said. The woman in yellow seemed the narrator of a tragic Orwellian opera. Behind her, gold letters beckoned on a large picture window: ARMED FORCES EXAMINING ENTRANCE STATION.

As dozens and dozens of draftees converged and filed into the entrance, I joined in, all the while listening to the young woman's heartfelt soliloquy. At the entrance to the induction center, I paused.

". . . Joseph Weinberg, 25 . . . Michael Sharp, 22 . . ."

As draftees passed by, I felt deeply agitated and bitter towards Presidents Johnson and Nixon for their crimes against humanity. How callous and misguided they seemed for continuing the bombing primarily because they did not want to be the first American president to lose a war. It was heart-wrenching enough seeing the slaughtered soldiers on both sides, but particularly traumatic were the news images of Asian children mutilated and killed by our napalm and bomb drops.

A battle raged in my mind as I stood at the doorway, listening to the woman's mezzo-soprano voice and its lament. A burning obligation to protest the killing mounted, compelling me to walk out on the pre-induction. But I knew if I did leave, I would jeopardize my CO case and likely increase the length of my prison sentence.

As a conscious act of civil disobedience, I started out the lighted doorway when an officer quickly stepped up and asked, "Where the hell do you think you're going? Get back in here and take a seat!" The nearby draftees stared, waiting for my reply.

"In conscience, I can't stay . . . I . . . I won't stay . . ." I stumbled.

Outside, I took a deep breath, and even though the woman in the yellow dress was oblivious to my presence, I nodded a thank you to her for her courage and service. The woman's spiritual strength moved me, so much so that I felt compelled to take her picture.

I fetched my camera from the trunk of my car, returned to the induction center, and photographed the woman as she read the names. I also took photos of the recruitment windows behind her that glamourized war with posters and medals. One poster featured combat soldiers holding their rifles high in the air, their faces contorted with anger. The large caption read: LEARN TO LEAD.

Suddenly I remembered my promise to call Carol, my draft attorney. From a phone booth I dialed the number, then hung up before she could answer. I knew Carol wasn't going to like what I had done. Aware that my hesitation magnified my fear, I made myself redial. She came on the line and asked cheerfully, "So how'd it go? Smooth as silk, right?"

"Sorry, Carol, but I walked out."

"*What?* Why?"

"The war process . . . it's totally insane. When I got here, the first thing I saw was a woman reading the names of soldiers killed in Vietnam. So many . . . and for what? Can you hear the names?" I held the receiver out.

"Yes, I hear them. It's *terrible*, I know, but I need you to listen to me carefully. I want you to go straight back in that induction center!"

I sighed, one hand holding the phone, the other holding my head.

"Francesco, are you listening to me?"

"Yes . . . and to the names."

"*Please*," she begged, "I want you to hang up this phone and get back in there before it's too late!"

"I can't do that."

"For God's sake, go back in, or whatever slim chance you have now as a CO is going to be wiped out! Gone!"

I stared at the woman in yellow performing her onerous duty, her voice occasionally breaking with emotion. "I'm sorry, Carol, but I'm not going back in. I know it doesn't make sense on a practical level, but . . . well, it's my way of saying no to the killing."

I waited for her retort. Instead, she broke down and sobbed.

"Carol, you okay?"

"No, I'm not, and I'm not going to stand by while you throw yourself in jail! You need to get another lawyer." *Click!*

My head still spinning, I headed south to San Diego along the freeway. Not far along the drive, I came upon a huge Marine Corps Base—Camp Pendleton, which is comparable in size to Rhode Island. My weariness gave way to wide-eyed intrigue as a massive dust cloud rose from the hills of the base and darkened the sky.

Out of nowhere, a furious, thumping sound came louder and louder. The sound escalated, turned thunderous, and made my car vibrate. As I stuck my head out the window, a helicopter swooped so low that I almost swerved off the freeway. The copter sped off toward a distant hill where a battalion of infantrymen swarmed over a mound like ants. In the dimness beyond the soldiers, a sign made out of large white stones read: WAR IS OUR BUSINESS, AND BUSINESS IS GOOD!

Upon returning home, I sat down with Jane at the dining room table and broke the news that I had walked out on my pre-induction physical. Her jaw clenched. She gave me a look that could kill and said, "I can't believe you did that. So what the hell happens now? What did your lawyer say?"

"She dropped the case."

Angrily, Jane grabbed the paperweight beside her and hurled it through the dining room window. I flinched at the explosion of glass. "You're ruining our life," Jane moaned. A tear ran down her cheek, and I held her. Over her shoulder, I stared at the glass fragments on the floor, struck by a moment of clarity. I saw how much pain I was putting Jane through. And yet, despite the pain I was causing the person I loved most in the world, I knew I wouldn't back down from declaring myself a conscientious objector to war.

Our situation was impossible. Until my CO case was resolved, Jane would inevitably suffer the pain that I caused by my stand, and I would suffer the pain of guilt.

Woman reading the names of the Vietnam war dead at the Los Angeles Induction Center, 1969. (Photo: F. Da Vinci)

32

PRE-INDUCTION ORDER THREE— OAKLAND

(1969)

"Tempt not a desperate man."

- William Shakespeare

After I walked out on my pre-induction physical in LA, my new draft attorney suggested changing the site of my upcoming physical exam. "Now that you've become persona non grata at the LA induction center, I think it's best we transfer your physical to Oakland," he said. "The atmosphere there is different. Less hostile. The Oakland center is getting record numbers of guys refusing the war."

In May 1969, the Oakland induction center reported that out of 4,400 men ordered to report for induction, 2,400 did not show up.

The attorney continued, "Let's face it. Your two pre-induction calls at Ft. Holabird and LA were unmitigated disasters. You're already on thin ice, Da Vinci, so let's not walk out on this one." He tapped his head. "Nothing mishugina, okay?"

"I'll do my best."

"If you won't cooperate for yourself, then think about not making waves for your girlfriend and family. Otherwise, you're going to be behind bars for quite a while. You going to go with the flow this time?"

"I'll try."

"Try? Oy."

At the Oakland Induction Center, several hundred inductees, wearing only underwear, went from one long processing line to another. We were inspected like pieces of meat and stamped by Uncle Sam as either rejects or ready for war.

In the line to have blood taken, a tall, bulky guy in front of me fidgeted nervously, opening and closing his hands and wiping his beaded forehead. When he became next in line, he began swaying, forward and back, then toppled. I lunged forward, cupping my hands under his head to break his impact. We both hit the floor hard, and when I freed my arms from under his huge hulk, I saw that he was out cold.

Not one inductee around us offered to help. They simply held their place in line. I summoned an officer who looked down on the motionless draftee with annoyance. "He'll be alright. Leave him alone." Gradually the draftee came to, seemingly more embarrassed than hurt.

Like sheep, we were herded along a thick line of gaffer tape on the floor. A long-haired draftee looked at me as if he sensed my skepticism of the whole process. "We're all just a bunch of numbers, aren't we?" he asked.

I nodded and smiled. Near the end of the ordeal, a doctor gave me a cursory exam. Weary and fresh out of tact, I said, "Would you agree, this whole thing is pretty nuts?"

He put aside his paperwork and looked me dead in the eye. I wondered if he was going to freak out and yell at me. Instead, he said, "It's only crazy if you *think*." I laughed, and he asked, "Any medical problems?"

"No."

"How about back problems? Looks like you might have a little scoliosis . . . curvature of the spine." His eyes held mine, and he added, "Back problems can be *very* debilitating." I stood silently, absorbing the Faustian bargain.

For a moment, I entertained a sweet scenario: returning home to Jane with the news that we were finally free of the draft—forever. I imagined how easy our life would be in comparison to the daily insecurity and stress we endured.

A year ago, I would have instantly said *no* to the doctor's offer, but seeing Jane in constant psychic pain was wearing me down. The collective voices of Jane, my parents, and my eight past draft lawyers seemed to say in chorus: *You may never get a chance like this again! Take the deferment!* But a moment later, I felt disappointed with myself for even giving the offer pause.

"You won't have to do a thing," the doctor offered. "I'll take care of all the paperwork, and you'll be good to go."

"No thanks, that's okay," I said weakly.

The doctor must have seen my torment. "You *sure*?"

I didn't even want to hear myself say yes, so I waved thanks and moved on.

At the end of the maze, while waiting in a large common area to be dismissed for the day, I asked an officer, "What's that group of men across the room?"

"They're resisters," he answered. "They refused the draft."

About a dozen young men had been sectioned off from the rest of us like bad apples.

Philosophically, I agreed with 'resisters' and their passionate aversion to war, but I differed concerning total non-cooperation. As a CO, I believed in going on record and affirming my beliefs to my draft board rather than not allowing for dialogue.

The officer I spoke with looked at the draft resisters without judgment and said, "Everyone's gotta do what they gotta do."

I walked over to the resisters to offer my moral support. "I'm a CO," I began. The group's collective glum expressions blossomed into a wave of smiles. A few resisters stood and shook my hand.

"Don't talk to those cowards!" someone yelled. I turned, expecting to see a military officer. The order, however, had been issued from a tall, thin draftee with close-cropped hair.

A resister glared at him. "Does goin' to 'Nam make you a big man?"

"I can't wait to go!"

The resister's voice rose. "You gotta go, alright!"

"Oh, yeah?"

"Yeah!"

They were nose to nose when an officer shouted, "SHUT THE FUCK UP!!" The whole room went silent as the men backed away from one another. Shortly afterward, everyone was dismissed except for the resisters, who I knew would soon be behind bars. I took a last look at them before I left and thought, *For refusing one system of violence, they'll be thrown into another.*

When the mind-numbing induction process ended, I started the long peaceful drive from the Bay Area down to San Diego.

At a roadside scenic pullover that overlooked the transcendent coast, I meditated: *I'm going to use the year or two I have left before prison to work for peace.*

When I arrived home, Jane was just getting home from work. "How did it go?" she asked cautiously.

"Fine," I answered. "No walkout this time."

She threw her arms around my neck and gave me a big kiss.

I smiled, but in the back of my mind I wondered if I had endangered our relationship for the future by not taking the doctor's offer of a permanent deferment. Valuing my life, there was no way I would tell her about the doctor's proposal! But by hiding that offer, I uneasily asked myself if I was lying to her by omission and being a hypocrite to everything I was trying to stand for.

A key issue in my CO case was "religious" versus "non-religious but spiritual," so when Jane and I learned that the comedian Woody Allen would be debating the Reverend Bill Graham on national television, we made a point of catching the special.

I related to Woody's perspective of *not* relating to any particular organized religion. If I had to label my spiritual beliefs, I might describe them as Buddhist-like, agnostic altruism.

I figured most viewers of the Allen-Graham debate would regard it as a battle of non-faith vs. faith. But I looked at it as non-traditional faith vs. traditional faith. In the words of Woody, "To YOU I'm an atheist; to God, I'm the Loyal Opposition."

Woody asked Billy Graham what his favorite commandment was. Billy answered, "Honor thy father and mother," to which Woody replied, "That's my *least* favorite commandment."

Jane laughed and said, "My thought exactly!"

After the fun, thought-provoking parley, I commented to Jane, "Both Woody and the Reverend totally disagreed with each other, but they stayed civil and respected their differences. That's what America is supposed to be all about."

"Like you and Jerry," Jane said.

I felt the program did a great service by promoting tolerance of religious differences, so I wrote Woody a thank you letter:

> Dear Mr. Woody Allen,
>
> Many of our leaders seem to have forgotten that freedom of religious thought is one of the basic principles that our country was founded upon. I can't understand why so many people insist on being judgmental and hitting others over the head with their particular views. Freedom of traditional religion also means freedom of *no* traditional religion. Your debate with the Reverend Billy Graham will hopefully encourage Americans to not only *tolerate* each other's differences, but to *celebrate* them. Personally, I'm a conscientious objector with spiritual but non-traditional religious views. Following my beliefs, I would rather go to prison than be trained to kill my fellow human beings. Meanwhile, my best friend, a devout Catholic, is serving in Vietnam. Out of mutual respect, we've never let our strong differences sway us into animosity. Perhaps, if there were more courteous celebrations of diversity in America, such as your debate with the Reverend Billy Graham, there would be less prejudice and war. Thanks again for the mannerly exercise in democracy!"

To my utter amazement, Woody took the time to write back. By coincidence, his letter was dated October 2nd—Gandhi's birthday. I read the letter to Jane.

> Dear Mr. Da Vinci:
>
> Thanks so much for your letter. I really mean that. I've had quite a lot of mail about the Special and Dr. Graham and I haven't so far had a better one. I'm glad that you liked the show. You are the kind of audience that I aim for.
>
> With all best wishes.
>
> Sincerely,
> Woody Allen

My 'spiritual but non-religious' stand with my draft board made my CO case particularly difficult. When I first applied as a CO in 1968, conscientious objection had a narrow focus. You were expected to belong to an organized religion. Later, in *Gillette v. United States* (1971), a U.S. Supreme Court decision broadened the conscientious objection criteria to include anyone who "has deeply held beliefs that cause them to oppose participation in war in any form."

Prior to that decision, my Virginia draft board seemed to scorn my "personal religion of nonviolence and active love." As atheist humor writer Dave Barry put it, "The problem with writing about religion is that you run the risk of offending sincerely religious people, and then they come after you with machetes."

33

THE VIETNAM MORATORIUMS

(October 15 and November 15, 1969)

"All we are saying is give peace a chance."
—John Lennon

The concept behind the Vietnam Moratorium planned for mid-October was to ask people to take a day off from work to march for peace. Or, if they went to work, they were asked to raise the issue of the war at their jobs. Together with other local activists, I held a meeting to plan a moratorium march in San Diego.

I felt dismayed that so many in our group were pessimistic about the chances of pulling off a successful march against the war. As one prominent leader said, "It's a great idea, but I don't see how we'll *ever* get enough support to get it off the ground in *Navy Town USA*! And if we do put together a march, I can almost guarantee it's going to be so small it'll be an embarrassment to the peace movement."

"We've gotta try."

He looked at me skeptically. "You think this'll work, then prove me wrong."

That was all I needed to hear.

They say many difficult things are accomplished because the individual has no clue how arduous the task is at the outset. This was definitely true in my case.

My lack of organizational experience came in handy in my approach to the Vietnam Moratorium. I had a fresh, naïve outlook. I viewed putting together a moratorium in pro-war San Diego with the attitude, *How can it hurt to try?* The truth, however, was that I had absolutely no idea what I was getting myself into.

Since I was so tirelessly gung-ho, others were quick to hand me a ton of tasks that included mobilizing the press. I soon found out why the job of press liaison was so readily handed off. The general San Diego press wasn't 'difficult,' as I had been advised; they were hostile. A newspaper editor I queried about the moratorium snapped, “You’re talking to a WWII vet!” and hung up. Another problem was that San Diego was basically a one-paper town, which gave the *Union-Tribune* a monopoly on their pro-war interpretation of the news.

Relentlessly, I sent out press releases to the media on the upcoming Vietnam Moratorium, but few responses were positive or even neutral. Editorials belittled and scorned our call to stop doing business as usual in protest of the war.

Divisiveness, however, was not confined to the press. It also flared within the peace movement itself. For example, the week before the moratorium, I proposed that our moratorium volunteers hold a peace ceremony to honor Vietnam Vets a few days before the October 15th march. The idea was to promote a spirit of reconciliation and break down the polarization between those on the right and left. Instead, all hell broke loose.

At the first meeting to plan the ceremony, heated arguments erupted. A guy angrily shouted, “I don’t think we should have *anything* to do with a tribute to murderers!”

Someone countered, “We don’t have to agree with the vets to give them credit for risking their lives for their country.”

I added, “We’re not against the vets. We’re against the war.”

“Francesco is right,” a coed shouted. “I’m sick of all this ‘us against them’ bullshit rhetoric. Otherwise, when is this country ever going to come together?”

On the day of the ceremony at the University of California, San Diego, I felt outraged and ashamed that about a third of the invited students boycotted the event. Why? Because they were prejudiced against those serving in Vietnam.

The event, however, went on as scheduled. On an open plaza, faculty, students, vets, and La Jolla residents came together in silent prayer as a flag was lowered to half-mast to honor fallen soldiers.

After the ceremony, I joined a half dozen volunteers at a busy downtown intersection, where we held up peace placards to remind people of the upcoming moratorium. If passing motorists liked our peace messages, they’d smile or wave. If they hated them, they’d either lay on the horn or flip us off. The ambidextrous did both.

I told the volunteers, “Never return rudeness with rudeness. Rise above it.”

As I held up a sign that read Escalate Peace!, a dark official-looking car slowed and pulled over. The backseat window went down, and a military officer with salt and pepper hair, mostly salt, stuck his head out the window. His uniform was dark green with big gold buttons, rows of multi-colored service ribbons, and silver stars on each shoulder.

I half-expected the general to assault me with a barrage of familiar insults: “Commie,” “Hippy,” “Draft-dodger.” Instead, he calmly and respectfully said, “Son, I’m a general, and I actually admire you for standing up for what you believe. That’s the American way. But I want you to know something—as long as there are two people in the world, there will always be a war.”

Before I could respond, the general motioned for the chauffeur to drive away. I thought *People find what they expect to find.* As the saying goes, *'You look for your friends, and you'll find friends; you look for your enemies, and you'll find enemies.'*

I wrote Dad about my work on the Vietnam Moratorium, and to my surprise, he replied with a moving letter:

> Dear Francesco,
>
> My father, for whom I had great admiration, was a kind and gentle spirit. He had compassion for all people and saw every war as a crime against humanity. It's interesting that you, as his grandson, should be so concerned about the less fortunate and the lack of peace in the world. Were he living, he would be very proud of you.
>
> Affectionately,
> Dad

As the date of the first Vietnam Moratorium grew near—October 15th, 1969—I was constantly on the phone to help ensure a good turnout. So were activists in other major cities across the country.

Nationally, the moratorium drew two million participants, making it the largest demonstration in US history! Future U.S. President Bill Clinton, a Rhodes Scholar at Oxford, helped organize the demonstration in England—an effort later held against him in his presidential campaign. Another participant in the moratorium was John Laird, the son of the Secretary of Defense—Melvin Laird. President Nixon and Henry Kissinger criticized the Secretary of Defense for not keeping his son quiet, but Laird defended his son's right to free expression.

Jane and I marched in the moratorium near an anti-war veteran holding a sign that read, WAR IS HELL. ASK THE MEN WHO FIGHT IT. I felt proud of the turnout and our democratic system at work. *This is how we do things in America*, I thought proudly.

In reaction to the October Moratorium, President Nixon testily addressed the nation on November 3rd, 1969: "North Vietnam cannot defeat or humiliate the United States. Only Americans can do that." That scolding only made those of us organizing the next moratorium that much more determined in our protest.

As a follow-up to the first moratorium, we invited citizens to march on November 15th to make it crystal clear to the administration that we were not about to stop marching until the war ended and the soldiers were sent home.

At the local second moratorium site in downtown San Diego, Jane and I marched and passed out peace buttons to the cheering crowd on the sidelines. Along the way, an elderly man motioned to me and asked for a Work for Peace button. As I pinned it on him, he stood at attention. At first, I thought he was joking, but he stood motionless with great dignity, then saluted. "I proudly served in WW II," he said, "and now I'm proudly serving in the peace movement."

As Jane and I marched, we smiled at the massive crowds lining both sides of our route. Suddenly Jane clutched my arm, pointing to a wild-eyed silver-haired man who was running alongside us, screaming, "I come from South Vietnam! The communists are destroying my country! Get out of here, you damn traitors, all of you, get out!" Marchers veered away from him in alarm. "Death to the communists!" he screamed, leaning in on us. "Death to the communists!" I wanted to talk with him and have an exchange of ideas, but it was clear that he was beyond any two-way communication, that he had lost his humanity to his cause.

The local evening newscast reported that seven to eight thousand people had turned out for the San Diego march. *How things have changed!* I thought back to 1965 when it seemed the peace movement couldn't have one iota of effect on the government or the public. *Back then, my generation's efforts to bring an end to the war seemed an impossible dream. Today, the realization of that dream seems inevitable.*

34

KICKED OUT OF GRAD SCHOOL
(1970)

"It has been said that democracy is the worst form of government except all the others that have been tried.

—Winston Churchill

A controversial resolution reached the City Council of San Diego, and if adopted, would call for an end to the draft. Just the fact that such a measure was going to be considered in such a navy-based city indicated how far the anti-war movement had progressed. Though the resolution would be non-binding, it would make a *major* symbolic statement that would impact the nation.

There was no way I was going to miss this.

At the spacious City Council Chamber, packed to capacity, a cloud of cigarette smoke produced by the council members wafted about the room. Before the members, pro-draft and anti-draft forces were set for verbal combat.

Straightaway, one of the council members tried to table the resolution but was unsuccessful. Then an anti-draft advocate presented his argument for supporting the resolution. He noted that this year, 1970, there were nearly 335,000 American troops still in Vietnam, many serving completely against their will.

I studied the remote faces of the City Council members. They seemed terribly bored. The members sat behind a raised wood-paneled dais and only rarely made eye contact with the citizens testifying below them.

Those speaking for the draft, most of them elderly, said that President Nixon needed to have a "free hand" in Vietnam so as not to "jeopardize our boys." I was thinking, *What could possibly jeopardize our boys more than putting them directly in harm's way with forced conscription!*

The speaker at the podium complained, "It isn't the place of this city council to question foreign policy. We should only deal with *local* problems."

An antiwar speaker responded that the Vietnam War was justified "neither morally nor legally and that the draft and the war should be *everyone's* concern at *every* level." He added, "I'm speaking from a strict interpretation of the Constitution."

One of the council members lit up a cigarette, and the speaker said, "I can see I don't need to talk to the council members about pollution since five out of the nine of you are smoking." The member directly before the speaker immediately crushed her cigarette.

The pro and con camps shook their heads, skeptical of each other's *misguided* views. The woman on my right, for example, sighed aloud in frustration every time an anti-draft speaker took the microphone. Meanwhile, the anti-draft guy on my left groaned heavily with every statement for the draft.

A councilman said, "I have a mortal fear of nuclear attack from Russia. It could come at any time, even as we're speaking. At least the draft will make that less likely. It's a deterrent."

I shook my head hopelessly, catching the attention of the pro-draft woman on my right. She smiled, wagged her finger at me, and exclaimed, "That's right, young man!" I couldn't help but smile back.

Both sides cited drawn-out abstract legalistic arguments concerning the draft. Finally, Mayor Curran asked, "Are there any other comments to be made before I call for a vote?"

Impassioned, I found myself raising my hand and walking toward the podium. I was frightened of speaking before such a large crowd but felt I had to say *something* on a subject that had preoccupied my life for the last seven years. Petrified, I looked up at the impatient council members. Twice, I cleared my throat and faltered. Then I said the following (which was transcribed verbatim from a tape recorder): "I agree with those who described the draft as illegal and immoral. Young men of San Diego and across America are *forced* by the draft to join the military and fight a war they don't believe in. If that isn't a form of slavery . . . of involuntary servitude, then I don't know what is. I cannot stand by in good conscience while the killing continues. As council members, I urge each of you to rise above partisan politics and do the right thing—support this resolution. Do not allow the draft and this *undeclared* war to keep taking lives. The draft is immoral, it's un-American, and it's overdue that we end it. Take this important step today, and vote to stop the draft and the daily tragic killing *now*!"

The City Council Chamber exploded with fervent sustained applause. As I returned to my seat, the Mayor shouted, "Order! Order! Order!"

The City Council vote was taken. Incredibly, the vote came to a deadlocked tie! The Mayor himself had voted for the anti-war measure! I could hardly believe the results. Excited, loud buzzing conversations filled the room. I wondered if, and hoped dearly, this kind of hunger for an end to the draft and the war was a growing appetite throughout the country. The crowd picked up its cheering again while

Mayor Curran continually banged his gavel. "Order! *Order!*" Clearly annoyed with the outcome, he quickly called for another vote. This time the Mayor changed his vote from "for" to "against," and before you could blink, the resolution had been defeated.

With a smile of relief, the Mayor moved on to the next item on the agenda. Suddenly a well-dressed man stormed up to the podium. "I'm making a citizen's arrest of the Mayor!" he screamed. "While the Constitutionality and un-Constitutionality of the war is being argued, young men are *dying* in Vietnam!"

The Mayor banged his gavel again, and the speaker was led away by officers. Before moving on, the Mayor added, "The many young people here are to be commended for their orderly conduct."

Though I was disappointed in the Mayor's conduct, I told myself I had no right to be dependent on it. In the past, I had done enough blaming of others, like the President and Congress. It was the useless exercise in complaining that left me out of sorts. I reminded myself of Ralph Waldo Emerson's words, "Nothing can bring you peace but yourself."

Though Jane and I were proud to be American, we felt bitter regarding the legacy of lies from our government regarding the Vietnam War. From the Johnson administration to the Nixon administration, deceptions to Congress and the public were rampant.

The war, Nixon said, was "winding down" when actually it was escalating. A token number of troops would be withdrawn, but the bombing would increase. War losses were constantly hidden or minimized, and gains exaggerated. But one of the worst, horrifying deceptions finally surfaced over the evening news in 1969—the My Lai Massacre, which had occurred without public knowledge on March 16, 1968. The hushed-up story came to light due to the relentless search for truth by journalist Seymour Hersh, who won a Pultizer Prize for his reporting.

What had happened at My Lai was almost beyond belief. Army Lieutenant William Calley was charged with pre-meditated murder in a bloody massacre in South Vietnam. His soldiers murdered between 347 and 504 unarmed civilians, most of them women, elderly, children, and babies. Many of the victims were beaten and tortured. Girls and women were raped and mutilated before being killed. Calley himself murdered 22 civilians in cold blood and had the village burned to the ground.

The massacre ended only after Officer Hugh Thompson, an Army helicopter pilot, landed his aircraft between the soldiers and the retreating villagers. He threatened to open fire if the soldiers continued their shooting. Thompson and his crew flew dozens of survivors to receive medical care. A cover-up ensued and the horrific murders were kept secret.

While twenty-six U.S. soldiers were eventually charged, only Calley was convicted and sentenced to life in prison. But *the next day*, Nixon ordered Calley transferred from the army prison at Leavenworth, Kansas, to house arrest at Ft. Benning. As a result of Nixon's intervention, Calley only served three years.

Several congressmen denounced servicemen who had tried to stop the mass slaughter as traitors. They received hate mail, death threats, and found mutilated animals on their doorsteps.

Twenty years later, Thompson and two other members of his crew received the Soldier's Medal—the Army's highest award for bravery not involving direct enemy contact.

The press was reluctant to publish the news of My Lai, not to mention the fact that My Lai was not an isolated incident. Without an apology, *The New York Times* had reported the horror in My Lai as a "victory." Initially, when journalist Hersh tried to break the story of the atrocities, *Life, Time,* and *Newsweek* ignored it.

When the news about My Lai broke, Jane said, "I hear about something like this, and I want to give up on the human race. I was raised to look at *all* people as bad, as sinners. I didn't accept it, but that's what I was taught. So, when I read about something like My Lai or the Nazis, a little voice says, *Maybe they're right, maybe humans are basically evil.* And you know there are going to be protesters that are going to say ridiculous things like, 'See, all soldiers are murderers.'"

"My Lai doesn't speak for soldiers or humans in general," I said. "Just look at Jerry.

Most are like him. They're dedicated, and they care about people. It was a soldier—Hugh Thompson—that stopped other soldiers from killing more people. Humans are a mixed bag. I like what Dr. King said: 'There's some good in the worst of us and some evil in the best of us.'"

Another particularly gruesome aspect of the war was the CIA's "Operation Phoenix" program. Without trial, the CIA executed over 20,000 civilians in South Vietnam that were suspected members of the Communists underground. It wasn't until the mid-'70s that the program was outlawed. The Senate hearings that resulted from the CIA's massive assassination program raised important questions: In our democratic society, are we to remain silent in the face of terrorist activities sanctioned by our government? Second, do we accept a policy of 'any means necessary,' including torture and assassination, to 'make the world safe for democracy'?

My Human Behavior class at U.S. International University (now named Alliant University) was taught by the Dean of the College. Occasionally the topic of the war would come up. Today, when I called for an immediate end to the war and defended those who sincerely seek conscientious objection, the professor looked at me askance. He pursed his lips, then motioned to me and said to the class, "Make no mistake about it—the rock throwers are right here among us." I was stunned, particularly since I had made it clear that I condemned violence, whether it came from the left or the right. Unequivocally, I stood for nonviolence and reconciliation.

A brave classmate said to the professor, "I can't help but wonder if Francesco's views will jeopardize his grade?"

Immediately, I feared for the student, figuring *his* grade was now at risk!

The professor chuckled. "Of course not." But a week later, I received a terse letter from The Office of Admissions:

> We are sorry to inform you that you have been denied readmission to U.S. International University for the next semester. Any and all fees that you have paid for said semester will be fully refunded.

My grades were excellent, so it was abundantly plain that I was being punished for political reasons. I called the Dean's secretary and asked, "If I have excellent grades, how can I be dropped from grad school in the middle of a semester?" She said she didn't know. "Can I please speak to the Dean?"

"He's unavailable," she said. The only thing she knew with certainty was that I was no longer enrolled.

In desperation, I called the American Civil Liberties Union. They were sympathetic and took my case for free. In the course of their investigation, they requested that I obtain my file from the university. When I called the dean's secretary to ask for the file, she said, "Apparently, it's been lost."

I reported the response to the ACLU. They wrote directly to the Dean, stating that there was probable cause to believe that I had been discriminated against because of my conscientious objection and peace activism. The Dean was given a simple choice: "Immediately reinstate Mr. Da Vinci or be held accountable in a court of law."

Miraculously, a notice quickly came in the mail from the Office of Admissions: "You are hereby reinstated to the graduate program."

35

KENT STATE AND JACKSON STATE SHOOTINGS (1970)

"Violence and brutality of any kind, particularly at the hands of law enforcement sworn to protect and serve our communities, is unacceptable."

—Senator Bernie Sanders

In President Nixon's televised address to the nation on April 30th, 1970, he justified an invasion of northern Cambodia, which actually occurred in secret two days *prior* to the press conference. It seemed another abuse of presidential war powers. Following in Johnson's footsteps, Nixon continually side-stepped Congress.

Less than a week later, a tragic event shocked the nation—four unarmed students were shot and killed by the Ohio National Guard at Kent State University.

Here is a thumbnail sketch of the events that led up to the shooting. Ohio National Guardsmen had been called in to the university by Governor James A. Rhodes to break up anti-war demonstrations motivated by Nixon's invasion of Cambodia.

Shortly before noon on Monday, May 4th, the General for the Guardsmen made the decision to order the crowd of demonstrators at Kent State to leave. A university police officer made the announcement using a bullhorn. It had no effect, so the officer and several Guardsmen drove up to the protesters and ordered them to disperse. They were shouted down, and some protesters threw rocks at them. The men in the jeep retreated, and tear gas was fired into the crowd. The protesters moved up a steep hill and went down the other side onto a parking lot and an adjoining football field. The Guardsmen followed the students and faced rock-throwing and shouting. Then the guardsmen, after about ten minutes, went from the football field back up the hill. At the top, 28 Guardsmen turned and fired their rifles and pistols at the students, unleashing over 60 shots in 13 seconds. Some of the protesters stood their ground because they assumed that the Guardsmen *must* be firing blanks.

As a result of the firing by the Guardsmen, four Kent State students died: Jeffrey Glenn Miller, age 20, shot through the mouth; Allison B. Krause, age 19, died later that day from a fatal left chest wound; William Knox Schroeder, age 19, shot in the back and died almost an hour later in surgery; and Sandra Lee Scheuer, age 20, died a few minutes later from loss of blood due to a neck wound.

The nine wounded included Dean R. Kahler, who was permanently paralyzed from the chest down. In response to the Kent State shootings, 350 universities went on strike.

The famous photograph of the 14-year-old runaway, Mary Ann Vecchio, screaming over the body of the dead student, Jeffrey Miller, was taken by John Filo, a photography major at Kent State.

Three days before the shootings, President Nixon widened the polarization between hawks and doves, calling antiwar college protesters "bums," to which the father of victim Allison Krause stated on national TV: "My child was not a bum."

After the shooting, guardsmen and officers claimed that they had fired because they had feared for their lives. But an FBI investigation contradicted that claim. It stated the assertion by the National Guard "that their lives were endangered by the students was fabricated."

Protesters were routinely and callously scorned with demagoguery, partly because the Republican administration wanted to win over the blue-collar middle class that was traditionally Democratic. The slandering worked on a pragmatic level, but there was a societal cost. The dehumanization of young demonstrators fostered an unseemly ethic among many Americans—a cold indifference to the lives of the protesters. A Gallup poll taken in the wake of the Kent State shootings corroborated that ethic: 58 percent of those polled blamed the students for the Kent State shooting, while only 11 percent blamed the National Guard. One woman interviewed said, "They should have shot all of them." I thought, *What if your 19 or 20-year old daughter or son was among them?*

Only four days after the shootings, construction workers in New York City, cheered on by Wall Street traders, attacked nonviolent protestors and raised the American flag flying over City Hall. The flag had been lowered to half-mast to honor the four students killed at Kent State. Peter Brennan, the union chief who organized the vigilante action, received a congratulatory call from Nixon and an invitation to the White House. In the early stages of his second term, Nixon named Brennan Secretary of Labor.

Eleven days after the Kent State shooting, another needless tragedy ensued. During a demonstration at Jackson State College in Mississippi, white state police using shotguns fired 300 bullets into a dormitory of black students, killing Phillip Gibbs, 21, a junior at the college, and Alexander Hall, a 17-year-old high school senior. They had been watching the events from a window when the police opened fire. Twelve students were wounded. It struck me as a matter of racial bias that the coverage of Kent State was wide, while the coverage of Jackson State was relatively minor.

Due to the killings of unarmed protesting students at Kent State and Jackson State, President Nixon established the President's Commission on Campus Unrest, which issued its findings in September 1970. The report concluded that the shootings of students were "unjustified." The report stated: "Even if the guardsmen faced danger, it was not a danger that called for lethal force." It issued a strong recommendation: the tragic May 1970 shootings "must mark the last time that, as a matter of course, loaded rifles are issued to guardsmen confronting student demonstrators."

The extreme polarization in America was also addressed: "The crisis on American campuses has no parallel in the history of this nation. This crisis has roots in divisions in American society as deep as any since the Civil War."

Though the massive violence from the government and state authorities dwarfed the violence from so-called 'peace groups' on the fringe, the vast majority in the peace movement never viewed violence as justified. In 1970, however, student violence was on the increase. During the first ten days of May, ROTC buildings were fire-bombed at more than thirty colleges/universities around the country, including my alma mater, the University of Maryland, College Park, and Jerry's alma mater, the University of Virginia, Charlottesville.

I felt a duty to condemn the student violence. It seemed extremely hypocritical for those of us in the peace movement to ignore it. As I said to my draft board, what good does it do to replace old tyrants with new tyrants?

It was a difficult, stressful time in America, with the country steeped in divisiveness that was unprecedented in modern history. Shootings of unarmed students and the targeting of minorities continued extensively across the nation, causing Jane to say, "Every day, everywhere we look, there's so much hate and violence. What can we do against The System?"

"Remember when I kept saying that someday I want to start a peace group that stands for nonviolence? Well, I'm tired of waiting. I'm just going to do it."

"A peace group is about the *last* thing *Navy Town USA* wants to see. I'll support you if you really want to do this, but it's going to be like pushing civil rights in the South. You better be prepared for a lot of hate."

The more I voiced my beliefs in public, the more confidence I developed to make a stronger commitment to nonviolence on a community level *and* a personal level. I particularly liked the nonviolent principle of means and ends—making the way you do something just as important as the goal you seek.

This new commitment, my private revolution, came out of my search for truths deeper than I had ever explored before. It also came out of reading a short novel that influenced me and many in my generation—*Siddhartha* by Herman Hesse. I related to the main character, Siddhartha, who leaves a life of privilege to seek spiritual fulfillment. Siddhartha felt compelled to search for true meaning, something that I searched for and found recently in the philosophy of nonviolence. The river in the story seemed to symbolize unity of spirit with the larger world, which was partially what my favorite reef in La Jolla represented for me—a connection with something larger than the polarization of the draft, the war, and politics—a connection to humankind's commonalities—a connection to the positive force of love—and ultimately a connection to the cosmos.

Then I became as obnoxious as a newly converted non-smoker who feels compelled to subject smokers to the cruel and unusual punishment of lecturing them to death. I went through a self-righteous stage of preaching the gospel of nonviolence to the unenlightened. By the time I finished my morally superior lectures, I had inadvertently motivated my victims to contemplate violence!

In addition to my sermons, I became a vegetarian. First, I stopped eating meat, then fish as well. I did not do this for my health; I did it for the health of the animals. It was not easy. I missed being a carnivore but held to my new diet for five years. In addition, I stopped wearing clothing made from the skins of animals. My leather belt and shoes were replaced with stiff, inflexible artificial leather products.

Jane noted my ascetic fanaticism. "What's next?" she asked. "Starting a Church of Nonviolence?"

Legal counsel suggested that I had about one year before facing prison. Determined to use that time to work for peace, I focused on how I would put Gandhi's principles of nonviolence to work here in San Diego. If I ever faltered in resolve, all I had to do was glance at the images of Vietnamese children covered with napalm.

I cautioned myself not to take on too many issues at once to avoid spreading myself too thin. My passionate interests included supporting civil rights, migrant farm worker rights, lowering the voting age to 18, women's and gay rights, outlawing land mines, an environmental campaign to create an "Earth Day," and ending capital punishment along with the draft and the war.

I meditated on which issue to start with. Since Cesar Chavez was one of my main role models for nonviolent activism, I began to focus on the plight of migrant farm workers. They had suffered shootings, beatings, deportations, and false accusations of being "unpatriotic troublemakers"—like COs. Chavez, and his co-leader Dolores Huerta, led the farm workers in their fight to unionize and further inspired my efforts to organize a peace group.

Cesar was the son of struggling migrant laborers. He quit school in the seventh grade because he did not want his mother to have to work in the fields where he saw workers experience conditions comparable to slavery. Later, a priest introduced the methods of Gandhi to Cesar, and in 1962, Cesar began organizing California grape pickers to demand higher wages and better living conditions.

Around my grad school studies, I volunteered to work with the farm workers at the Cardijn Center office in Old Town, San Diego. By gathering food and clothing for the migrant workers, I also gathered self-satisfaction and pride for myself. What a joy I found serving others and promoting social justice. When we leafleted, however, it was not always pleasant.

As I passed out flyers at the Mission Valley Shopping Center and various Safeway supermarket stores, the response from shoppers ranged from the good, to the bad, to the ugly.

The *good*: those already in our camp told us to "keep up the good work." Some volunteered to help.

The *bad*: those that sneered at us, ignored us, or quickly wadded up our leaflets and threw them away.

And the *ugly*: the haters—those who cursed us and ranted loud with no respect for themselves or us. "You goddamn hippie agitators aren't fooling anyone! Everyone knows that Cesar Chavez is a (insert curse) commie!"

One afternoon I told Carlos, an organizer at the Cardijn Center, that I had a burning desire to form a peace group dedicated to nonviolence and to focus it on helping to end the draft and the war. Carlos responded, "There's a *huge* need for that, especially here in San Diego. What are you waiting for? As Cesar and Dolores would say, '*Si, se puede*'—Yes, it can be done. I might be able to help you with an office. Cesar is coming down from Delano to visit next month. I'll tell him about you, and maybe he'll let you work here 'til you find your own place."

"Thanks, buddy. That would be huge."

"He travels a lot in California, and I'm worried for him," Carlos said. "Everywhere he goes, his life is threatened. We try to get him to be more careful, but he just says, 'I have my life to live,' and goes on with his work. I pray for him."

That evening Carlos called me at home.

"Good news, my friend. Cesar would like to meet with you to talk about your peace group."

36

THE BIRTH OF NONVIOLENT ACTION
(July 4, 1970)

Si se puede! (Yes, we can!)
—Cesar Chavez

As Cesar Chavez entered the Cardijn Center, it seemed someone had just brightened the lights. There was something luminous about his presence. Even at forty-nine, he had an intense youthful aura about him, similar to the positive energy I felt meeting Bobby Kennedy. Both men exuded compassion and courage.

My friend Carlos introduced me to Cesar. "Carlos tells me you're a CO," Cesar said, "and that you're doing some fine work here."

"Thanks, Cesar, but I'm just doing what everyone else here is doing. I'm so honored to meet you. You inspire people everywhere. When I look at what you've done, I think anything is possible."

Cesar smiled. "Carlos says you'd like to work for peace. That's a noble cause, and we're happy to welcome you here to help you get started."

"I'm very grateful for that."

Cesar nodded and started to walk away. Then he paused and turned. "Nothing will stop peace and justice, will it?"

"Nothing," I answered.

Cesar left as gracefully as he had entered, and I stared at the space he had stood in only moments ago. As an agnostic and a devotee of scientific inquiry, I wasn't one to indulge in magic and mysticism. Yet, part of me felt Cesar was still present in spirit as if he was joining other inspirational apparitions in my life, among them Thoreau, Helen Keller, Gandhi, Einstein, Martin Luther King, Jr., Neil Armstrong, and the Dalai Lama. They, and others who lived an exemplary life, made up my spiritual support group. Frequently I read about and reflected on the lives of these mentors in my endeavor to establish a new peace group, undaunted that I was trying to do so in one of the most militaristic cities in the world.

Before I formed my peace group, I wanted to make sure that I would not be duplicating the efforts of existing anti-war organizations. Every week I met with leaders of local groups to seek their advice on how we might complement each other's efforts. I had expected resistance and resentment from the pro-Vietnam war community, but surprisingly I encountered a great deal of resistance from members of the peace movement. In their eyes, I was invading their territory.

Everyone I spoke with seemed to have a "San Diego mindset"—the attitude that viewed peace work in San Diego as acceptably limited. Without exception, every group leader said it was either "unnecessary" or "impossible" for me to form a meaningful new peace organization in a city that was traditionally hostile to progressive causes. But the opposition was more than practical. Many took my efforts as an indirect admonishment that they were not doing enough. I nodded politely to all the naysayers, not about to accept the status quo.

One leader warned I might face danger. "You even *try* to set up a new peace group and you'll be subject to harassment. Activists in the past were subject to fire-bombings, threatening phone calls, property destruction, police raids, and FBI intimidation. And these were people like you, committed to nonviolence." Several activists cautioned that there might even be attempts on my life. "Not that long ago," said one organizer, "an antiwar student leader had a hand-grenade thrown into his home. Fortunately, it failed to go off. All I'm saying is that if you go through with this, you're going to be wearing a target on your back."

I was torn on whether to share these warnings with Jane or whether to keep them to myself. Would it be dishonest, or would it be the kinder way, sparing her unnecessary worry? I concluded that I'd try for the middle. I'd tell her what I had learned but without emphasizing the risks. The balance I sought was to be open yet considerate—not an easy tightrope to navigate.

In early July 1970, I posted an ad in the local papers to recruit volunteers for my new peace group.

Seven people responded; three showed up. One of the three was Jim, a clean-cut college student at the University of California, San Diego. He was brimming with contagious enthusiasm. "I can't believe there's actually a nonviolent group like this! My family is completely divided on the war. My dad is an admiral; I'm anti-war. This peace group is just what I've been looking for."

"Great. Welcome aboard."

Then there was Ben, a particularly articulate vet, who had pitch-black shoulder-length hair, a deep bronze tan, and an athletic build. He wore an olive army surplus shirt over blue jeans.

Norie, in sharp contrast to Ben and Jim, looked like a working professional. She wore an Ann Taylor outfit and seemed to epitomize young, corporate America.

"By the way," Jim asked. "Where's everyone else?"

I paused. "They're on their way. They just don't know it yet."

With the same painstaking care of naming a child, I decided to call my peace group Nonviolent Action. I wanted to shatter the stereotype that nonviolence is passive and that it simply means not being violent. I agreed fully with Gandhi—nonviolence is an *active* force.

Several new volunteers telephoned over the weekend. A few calls came late into the evening, and Jane became irritated. I tried to assuage her. "Isn't it great that they want to do something for peace?"

She smirked. "And at *all* hours."

On July 4th, 1970, Jane and I held a potluck dinner to kick off the formation of Nonviolent Action. A dozen volunteers enlisted. The gathering was meant to be an informal prelude to our official opening on August 6th, Hiroshima Day. A week and a half later, our volunteers increased to twenty-five. We worked out of the farm workers' office to build our peace group, and at the same time, supported the United Farm Workers.

We named our first nonviolent campaign The Farm Workers Project, and by September, we were leafletting at Safeway grocery stores in support of the lettuce boycott. Our leaflets called on growers to negotiate contracts with farm workers for decent wages and working conditions.

Nonviolent Action's leafleting and interaction with the public was an invaluable experience. We developed a Goldilocks approach through trial and error—not too much communication with shoppers and not too little. Bottom line—respect people's feelings while spreading the word about the plight of impoverished farm workers.

Within two weeks, we were able to thank Cesar for his generous hospitality and move our office to a small house in Southeast San Diego. We continued our Farm Workers Project, leafleting at grocery stores, days and evenings.

When a few more volunteers joined Nonviolent Action (NVA for short), we added another nonviolent campaign—The Draft Project. Since San Diego did not have an induction center, draftees were ordered to report to the downtown Greyhound Bus Depot at dawn to be shipped up to LA for processing. Very few draftees knew their legal rights, especially minorities. To give them more power over their lives, we gave out leaflets that listed the phone numbers of lawyers who volunteered to counsel draftees without a fee. I remembered how much draft counseling had meant to me in the early stages of my CO process and felt immensely gratified that Nonviolent Action was offering that opportunity to others. As one draft attorney said, "The price is right, the need is great, and it's good karma!"

My hat was off to these dedicated, unrecognized anti-war attorneys who gave draftees the chance to make critical life and death decisions with knowledge of their rights.

A week before Nonviolent Action's first draft leafleting at the downtown Greyhound Bus Depot, I dreaded an unwelcome announcement I had to make to the two dozen volunteers at our general meeting.

Anxiously, I cleared my throat and said, "I found out what time we'll need to be at the bus station—5:15 A.M." The ungodly hour was met with a loud chorus of groans. "In a way, it's good," I offered weakly. "That means the leafleting will be over before any of us has to go to school or work."

"How convenient," Jim said dryly.

Sensing mutiny, I said, "If the *Army* can get up at that hour, can't *we*?"

Norie and Ben nodded and strongly argued for support of the leafleting.

Jim, however, called for a vote on whether to abandon the Draft Project for another that didn't require the sacrifice of sleep.

"I have something to say before we vote," I interjected. "I feel this project is so important that I'm making a pledge right now—I give my word that I'll leaflet every single pre-induction and induction call in San Diego for one year solid—July 1970 through July 1971—and if I have to, I'll do it on my own. This project isn't a frill; it's a matter of life and death."

"Okay, let's vote," Jim suggested. "Who wants us to keep the project?"

Hesitantly, three-fourths of the members raised their hands. The Draft Project was a keeper. "Okay," Jim said with a sigh, "but everyone should know right now, I'm definitely not a morning person!"

Si, se puede! (Yes, we can!), Cesar's inspirational mantra.
(Photo: F. Da Vinci)

When I met Cesar for the first time, he said, "Nothing will stop peace and justice, will it?", San Diego, 1970.

37

DEDICATION OF NONVIOLENT ACTION—HIROSHIMA DAY

(August 6, 1970)

"Inhumanity begins with the contempt and neglect of the individual. The atomic weapon is the end product of this indifference towards the many individual, inexchangeable, and irreplaceable human beings."

—Tokie Uematsu, daughter of a Hiroshima bomb victim

At 5 A.M., I arrived at the mist-covered downtown Greyhound Bus Station for Nonviolent Action's first leafleting of draftees.

The depot had an eerie glow, its neon lights glimmering through a drifting fog like a macabre dream. With no sign of the Draft Project volunteers, I passed the time taking a few pictures. With my 35mm camera, I focused on two draftees slouched down in plastic chairs that offered the amenity of small pay TVs attached to the arms. The draftees left the TVs off in favor of catching a nap before heading to LA. I thought of what was ahead for them. In ten minutes or so, they would board their bus to the Los Angeles Induction Center. There they would sleep-walk through an early morning physical. Next stop would be basic training, where they would learn to kill. Then graduation to Vietnam, where 58,148 young American men would eventually die; 61% of them were younger than 21.

While I was at the coffee shop counter nursing hot tea, Norie arrived. As usual, she looked immaculate in her well-pressed blouse and slacks. Ben trailed in, wearing faded jeans and a work shirt. Jim, last to arrive, looked particularly bedraggled with his shirt buttoned completely wrong. He rubbed his eyes and said, "This feels like an out-of-body experience. I gotta grab some coffee." Jim motioned to the waitress behind the coffee counter. "Can I get a double shot of espresso?"

The waitress put her hands on her hips. "This is a bus depot, kid. Not The Ritz."

"Okay. Coffee. Black."

At the counter, I reviewed the ground rules for leafleting that we had rehearsed in previous meetings. "Be friendly and don't block anyone's path," I reminded. "If a draftee doesn't want to talk, respect that."

Norie took a stack of leaflets and said, "I'm still new to leafleting. Until I get used to it, I think I'll feel more comfortable by the side entrance instead of out front."

"I'll go with you," Ben offered.

Jim and I took the main entrance and handed out leaflets to the bleary-eyed draftees. Near the buses, a middle-aged draft board clerk with a clipboard checked off the draftees as they boarded.

A draftee kissed and hugged his girlfriend, then held her face tenderly. "I'll be back," he said. Tears streamed down the girl's face. Out of nowhere, a portly newspaper salesman suddenly screamed, "Teenager dies!" The couple flinched and stared resentfully at the newspaperman as he held the headline up high. "Teenager dies!"

The flow of draftees steadily increased, forcing Jim and I to leaflet double-time. I had seriously underestimated the number of leaflets we would need. When we ran out, Jim and I joined Norie and Ben at the side entrance.

Norie looked at us with a big radiant smile. "This is one of the best experiences of my life. What a nice way to wake up. The draftees are *really* glad we're here."

"Yeah," Ben chimed in, "they were comin' in here like zombies, but when they saw what we were all about, they came alive again."

Once the buses were packed with several hundred draftees, our NVA volunteers hurried around back to wave goodbye. Some, we knew, would not be coming back. As the last bus faded from view, the four of us hugged. Then Norie asked, "Will you walk me to my car?" At first, I thought it was for safety. Twice, however, she looked like she had something to say but stopped herself.

"What is it?" I asked.

She took a breath. "I want to tell you why I joined Nonviolent Action . . . why this leafleting is so important to me." She pursed her lips. "I'm a 22-year old widow."

I absorbed the shock, then said, "I'm sorry."

"My husband was killed in Vietnam six days before he was supposed to come home. A taxicab pulled up at our house, and I was handed a damn telegram. It said, 'The Secretary of the Army has asked me to express his deep regret . . .'" Norie wiped away a tear. "I couldn't believe it. There were only six *days* left! Since he'd been in for two years, I figured nothing would happen to him. They said he died in a 'firefight,' like I'd be pleased with that. He *hated* the war, but he thought he had to go." Her eyes began to tear and her voice broke. "I just wanted to let you know why this peace group means the world to me."

I officially launched Nonviolent Action on August 6th, Hiroshima Day. It was a day in history symbolic of the dire need to replace methods of violence with methods of nonviolence.At our new headquarters, the Peace House, Jane and I held a coffee and pastries get-together to welcome the new volunteers—thirty-four peace-hungry people, mostly college students. Among the volunteers were the first three members of NA: Jim, Norie, and Ben. They were all smiles with the steady growth of our peace group. "Hey, man," Ben said. "Looks like we're doin' it. The revolution is on!"

Norie and Jane hit it off. After everyone got to know each other better, the conversation turned to the significance of Hiroshima Day and the research I had gathered about the two atomic bomb drops on the civilians of Hiroshima and Nagasaki.

The first bomb that dropped on Hiroshima bore the nickname *Little Boy.* It killed between 90,000 and 166,000 Japanese men, women, and children and left thousands maimed and slowly dying of radiation poisoning. Three days later, we dropped a second atomic bomb, nicknamed *Fat Man,* on Nagasaki, killing between 39,000 and 80,000.

Whether it was necessary to drop atomic bombs on Japan to shorten the war and save lives still begs to be answered. Many cogently argue that the bomb drops killing at least 150,000 innocent civilians were unnecessary, that they were acts of genocide.

Before the bomb's development in America, Einstein wrote a letter to President Franklin Roosevelt urging "large-scale experimentation to ascertain the possibility of producing an atom bomb." Later, in 1952, Albert Einstein stated in an essay, "I was well aware of the dreadful danger for all mankind if these experiments would succeed. But the probability that the Germans might work on that very problem prompted me to take that step. I did not see any other way out, although I was always a convinced pacifist. To kill in war time, it seems to me, is in no ways better than common murder." He said that he was sure that President Roosevelt, unlike President Harry Truman, would have forbidden the atomic bombing of Hiroshima and Nagasaki. Later, Einstein wrote, "I have always condemned the use of the atomic bomb against Japan."

Seven decades after World War II, new evidence emerged that another country, in addition to Germany, had a secret program to build an atomic bomb—Japan. In 1945, Japan's navy and army were diligently developing the bomb, but they lacked sufficient materials. In May 1945, about two and a half months before the atomic bomb was dropped on Hiroshima, a Nazi submarine was captured by a U.S. destroyer escort. The sub contained 1,200 pounds of uranium oxide intended to be shipped to the Japanese military. It had been ordered to Japan shortly after Hitler committed suicide. Historians speculate that the confiscated uranium ended up in the American atomic bombs.

After the war, a Japanese atomic scientist was reported to have said to his wife, "If we'd built the bomb first, of course, we would have used it."

While passionate arguments regarding the pros and cons of dropping the bombs on Japan continue to this day, there remain, in the aftermath, timeless haunting images that, for many, have had more impact than all the scholarly debate. In the Hiroshima Peace Memorial Museum, a poignant symbol of the horrific reality of atomic war is a melted, charred tricycle that belonged to Shin, a three-year-old boy who died in the blast while at play. Shin's parents survived and buried their son on the grounds of their home.

After our formal launch reception for Nonviolent Action, Jane turned in early. But I couldn't sleep. Excited about my new peace group, I went to the reef at Windansea to mediate and watch the stars come up. Walking barefoot along the shore, I expressed my gratitude and hopes for Nonviolent Action. I intended NVA to become a beacon for those who wanted to end the seven years of senseless bloodshed in Vietnam.

President Nixon's cold hubris regarding the war was beyond my comprehension.

An example of his chilling callousness is revealed on a White House tape recorded on April 25th, 1972. With vitriolic fervor, Nixon was obsessed with winning the unwinnable war in Vietnam no matter the cost. In this tape, we hear the exchange between President Nixon and his national security adviser Henry Kissinger. Even Kissinger, who was a super-hawk on the war, had qualms about Nixon's almost sociopathic indifference to human life.

PRESIDENT NIXON: "I still think we ought to take the [Vietnam] dikes out now. Will that drown people?"

HENRY KISSINGER: "About 200,000 people."

PRESIDENT NIXON: "No, no, no . . . I'd rather use the nuclear bomb."

HENRY KISSINGER: "That, I think, would just be too much."

PRESIDENT NIXON: "The nuclear bomb, does that bother you? . . . I just want to think big, Henry . . ."

In a later exchange, Nixon acknowledges that he and Kissinger disagree in regard to the bombing.

PRESIDENT NIXON: "You're so goddamned concerned about the civilians, and I don't give a damn. I don't care."

HENRY KISSINGER: "I'm concerned about the civilians because I don't want the world to be mobilized against you as a butcher."

My deepest hope was that Nonviolent Action would become a strong voice for those without a voice, whether migrant farm workers, draftees, or disillusioned and traumatized vets returning home from Vietnam. Yet, I knew hope was not enough. My peace group would need to define itself in action.

The antiwar movement had steadily gained momentum, but less than a month after I opened Nonviolent Action on August 6th, 1970, a tragic event happened that many called "the death of the peace movement."

Early morning, August 24th, 1970, a van loaded with explosives was detonated at Sterling Hall on the University of Wisconsin-Madison campus by four students (led by Karl Armstrong) as a protest against the Vietnam war and the university's research connection with the U.S. Army. Accidentally killed was 33-year-old researcher and father of three, Robert Fassnacht. He had gone to Sterling Hall lab to finish up work before leaving on a family vacation. Armstrong went on the run but was eventually caught in Toronto. Upon his release after serving seven years in prison, he returned to Madison and became friends with Fassnacht's widow, Stephanie, and daughter, Heidi.

Groups like the Weather Underground justified bombings to protest the Vietnam war and thought of themselves as politically effective. What they did effectively, in my view, was to discredit the hard work of the peace movement. We had built up serious momentum and reached across class boundaries with our call for an immediate end to the Vietnam war. Things were hard enough after the assassinations of JFK, Dr. King, and Bobby Kennedy. The last thing we needed at the start of the '70s was guerrilla warfare. Leftist violence gave the FBI an excuse to bump up harassment and persecution of anti-war activists in general. It also played into the hands of those on the right who consciously stereotyped activists as 'violent troublemakers.' The public bought the myth and made no distinction between the small minority of violent students and the vast majority of nonviolent students.

Especially troubling to me was the tossing around of the word 'violent' and having it habitually land on descriptions of students without examining the massive amount of violence in Vietnam perpetrated by the Johnson and Nixon administrations.

Every time I read about a bombing or a slandering of the peace movement, it made me that much more determined to go forward with Nonviolent Action.

Although Jane felt that my peace group was very much needed, she was basically indulging me. With the bombings and the bias in the media in favor of the mounting call for repressive 'law and order' she would say, "You're not dealing with reality."

And I would say, "You're right. I'm not."

Draftees in TV chairs at the Greyhound Bus Depot. (Photo: F. Da Vinci)

38

LEAFLETING DRAFTEES
(1970)

"Never think that war, no matter how necessary,
nor how justified, is not a crime."
—Ernest Hemingway

As NVA volunteers steadily increased, the new members included more and more Vietnam vets, who had initially viewed the war as noble. Today they viewed it as misguided, at best. I felt very gratified that they were now supporting NVA's call for an immediate end to the war and were serving their country in opposition to the mass violence being rained on Vietnam. NVA welcomed our new vet members and respected their reluctance to talk about their traumatic battle experiences.

One afternoon after a general meeting at the Peace House, I went with a half dozen vets to a casual cafe in Pacific Beach. We pulled two tables together, ordered pizza, and rapped about the war. Ben, who had been with NVA from the start, said, "At this point, if we really want to win in 'Nam," we should declare peace and get the hell out. Otherwise, it's a meaningless, endless quagmire."

Another vet chipped in, "Right on, brother. WWII was one thing. It was worth dying for. But Vietnam—it sure as hell isn't my dad's war for freedom."

Ben mentioned how incredibly bored and frustrated he would get while out at sea, and I asked, "Did you ever get to the point where you actually looked forward to combat?"

"Oh, yeah! That's exactly the way it was with a lot of us." The other vets nodded.

One vet said, "That's why we joined—to defend freedom and see some action."

A stocky sailor with dark brown wavy hair and tortoise shell glasses said, "In my case, I didn't want to kill the North Vietnamese as much as I wanted to kill the Navy." I asked him what he meant, and he said, "I was so fucking bitter about all the bullshit coming from the Navy *and* from Tricky Dick that I was always on edge.

When I signed up, I bought the bunk that we were in 'Nam to fight the Commies. But after I was in, I figured we weren't really protecting Saigon; we were settin' it up so we could control it and grab stuff like oil and tin along the way. The brass and the government were using us big time. It made me super bitter. Any little thing could make me wanna freak out. I felt like I was headin' for a nervous breakdown. Yet, *I* was one of two guys on my ship in charge of a nuclear key, which shows you how bad the Navy's judgment was!"

"How does that work," I asked, "having a nuclear key?"

"They pick two guys to wear keys that can activate the nukes. I wore it around my neck day and night. Out of spite, I tried to talk the other guy carrying a key to help me launch. I didn't want to hurt anyone. I just wanted to sabotage the Navy. Pretty sick, I know. That's when I told 'em they'd better find someone else."

"Good move," Ben said with a grimace. "Personally, the military was a good thing for me. I got the discipline I needed, and for the first time in my life, I had a sense of purpose. I felt proud to serve . . . 'til 'Nam."

I asked, "Before you joined NVA, did you have any stereotypes about guys like me who protest the war?"

"Plenty," Ben said. "I had a *big* problem with protesters. I thought of 'em as spoiled rotten, smelly hippies on drugs."

Another vet quipped, "You mean they're not?"

We laughed, then a vet asked in a serious tone, "Francesco. I know you're applying as a CO 'cause you don't believe in killing. But what would you have done in WWII?"

"Good question. I can't honestly say. Ever see the movie *Friendly Persuasion*? It's about a family of Quakers who thought they'd never raise a gun to anyone. They couldn't even imagine being part of a war and killing. Then their family faced the Civil War. First, the son and then the father ended up grabbing guns to survive. They turned to violence because they thought it was their last resort. So, if I was faced with WWII, I *think* I'd fight nonviolently, maybe try to smuggle Jews out of countries that the Germans occupied, or maybe be a medic. But who really knows. You ask a hypothetical question and you're going to get a hypothetical answer."

Sam, another vet, looked at me skeptically. "Come on, Francesco. The only way to *save* lives in a time like WWII is with kick-ass military power."

"That's not the only way. Look at the nonviolent resistance of Gandhi. He sacrificed and suffered to free India from the British without using violence. I'm not saying that military power isn't necessary sometimes. I'm saying that whether it's soldiers or COs, both can fight evil in their own way. The worst thing is looking the other way and doing nothing."

"Damn straight," Ben exclaimed. "So, how about you guys pitching in and helping NVA with leafleting at the bus station? What do you say?"

Everybody nodded yes, then put their hands in the center of the table, one on top of another. In chorus, the vets yelled, "Yeah!"

"Here, here," Ben said, lifting his beer. "To Nonviolent Action!"

At 5:30 A.M., the downtown Greyhound Bus Depot was enveloped in a dark gray, misty shroud. I welcomed the five vets that joined our leafleting this morning and marveled at how they could muster so much enthusiasm at such a disgustingly early hour.

It was NVA's third leafleting, but this one was totally different from the previous two. Many of the draftees this morning appeared nervous and fearful. Some were hostile and handed our draft counseling leaflets back. As a draftee tore a leaflet up into tiny pieces, I hoped his reaction wouldn't discourage the vets who had recently joined NVA.

While Ben and I leafleted at the depot's main entrance, a few draftees stopped to talk. Politely, Ben asked one of them, "Do you *want* to go to Vietnam?"

The draftee shook his head. "Not really."

"Then you might think about doin' something about that before it's too late. I'm speaking from experience, buddy. I've been to 'Nam."

"You puttin' me on?"

"I'm dead serious. If you go, I can *guarantee* you that the *only* thing you're gonna be thinkin' about is gettin' back home alive. This war is bogus all the way."

After I offered a leaflet to a lanky, bony guy I thought was an inductee, he hollered, "I sell newspapers here, and I'm not *about* to go into the Army!"

"We're not recruiting," I explained. "We're offering draft counseling."

"Stick it up yours!" he shouted. "I don't want any of that *crap*. I wouldn't go in for anything!"

"It's *alternatives* to the draft," I persisted.

He flipped me off. "I'm not going in!"

"Fine," I said, giving up on him.

I turned my attention to a draft clerk who was giving me a suspicious gaze. "We called the draft board yesterday to let them know we'd be here leafleting," I said. That led to a mutually respectful rap on the merits (her view) and the folly (my view) of the war. She didn't make much eye contact but lowered her head and listened intently when I spoke. When I thanked her for the exchange, the glimmer of a smile came to her lips. It made my morning.

Ben and I walked over to the station's side entrance to check on Norie, Jim, and a couple of vets.

Jim said, "Tense morning. This one guy wadded up a leaflet and threw it in my face. I said to him, 'Have a nice day,' and that drove him even more nuts."

Norie added, "The guy was so freaked out that he kept yelling as loud as he could at Jim until someone told him to cool it or they'd call the police. Then he split. The whole time Jim was unbelievably calm."

"Good man," I said.

I led our NVA volunteers to the back of the bus station to wave goodbye to the three hundred-plus draftees. A prim middle-aged couple joined us. They looked over-dressed for the squalid bus station in their bright, expensive clothes. "My son is on one of those buses," the father said, "and he has a *terrible* knee injury."

His wife shook her head indignantly. "I saw another young man actually hobbling onto the bus."

The father wagged his finger as he spoke. "Now, if my son isn't deferred, I'm writing letters to senators and congressmen!" He looked at us as if we should be impressed. "I mean it! I'm going to do it!"

Norie looked at him squarely and said, "I lost my husband to this stupid war. Just do *something* before it's too late."

Today marked the third induction call this week. When my alarm went off at 4 A.M., I thought, *There's no way I can make this one. I'll tell everyone I overslept. No, that's not good enough. I'll tell 'em I have the flu. Yeah, that sounds more legit.*

Then, reluctantly, I reminded myself that the war was a life-and-death matter and not something to be avoided for my convenience. Also, I had made a *promise* to leaflet *every* draft call for one year. *If you break a promise now, it'll be easier to break others in the future. Don't start down that road.*

Just getting dressed seemed a major task.

As I arrived at the bus depot amid a dreary, thick fog, six NVA volunteers met me to leaflet. Two of the first people we leafleted were Mexican-Americans. They glanced down at our leaflets and looked up in bewilderment. "*No comprende.* No English."

My pathetic Spanish only elicited shrugs from the draftees. God only knows what I was saying to them. Determined to communicate, I asked a draft clerk, "Do you speak Spanish?"

"Of course. It's my native language!" she snapped.

"Do you think you can translate this leaflet?"

She snatched the leaflet out of my hand, and with obvious pride, began a rapid read in fluent Spanish.

The draftees nodded and looked at each other with raised eyebrows. "*Si, si*!" one muttered.

Suddenly, realizing the content of what she was reading, the clerk's eyes widened. "I should *never* have read this!" She stormed off, leaving our volunteers and on-looking draftees doubled over with laughter. Though it added a welcome touch of levity, I felt negligent. The lesson learned was to make all our leaflets bilingual.

As dozens of draftees were instructed by the draft clerks to form a long line and file onto the buses, I stared with a tinge of melancholy at the sign printed beside the bus doorway: DISCOVER GREYHOUND AMERICA.

At the next leafleting, on a Monday morning, I made a point of saying hi to a thirtyish draft board clerk who always wore her hair up in a bun. I wanted to break the ice so we wouldn't be looking at each other with mistrust. As she mechanically checked off the arriving draftees, I nodded hello. She lowered her clipboard and said, "I can tell there aren't going to be as many men here today as there's supposed to be. Bet you're glad."

"I am," I said.

"I really don't know why I'm in this job," she muttered, surprising me.

"What about looking for a different job?"

She paused. "Maybe." She almost missed a draftee who walked by and panicked. "Don't talk to me now. I have to count the men." I started to turn away, and she said, "Wait!"

I turned, and she glanced around as if to see if her supervisor was watching. "I *am* thinking about leaving."

"Maybe I can help you find another job?"

Under her breath, she muttered, "I'd like that if the job was stable."

"What's your name?"

"Robin."

"I'll see what I can do, Robin." We exchanged a smile as the bus driver boarded his bus and covered his flattop with a cap. Spontaneously, I decided to follow the driver onto his bus. The driver got behind the wheel as I stood in the aisle and looked out at the gallery of sad and anxious draftees that were bound for war. There wasn't anything I felt I could do except lighten the tension in the air.

"Excuse me," I said to the driver so loudly that even the draftees in the back could overhear. "Is this the bus that goes straight to Canada?"

There was a split-second of silent shock, and then the men erupted into a roar of applause and cheers. Even the bus driver laughed. I flashed the guys the peace sign and hopped off the bus only to be greeted with a stern look from Robin. "*Please*," she said, "don't *ever* do something like that again! You could get me fired."

"Sorry, Robin. I won't do it again. I promise."

In 1970, the FBI's director, J. Edgar Hoover, was engaged in a no-holds-barred war with America's civil rights and peace movements. Hoover's attacks on those he politically disagreed with were not new. Even President Truman complained that Hoover had turned the FBI into his private secret police.

For years, J. (John) Edgar Hoover had exceeded the jurisdiction of the FBI. He amassed secret files on political leaders, including presidents, and sought to undermine activists by collecting so-called evidence by illegal means. His methods included intimidation, threats, wire-taps, harassment, and unfounded smear attacks leaked to obliging media organizations. Additionally, the ACLU revealed that various undercover FBI agents impersonated journalists. The Associated Press called it "improper and inconsistent with a free press." This secret practice included the censoring and halting of information from whistleblowers. Such covert policies seriously damaged our democracy and our system of checks and balances.

For decades, from 1924 to 1972, the Hoover-controlled FBI ruled without accountability. What a striking contradiction—when We, the People and our legislators, allow our democratic society to be ruled by secrecy and deceit. Of course, the positive things that the FBI does should be recognized, such as protecting our country from domestic and international terrorism. But when the FBI treats political dissent in America as terrorism and devotes disproportionate resources to surveillance of nonviolent civil rights and peace activists, then the rights guaranteed in our Constitution are wantonly violated.

Integration of the bureau under Hoover was shamefully low. In his book, *1968 in America,* Charles Kaiser wrote, "When Bobby Kennedy had asked the director how many black agents worked for the FBI, Hoover told him truthfully that there were five—without mentioning that all of them were his personal servants."

Like the tides, glimmers of hope for ethical leadership in the bureau flowed in, but all too soon flowed out again. Occasionally, the FBI admitted to wrongdoing. For example, forty-plus years after Hoover vengefully targeted Dr. King, director of the FBI, James Comey, placed a copy of the letter authorizing the surveillance of Dr. King on his desk. In his memoir, Comey said it served as a reminder of the "shameful" history of the bureau's politically motivated excesses. Despite this acknowledgement, Comey increased monitoring of the Black Lives Matter movement while investigation of widespread police misconduct and brutality was treated as a relatively low priority.

As a conscientious objector and peace activist in 1970, I was aware of Hoover's excessive tactics, but I pushed them to the back of my mind—until the FBI called me . . .

Leafleting draftees at the Greyhound Bus Station. L-R: Francesco, draftee, draft clerk.

I'm talking about the war with a skeptical draft board clerk, 1970.

39

THE FBI CALLS
(1970)

"Justice is incidental to law and order."
—J. Edgar Hoover

Cruising south on the San Diego Freeway, I cranked up the radio as the Moody Blues questioned hate and death and war.

The thick fog made the station particularly grim as I arrived at the downtown Greyhound Bus Depot to leaflet draftees. Instead of the usual translucent mist, an opaque, massive cloud cloaked the entire depot. A murky gray mantle slowly drifted across the blinking neon lights. Harsh vivid colors flicked on and off the somber, ghost-like draftees as they slowly plodded toward the waiting buses.

The tall thin newspaper salesman who had hassled me in the past gave me a smiling nod. Instead of his usual ranting, he politely said, "I got no beef with you, man. Just, please, stay outta my way so I can sell my papers."

"No problem," I said. "What's your name?"

"Kevin. I wanna go back to school someday, but I don't have the dough." He looked down sadly, then snapped his head up. "Tomorrow's my birthday. I wanted off, but the bastards wouldn't let me have it. You know what?" he asked with a sly smile. "I think I feel a *real* bad cold comin' on." Suddenly, he exploded with a painfully loud goofy laugh.

Nearby I noticed a cab driver pulling over with a male passenger in the rear seat. The back window rolled down, and two slim young women wearing open blouses, short shorts, and spiked heels leaned down to negotiate with the potential john.

The draftees trickled in, then poured in heavy, the vast majority with expressions of weary resignation. As I leafleted with a half dozen NVA volunteers, a rough-faced man with the mangled nose of a boxer approached fast with one of our leaflets clutched tightly in his hand.

He pointed to the peace sign on the leaflet. "Do you know what that means?"

"It's the peace sign," I answered.

"It's the sign of Satan, and you're helping the godless communists by using it!"

"I heard that the sign represents the semaphore signals N and D for nuclear disarmament. The N is a signal in the shape of the upside-down V, and the D is the straight line."

"Wrong! It's a broken cross, and I'm the one with intelligence here, so don't tell me anything different!"

I tried to lighten his mood. "This is America—what do you say we agree to disagree?" I held out my hand to shake.

"You're nuts, just like your long-haired friend over there." He pointed to Ben. When I turned my head, he shoved the leaflet against my chest. "Here! Wipe your ass with it. That's all it's good for!"

He stomped off, and I said to Ben, "Sometimes when I meet someone that rude, I just want to take a leaflet and shove it in their big mouth."

Ben looked at me in shock. "Really?"

"Really." We laughed, then leafleted again. Just when the morning seemed to be mellowing, a bright light blinded us. "Hold it right there," a police officer yelled. "I want you two to answer a few questions." He raised the powerful light right in front of our faces.

"Could you cut the light first?" I asked, shielding my eyes.

He flicked it off and asked me, "Did you ever serve in the military?" I shook my head no, and he exclaimed, "I didn't think so!"

"Why would you ask that?" I queried.

"I'll ask the questions," the officer said gruffly. "When you leaflet, you'd better not block any entrances. That's breaking the law."

"We're careful about that," I said. "I called the police this morning and told them we'd be out here."

"Sure you did."

"Call headquarters if you like and ask if someone from the peace group Nonviolent Action called."

"Yeah? Well, I'll call right now, and we'll see about that, won't we?"

He called, and to his dismay, my story was verified. "Well . . . make *sure* you don't block any of the entrances," he repeated.

I joined Jim and Ben at the side entrance. "What an off day," Jim said.

Ben agreed. "Yeah, everybody is super cranky. Bummer of a morning."

A man in a gray suit behind Ben was listening in. "Just the opposite, my friend. Not a bummer morning at all. It's a *great* morning," he beamed, giving us a thumbs-up sign. "I just made a *ton* of sales!"

"Sales?" Jim asked.

"Life insurance for the future troops. Just in case." He walked off with a swagger, and we looked at each other grimly. I thought of the stone sign I saw on the hill at Camp Pendleton: WAR IS OUR BUSINESS AND BUSINESS IS GOOD.

Exhausted, I went home and got in bed to get some sleep before my grad school classes. Two hours later—about 9:30 A.M.—the phone jarred me from a deep slumber.

"Is this Francesco . . . Francesco Da Vinci?"

"Yes."

"I read your ad in the paper," the gravelly voice said. "Tell me about the leafleting. I want to help."

I paused. Something didn't seem right. The voice was middle-aged and without emotion. Then again, I thought, maybe it's his first time volunteering and he's nervous. "We leaflet draftees at the bus depot and sometimes at the draft board. It's so they can get counseling on their legal rights."

"Who are the lawyers you work with?"

I was silent, taken aback. No volunteer had ever asked that kind of question. Then, I picked up the buzz of indistinct voices in the background on his end.

"Are you calling from an office?"

He paused. "Yeah, the Resistance."

My brow furrowed as I wondered if he was mental.

"Actually, this is the FBI," he said solemnly. "I'm agent Earl Wood. If you don't believe me, you can call information for the FBI headquarters in San Diego. Get the number and call me back."

Earlier this morning, a police officer at the bus depot had made a call to his station to verify my story. Now I was the one verifying a story. What a bizarre Kafkaesque morning! I hung up, dialed 411, and got the FBI number. "Agent Earl Wood, please." Sure enough, I was connected.

"Earl Wood," he said coolly.

I felt ticked off by the agent's earlier deception. "Why not tell me who you are from the beginning? It would've been a lot more honest and direct, don't you think?"

"Then you wouldn't give me any information and I wouldn't be able to do my job, which is to put certain people in jail."

The thinly veiled warning shocked me, but I wasn't about to give him the satisfaction of sensing alarm in my voice. Resentfully, I wondered why they were wasting their time on a law-abiding citizen who was just as patriotic as they were. "Is that supposed to be a threat?"

"It's a statement of fact, that's all."

"I'm not doing anything illegal. I'm against the draft and the war, like a *lot* of people."

"Do you know anything about sedition?" His tone was brittle.

"We're not trying to overthrow the government," I said. "It's just the opposite. We're leafleting draftees because we want draftees to know their rights."

"If I were you, I'd bring those leaflets you're circulating down to my office. I want to interview you."

"Sorry, but I'm not interested in that."

"Then I might drop by while you're leafleting."

"Fine with me."

He paused. "I've got no good reason to suspect you of anything now, but you can bet we'll be watching you."

He hung up, and a stream of paranoid thoughts raced through my mind: *Did the FBI have a hand in my CO case? Did they want to make certain I would go to prison as soon as possible for being a CO and an activist?*

The next thing I knew, I was taking the phone apart to see if it was bugged. Nothing there. *Maybe the whole apartment is bugged? My God, maybe even the bedroom is being monitored. Was my lovemaking with Jane on a tape in some FBI bin?* A torrent of worrisome scenarios played out in my mind. I calmed myself and tried to take a reasonable middle approach—concern without paranoia.

Suddenly I remembered—for weeks, all our mail had arrived torn open. I complained to the Post Office to no avail. *Was it the work of the FBI, and if so, did they* want *me to know they were watching?*

I sat at my desk feeling that my privacy and Jane's had been violated. After all, the bulk of my time and energy was spent trying to better my country nonviolently. I didn't deserve to be treated like a criminal. The stack of draft leaflets atop my desk caught my eye. I mused on the epigram at the bottom of our leaflets, words I had written to stay strong and positive through my CO ordeal: HATE IS OUT OF FEAR. IF WE ARE TO FEAR, LET US FEAR HATE. LOVE IS FROM COURAGE. IF WE ARE TO BE COURAGEOUS, LET US LOVE.

Don't let them intimidate you, I ordered myself. But I *was* intimidated, and I knew there would be hell to pay with Jane. I wanted to hide the fact that the FBI called, but this was way too big to bury. She had a right to know. *When I break the news, is this going to jeopardize our whole relationship?*

When Jane returned home from work, she read the concern on my face and asked, "What's going on?"

"Well . . . the FBI called."

"What?"

"The FBI called. They don't like the leafleting at the bus station, but NVA has every right to do it. I don't know why they're hassling me."

"What did you expect?" Jane asked. "You start a peace group in *Navy Town USA*, and you're just asking for trouble. Of course, it's going to grab their attention." She folded her arms, her emotional road sign that said loud and clear *Don't even think of holding me now.* After a few moments, her tone softened. "I'm afraid."

"We're not doing anything wrong, so let's just ignore 'em. We've gotta stick together on this."

"We're *not* together on this," Jane said. "We were already going through hell with your CO case, and now this. I've had it. I can't even stand to look at you now." She went straight to the bedroom, returned with a pillow and a sheet, and tossed them on the living room couch.

"I really feel bad about this, but . . ."

"Well, it's too little and too late!" She slammed the bedroom door shut with a bang.

The next morning, I was abruptly awakened by a rant. I opened my eyes, and Jane was overhead talking to me as if I was wide awake. "I've been putting up with a lot, but no more," she said firmly. "That call from the FBI was the last straw. They're probably listening to us right now . . . in our *home,* Francesco! All because of you! I thought hard about this last night. I'm thinking of leaving you."

"Jane," I said, shocked. I reached for her hand, but she backed away.

"I'll give you a few days to make a choice. Either drop NVA *and* being a CO, or I'm leaving for good."

We had clearly reached the most precarious point ever in our three-year relationship.

I didn't know what I wanted to do. I only knew that I didn't want to make a hasty decision that would forever plague me with regret. Just before Jane went off to work, I said to her, "I decided I'm going to drive up to the Bay Area to meditate on everything."

"That might be good for both of us," she said. "It'll give us time to think in private."

Jane, c. 1970. (Photo: F. Da Vinci)

40

JANE'S ULTIMATUM
(1970)

"We are afraid to care too much, for fear that the other person does not care at all."

—Eleanor Roosevelt

The first stop on my retreat north was at the home of a family friend, Melvin Powers. Melvin was one of Dad's self-help book publishers. He showed me in and said, "I'm Jewish and you're Italian. We *have* to eat something!"

Over coffee and cheesecake, I told Melvin about my conflict with Jane, and he said, "I'm not surprised that she's thinking about leaving. What surprises me is that she's still there!" Melvin smiled. "I suspect most people don't understand your position, and quite a few *hate* what they don't understand. Am I right?"

"True."

Melvin refilled my coffee and continued, "Your father is wealthy. He could easily pick up the phone, call a senator, and have you out of the draft in a heartbeat. But he tells me you won't accept that. Why?"

"I'm just being what I am—a CO."

"You're anti-war?"

"I am, but I don't just want to be *anti*-things. I'm trying to stand for alternatives to violence. That's why I formed a peace group in San Diego—Nonviolent Action."

"What does the peace group do?" Melvin asked.

"We've got two main projects. We support the farm workers and we leaflet draftees with a list of free draft lawyers."

"Wonderful. I've got to say, it's admirable the way your generation is focused on helping others. I respect that, and I respect that you're a CO, but I wonder if you think it's wise to go to jail on principle?"

"I don't know about wise, but I can accept it if things come down to that." I paused. "Do I seem pig-headed?"

"Very! If I were in your position, I'd pick up and move to Canada."

"I think if Jane and I moved there just for her sake, I'd always resent her, and that wouldn't be good for either of us."

"You've got a point there, but I don't think you stand a chance with your draft board. If you don't compromise, you'll probably wind up in jail . . . and no more girlfriend."

When we finished our cheesecake, Melvin walked me to the door and gave me a fatherly hug.

As I headed north on the freeway, I sensed that whatever decision I came to in the Bay Area would mark a turning point in my life.

When I reached northern California with its scenic views of the Santa Cruz Mountains, I stopped by the Institute for the Study of Nonviolence. I had hoped to say hello to Joan Baez, but the staff said she was traveling. Kindly, they offered me a room for the night, and I took them up on it.

Bright and early the next morning, I took a long quiet walk in the wooded area surrounding the institute and mulled over my rocky relationship with Jane. As I strolled down a dirt path that cut through the woods, I thought, *Doesn't real love come down to mutual growth? Why should I feel guilty for following the path that's right for me as a CO? But I do, dammit. There are real differences between Jane's outlook and mine. Jane's main goal is security—a stable, happy home. She would like to see me manipulate my way out of the draft and take a nine-to-five job. My priority is to continue my peace work with NVA and make a moral statement as a conscientious objector. I won't turn my head from the social injustice at home or the war abroad. I'm happy that Jane feels fulfilled helping people as a social worker, but not happy when she tries to change me into somebody I'm not. On the other hand, I recognize that she's put up with a helluva lot out of love.*

I drove into San Francisco and attended the launch of a Bay Area project called "Draft Refuser Support." When I compared the liberal San Francisco community with staunchly conservative San Diego, it seemed I'd traveled to another planet! At the meeting, I was told that Bay Area civic leaders actively support draft refusers and their families before, during, and after trial. People smiled at the shock on my face. And whenever I was introduced as a CO, most people would say something like, "Thanks for the stand you're taking. We owe you."

At the Draft Refuser Support meeting, one man said, "I served as a CO medic in World War II. What most people still don't understand is that it takes at least as much courage *not* to kill as it does to kill."

Heartened from the meeting, I visited the draft counseling office at the University of California, Berkeley. Greeted by the head counselor, I explained my dilemma—whether to drop being an activist and CO or whether to break up with Jane. She said, "In a few minutes, I'm meeting with young people who are in training to help draftees like yourself. If you don't mind, it would be wonderful for them to hear your situation."

I obliged, and she opened the door and showed in two dozen trainees. We sat in a circle on the floor, and I said, "First, I'd like to thank all of you for choosing to spend your free time helping draftees. You're not just counseling; you're saving lives."

Larry, a Vietnam vet officer turned CO, said, "I was in the brig for over a year. Sometimes I would regret that I was a CO. Looking back, I think if I had to do it over again, I'd split to Canada."

One of the counselors-to-be said, "I don't know if it's such a good idea to give your opinion in front of Francesco. We should be more objective."

"Personally," I interjected, "I'm glad he's not holding back. I like to hear how he thinks as long as he doesn't *order* me what to do!" Everyone laughed.

"Good," another guy said, "'cause I'm gonna tell you how *I* feel." Everyone laughed again. "I *wouldn't* go to Canada. There's so much to do in America. I've grown up here, and I know it best. But I wouldn't go to prison either. I'd get out with a fake deferment and work for peace. You can't do much in prison."

I said, "I'm not comfortable taking a fake deferment *or* with going to Canada."

The trainee looked at me, perplexed. "Why not?"

"Means and ends," I answered. Several people nodded. "My girlfriend gave me an ultimatum—she wants me to drop being a CO and stop my peace work, or she says she's leaving. I don't want to lose her, but I don't want to give up my stand either. Whatever I end up doing, I'm glad I met all of you and that we shared this time together. It means a heck of a lot to me."

I stood and asked the counselor hesitantly, "Do you mind if I say goodbye by asking everyone to join hands?" I feared I was making a fool of myself, that it would be too much of a 'touchy-feely' idea that would unnerve everyone. But before she could reply, everyone stood and clasped hands. Quaker-style, we closed our eyes in silent reflection. Shortly afterward, my CO dilemma was answered. What vividly came to mind was Shakespeare's adage in *Hamlet—This above all: to thine own self be true.*

At that moment, with a new sense of certainty, I knew what I had to do—go forward as a CO and keep NVA going, even if it meant the painful end of my relationship with Jane.

Stoically, I left Berkeley and drove south along the coast, dreading what I knew I had to say when I returned home.

41

RESOLUTION
(1970)

"First best is falling in love. Second best is being in love.
Least best is falling out of love. But any of it is better
than never having been in love."

—Maya Angelou

Once I returned from the Bay Area, I sat with Jane on our couch, holding her hand. I couldn't move. I couldn't speak. Then I pushed the words out and said, "I can't stop being a CO, and I can't stop working to end the war. If I did that for your sake, I'd just end up resenting you, and we'd both be miserable."

In the silence that followed, I thought back to the first time we had met on a blind date. *In our three years together, we've shared so much . . . and now it's over.* I half-expected her to pull her hand away, but she left it in mine.

"While you were away," she said, "I changed my mind. I decided that even though I hate what you're putting us through, I don't love you any less. I respect and love you so much, Francesco. I figured that instead of going back and forth on our relationship, I'd commit to it all the way. Even when you're sent to prison, I'll get a job in the area to be close."

I stared in joyful shock. Over my tears, I said, "You're amazing. It takes so much to do what you're doing."

After almost losing our relationship, the bond between Jane and I seemed stronger. We spent less time fighting and more time united on how we would handle the draft and the threat of prison.

After a romantic dinner at home, Jane announced, "I'd feel better if we were engaged. I think that commitment will keep us close, even while you're in prison."

I smiled. "I'd like that."

The site I selected for my proposal was The Cove, a breathtakingly gorgeous park in La Jolla. With the ring hidden in my jacket, I took Jane's hand and led her onto a grassy expanse that overlooked the tranquil Pacific Ocean.

"What a beautiful day," Jane said.

"It is," I said, and I got down on one knee and proposed. "Will you marry me, Jane?"

She put her hand over her mouth and said, "Yes! *YES!*"

When I slid the ring onto her finger, her face glowed with joy. It had been so long since I had seen such an unrestrained smile on her lips. Jane wiped away a tear, and we hugged. My second gift to her was a magnifying glass.

"What's this for?" she asked.

"To see the diamond."

With the growing number of volunteers at Nonviolent Action, we expanded our leafleting from the bus depot to the draft board as well. We not only leafleted draftees, but we also made a point of talking with the draft board clerks about the war. The best time to converse with them was in the early morning, just before they entered work. We never *told* the clerks to do anything. But if they expressed qualms about the morality of their work—forcibly sending young men off to a war they did not believe in—we heard them out. And, if they *really* wanted out from the draft board, we brainstormed with them about alternative work.

Early this morning, we greeted clerks Robin and Sandy in the parking lot of the draft board and offered them coffee. The ladies gladly accepted, then sat in their car and smoked, waiting until the last possible moment to go inside. "We were placed here by Civil Service," Robin explained. "The pay is real low, but the personal satisfaction *more* than makes up for it," she snickered.

"Do a lot of clerks come and go?" I asked.

"No, but when someone does quit, it takes a long time to find a replacement. It's not just 'cause the war is so unpopular—the job is *boring*."

"There's a big generation gap inside," Sandy added. "The younger clerks are more lenient. They'll try and help guys who want out. Sometimes it affects the way their files are processed."

"What do you mean?"

"Let's say a file containing a request for a deferment happens to be near the top one day, and it happens to be seen by a clerk who is sympathetic. Then that draftee might not have such a problem getting the deferment and getting it fast."

"Really!" I exclaimed.

"Oh, yeah. And sometimes, the paperwork that speeds up a draftee's induction call is conveniently left undone. The clerks that do that are usually young. But if an older gung-ho clerk sees that same file, it's the other way around. Even though legitimate deferments are allowed and are *supposed* to be granted, some of the clerks don't believe in deferments. What they'll do is see to it that the draftees go into the Army right away, no matter what deferment they should get."

I stared in shock. "Amazing. I appreciate that you shared that."

I thought back to when I first met Sandy and Robin. There was such an emotional wall. Now they were opening up more than I could have ever imagined.

Robin glanced at her watch, snuffed out her cigarette, and nudged Sandy. "We should get going."

"I'm still working on lining up a new job for you," I said.

Robin looked at me hopefully. "I'm just working here for the money, and that's not much. I'd quit this job in a snap and even consider draft counseling on the side."

"Now I'm *really* going to work on it."

Sandy started toward the door. "We'd better get in there, Robin."

All afternoon I called for a job for Robin but only came up with one lead—a florist shop. The pay was so low I didn't think Robin would go for it. I passed on the info just the same but never heard from Robin after that.

A week later, I showed up early at the draft board and greeted Sandy as she arrived for work. "Where's Robin?" I asked.

She smiled. "She's working at the florist shop and doing draft counseling. She's super happy."

I grinned ear-to-ear, then stared at Sandy as if to ask silently if she wanted to do the same thing. She crushed her cigarette in the car ashtray and said, "I'm not ready to quit cigarettes *or* my job, even though both are killing me."

In my second year of grad school, I faced the task of writing my Master's Thesis. The topic I decided on was conscientious objection to war and my work with Nonviolent Action. But sadly, no faculty member would sponsor my paper. I shouldn't have been surprised. Faculty and administration viewed me at best as an outcast and at worst as an anarchist.

Finally, with persistence, I found a faculty member who would at least consider my controversial topic. Dr. Campisi, my sociology professor, asked uneasily, "What do you want to call your paper?"

I stifled "The Insanity of War" and went with the more academic, "The Dynamics of Conscientious Objection and Nonviolent Action in America."

Dr. Campisi grimaced. "I agree the peace movement and its facets are a very important subject, but there are certain personal factors that I need to consider. Let's face it, Francesco, that topic will be *anathema* to the administration. Everyone around here knows that you're a CO and activist . . . that the Dean expelled you . . . illegally, of course . . . and was then forced to bring you back. While I understand that his actions were blatantly unjust, I need to be careful to safeguard my career. Can you understand my reluctance to be associated with you?"

I looked directly at the professor. “You’re my last hope for a thesis, Dr. Campisi. I understand that you’re hesitant, and for good reason, but maybe you won’t let that stop you.”

The professor avoided my gaze, needlessly shuffled the papers on his desk, and said, “The only way I could even *think* about being your sponsor would be if you picked a topic less controversial. It may seem hypocritical but consider this. I’m up for tenure soon, and I’ve got a family to think about. So, if you can come up with another thesis subject that’s less controversial, I’ll consider being your sponsor.”

“I understand,” I said. “I like the idea of changing our dysfunctional educational system. How about a thesis that compares different systems and teaching methods?”

Professor Campisi hemmed and hawed. “I’m still having second thoughts. It’s not the topic . . .”

“I’ll respect whatever you decide, but like I said, you’re my last hope for getting my thesis. You turn me down, and the university wins with their discrimination.”

Campisi looked out his office window pensively and then said, “Oh, screw it. This is against my better judgment, Francesco, but I’ll be your sponsor. Maybe that charge-the-windmills virus of yours has infected me!”

I grinned with relief and said, “I admire you for doing this.”

“Now you’ve got me smiling, and I shouldn’t be!” We laughed.

After completing and receiving approval of my Master’s Thesis on education, the thesis was bound and placed in the university library. I wrote my parents, and they were delighted. However, shortly afterward, I received a shocking letter from the University that put my two years of grad school work in jeopardy.

42

PEACE WORK FULL-TIME
(1970)

"You always have two choices: your commitment versus your fear."
—Sammy Davis, Jr.

I figured that the new letter I received from my grad school was to congratulate me on the approval of my master's thesis. Instead, it said that upon further review of my records, it was discovered that I lacked credit in a certain required statistics course. The letter stated that even though my master's degree had been approved and placed in the university library, it was now "invalid."

I called the admissions office secretary. "Why did you wait until now to tell me about this? You had my records for two years, and no one ever said anything about a required statistics course."

"We just noticed it."

When I hung up, I couldn't be absolutely sure that this was once again a case of political intolerance, but it certainly appeared to be. It gave me a taste of what women and minorities sometimes go through—suspecting discrimination, and not being in a position to prove it without a lengthy and expensive court battle.

The first time the university kicked me out for my political views, it was obvious what they were doing. This time it was for a technicality they could claim was an innocent error. Discrimination would be much harder to prove, so I considered dropping out of grad school and foregoing my Master's Degree. I had no interest in taking the statistics class and figured that even if I did, the university might just come up with one more reason to deny my degree.

I asked myself, *Which is more important, your studies or your peace work?* Easy answer—Nonviolent Action. Clearly, my aversion to the war and my passion for peace superseded the value of being sequestered at the university. It had long been a dream of mine to be a full-time peacemaker. Here was my chance to realize that dream.

I consulted Jane about the choice, and, surprisingly, she supported that I work for peace. "I know how much the peace work means to you," she said. "Besides, you don't have that much time left before prison."

The news that I was dropping out of grad school didn't go over well with my folks. Instead of the steady generous checks that came from home, financial support all but dried up. Dad gave me a clear message: *You won't do things our way and get your Master's Degree, then you pay the price. You and Jane are on your own.*

To give me at least six months of uninterrupted peace work, I sold my car with Jane's approval, and we agreed to share her VW Bug. Far more than I had ever applied myself in grad school, I *plunged* into peacemaking. I began with research—studying the works of American nonviolent activists. For example, in 1846, Thoreau was arrested by the local sheriff for failure to pay a poll tax. He believed the tax supported the Mexican-American War and the expansion of slavery. Thoreau's protest inspired me to withhold my phone tax from the government, a tax that I believed was being used to support the Vietnam war.

The following is the letter I sent to the telephone company:

> Dear friends,
>
> I am deducting the federal tax from my telephone bill payment because, essentially, it is a tax for war. I am against the Vietnam war, and all wars for that matter. Day by day the loss of lives increases. If I were to pay the federal tax I would hold myself complicit with the killing. I am not doing this to make trouble for you. It is simply a matter of conscience.
>
> Sincerely,
> Francesco Da Vinci

Not long after I withheld my phone tax and wrote the phone company, I stopped in at my Security Pacific bank in Pacific Beach to make one of my customary paltry withdrawals. The manager frantically motioned me over to his desk. "Francesco, you troublemaker, you," he said with a mischievous smile.

"What do you mean?"

He looked around and lowered his voice. "You're not paying your phone tax, are you?"

"How did you know that?"

"Two FBI agents came in here yesterday and told me that they were taking the money out of your savings account. I think it amounted to three dollars and sixty-six cents! Three lousy dollars and change! Nothing!"

"I don't pay it because the money goes for the war."

"I get it. The war sucks. When the agents told me what they were up to, I thought to myself, *Don't you guys have* better *things to do than this?"* The manager

EXPLANATION OF OTHER CHARGES AND CREDITS ~~ON~~ OFF YOUR TELEPHONE BILL

714 291- 806([illegible]73) FINAL B DEC 07,1970 PAGE 1

DESCRIPTION	MONTHLY RATE	PERIOD FROM	PERIOD THROUGH	CHARGE OR CREDIT
CREDIT FOR SERVICE PREVIOUSLY BILLED	525	NOV 23	DEC 12	333CR
US TAX				33CR
			TOTAL CARRIED TO BILL	366CR

I have deducted the US Taxes for war from the enclosed bills.

in peace,
frank

laughed. "You're quite the troublemaker." He looked over his shoulder again. "Keep up the good work, my friend. This war is an abomination."

"Do you know one of the main reasons I decided to bank here?" I asked.

"No, why?"

"The name of your bank—Security Pacific. Indirectly, it tells your customers 'Real security is in peace, not war.'"

"Hey, I never thought of it that way. *Security . . . Pacific.* Cool!"

43

MARRYING JANE
(1970)

"One word frees us of all the weight and pain in life.
That word is love."
—Sophocles

On Christmas day, Jane and I were married outdoors on the majestic cliffs of Torrey Pines State Preserve in La Jolla. We stood on a plateau high above the ocean, the blue water sparkling below.

Ralph flew out from the east coast and served as Best Man. He wore bell-bottoms and a colorful paisley shirt under an open vest. My brother looked pretty much the same as when I last saw him about a year and a half ago. The only noticeable change was a thick, dark brown mustache that reminded me of musician David Crosby's.

As a thank you for coming to the wedding, I gave Ralph my favorite photo book—*The Family of Man.* It contained an international collection of images that showed the commonality of people around the world. The curator, Edward Steichen, described the book as a mirror of the essential oneness of humankind. Inside the cover, I wrote, "To Ralph, my dear brother: One day may the vast majority of men and women on Earth look at each other as brothers and sisters."

I gave Ralph a big hug, then turned to greet the other guests. Ralph tapped me on the shoulder. "By the way, you don't have to worry."

"About what?"

"I'm not gonna get high or drunk at your wedding."

I nodded thanks, and Ralph joined 22 of our friends from NVA who stood in a semi-circle around Jane and me. Among them were Jews, Christians, a Muslim, a Buddhist, agnostics, and atheists. Unfortunately, neither Jane's parents nor mine flew out from the east coast because they disapproved of my CO stand. The absence of our folks hurt us, but we had become somewhat accustomed to the family at a distance.

We were particularly isolated from Jane's family. Her parents, devout Catholics, frowned not only on my conscientious objection but also on the fact that I did not belong to the church. Though Jane had broken from Catholicism long before we met, she hid that fact from her family. In their eyes, I was the heathen corrupting their daughter. It was a rough way to begin our marriage, but perhaps the parental adversity ended up bringing Jane and me even closer.

With the ocean's serene sounds in the background, Ralph handed me the wedding ring. I slipped it on Jane's finger as a symbol of our love. Jane never looked lovelier, her face glowing with joy. A circular wreath of small flowers adorned her hair. Her dress was sky blue accessorized with a thin white sash around the waist. I wore dark brown pin-striped bell-bottoms and a light brown tunic over a white shirt with a Nehru collar.

Once we exchanged vows, we sealed the ceremony with a kiss. Ralph and the NVA volunteers enthusiastically applauded and cheered.

At the close of the wedding, Jane presented me with Gandhi's *An Autobiography*. Inside she had inscribed a poem by Stephen Spender that she asked Ralph to read aloud to everyone:

Why cannot the one good
Benevolent feasible
Final dove, descend?
And the wheat be divided?
And the soldiers sent home?
And the barriers torn down . . .
. . . Love's need does not cease.

Our romantic honeymoon took place in idyllic, snow-covered Lake Tahoe. We had saved enough money to rent a charming two-story pine cabin. After a candlelit dinner, we made love in front of the rock fireplace. The lovemaking resumed the next morning but was sharply interrupted when the maid knocked on the door and quickly started to enter the room to clean. Jane and I, in the throes of passion, yelled, "Wait!" In our hurry to get on the floor and hide, the couch flipped on top of us.

The maid called out, "Ai-yai-yai! Need help?"

Jane and I stopped laughing long enough to answer in unison, "No! No help!" Shortly after we returned from our honeymoon, a rude reality-check impinged on our bliss. A new draft card arrived in response to my appeal in Oakland. Once again, Uncle Sam failed to recognize me as a CO and classified me 1-A, ready for war. I imagined my future life behind bars—the loss of freedom, the daily dull routine, the authoritarianism, and especially, life without Jane.

That evening I nervously waited until Jane came home from work. When I told her that the draft board would soon order me to report for induction, a faraway look came to her eyes, and she murmured, "Just hold me."

Our Wedding Day, La Jolla, Christmas 1970.

44

NVA GAINS MOMENTUM
(1971)

"War is the slaughter of human beings,
temporarily regarded as enemies . . .

—Jeannette Rankin

Amid my CO ordeal, and with the February 8th U.S. invasion of Laos, a massive peace rally was planned at the University of California, San Diego (UCSD). The angered students were protesting the widening of the war and the merciless bombing.

Organizers of the protest knew about the peace work of Nonviolent Action, and I was invited to be one of the main speakers. When I was informed that the audience would be about two thousand students, I got the jitters.

I entered the jam-packed venue, and my eyes widened as I scanned the daunting throng. An organizer of the event tapped me on the shoulder, startling me. "You're going on third."

The first speaker, a Students for a Democratic Society (SDS) member, began his talk with a touch of levity. "Early in Nixon's career, he applied to work for the FBI but was rejected. That was probably the best decision the FBI ever made!" However, the rest of his speech was filled with hateful rhetoric, making a scapegoat of Nixon.

The next speaker went on about the evils of Nixon, calling him "perversely paranoid" and a "pathological liar." The attacks were personal, with no mention of alternatives to Nixon's policies.

Then a vet against the war introduced me. "And now, the founder of Nonviolent Action."

As I approached the microphone, I made up my mind to stress what students could do here and now to help draftees, rather than simply rant about the failings of Nixon's foreign policy in Vietnam.

Anxiously, I looked out over the crowd. I felt passionate about speaking for peace, but I had never before talked to so *many* people. I told myself, *Don't fret about the size of the crowd or how they'll react. Focus on the war and what you want to say.* If I screwed up, I'd not only be letting myself down; I'd be letting down NVA. Somewhere out there in the crowd were my friends from NVA—Norie, Jim, and Ben—ready with clipboards in hand to sign up anyone who wanted to help.

To no avail, I scanned the swarm of students hoping to spot Jane. She *had* to be out there somewhere. Then, unexpectedly, near the front and off to the side, I spied Jane's smiling face. I smiled back, and a wave of calm and comfort came over me.

As if Jane sensed my nervous hesitation, she gave a little nod.

I took a breath and tried to find common ground with the crowd. "I know most of us here are deeply concerned about the policies of President Nixon."

"Damn right!" a guy yelled.

For a moment, I forgot what I was going to say. "Yeah, but what good does it do to just complain about Nixon?" That question seemed to offend. Silence. "Why not use our time and energy to do something positive right here in San Diego, like fighting today's modern-day slavery—the draft! The draft is taking the lives of young guys who have no idea what they're fighting for in Vietnam! I don't know what we're fighting for myself, do you?"

"No!" came the reply in chorus.

"Our troops are being maimed and blown to pieces for a cause that they, and most Americans, don't believe in! We've got to help stop it!" *Applause.* "The peace group that I represent, Nonviolent Action, needs you to help us end the draft and the war. Are you with us on that?"

"Yes!"

"Here's how you can help: Join us when we leaflet at the induction calls. Most draftees don't know their rights. Because of that, they're not getting the deferments they're supposed to get. Our leaflets give them the names of draft lawyers that will counsel them for free. So, if you help, you're giving draftees access to their rights, *and* you're saving lives! Let's show 'em that we care about 'em! Are you with Nonviolent Action on this?"

"Yes!"

"We've been *talking* a lot here at this rally about the war; now let's *do* something about it! Will anyone here help us to help others? Let me hear you!"

"YESSS!"

"Great! Nonviolent Action volunteers are circulating through the crowd with sign-up sheets. Put your name down, and you can be proud that you didn't just stand by, that you were a part of the movement to put a stop to the slaughter on both sides. Be a peacemaker!"

At the next induction call, fourteen new UCSD students showed up at the downtown bus station and helped us leaflet draftees. Then along came Spring

Break. With more free time and less study pressure, 11 more students were willing to make the sacrifice of getting up at the ungodly hour of 5 A.M. to leaflet.

Before we knew it, the total ranks of NVA swelled to over 100 members! The buildup was partly because dissent to the war was now being accorded a new level of respect. It became *popular* to be against the war. In the next few months, our grassroots movement grew and *kept* growing. It was an exciting time, and due to the increased media coverage, NVA became the talk of the town.

Once we were up and running with the Farm Workers Project and the Draft Project, a charismatic visiting history professor from M.I.T. contacted us.

Eric had a full red beard and a vibrant, captivating speaking voice. He had formed a study group at UCSD to discuss nonviolence. When he learned about NVA, he and a dozen of his students joined our ranks.

Eric and I quickly became friends, balancing each other's strengths. As a professor of history, Eric was more the academic, always steeped in research; I was the doer, pushing for social change and peace through nonviolent action.

The professor had an incredible talent for thorough, detailed research on the war. He calculated the incredible waste of resources that were required to wage war in Vietnam. Fastidiously, he checked and rechecked his facts. For example, he called attention to the fact that aircraft carriers deployed to Vietnam were used by the Johnson and Nixon administrations to perpetuate the heaviest bombing war in history. Eric illustrated how our technological nation was unleashing savage power against non-technological Vietnam and other small countries.

My skill was in applying Eric's research as a foundation for our nonviolent activism. As an anology, the professor was the designer of an aircraft; I was the test pilot. We printed Eric's research on flyers, then I organized leafleting campaigns at grocery stores and shopping centers, conveying Eric's latest fact-finding.

Eric was kind enough to offer me a part-time position as his teaching assistant in the History department of UCSD. The subject of the course was close to me—*The History of Nonviolent Action in America.*

Even the history of UCSD was fitting for our course. The founding chancellor of the university was Herbert York, a renowned physicist who helped develop the atomic bomb and later changed his perspective and became a passionate champion of arms control.

I felt especially grateful to Eric for offering the teaching assistant job because Jane and I badly needed extra money while I worked for peace full-time. A secretary in the administrative office summoned me to campus to sign my contract. When I arrived and filled out the forms, she said, "Good. Now you need to sign the loyalty oath."

"Why would the university assume that loyalty can be measured by an oath?" I asked, smiling. "Have you ever heard someone say, 'Hey, I'm not going to sign this because I have no intention of defending America against foreign and domestic enemies!'"

She gave me an amused look. "No, I haven't." She pointed to the document. "Sign here."

"But it says that I've read the California Constitution in its entirety. It's *humongous*! I haven't read it. All I know about it is that it goes back to gold rush times, and it prohibits slavery. You must have signed the oath. Did *you* read it?"

She winced. "Actually, no."

"Has *anyone* you've known at the university ever read it?"

"Mr. Da Vinci, it would be much easier for everyone concerned if you just signed."

"Seriously though, it seems somebody should protest this requirement. The only way I'll feel comfortable signing it is to add a reservation, telling them that I haven't read the California Constitution in its entirety."

"Just as I've never heard of anyone who has read the California Constitution, I've also never heard of anyone challenging it," she said. "But let me warn you—if you add reservations when you sign, it's *very* likely they won't accept it that way. I can almost guarantee their reply—'No oath, no pay.'"

In a few days, the secretary called. "Because of the reservation you added stating that you haven't read the California Constitution in its entirety, I'm afraid that you will not receive a salary as a teaching assistant."

On the first day of the class on nonviolence, Eric and I were amazed that the course drew a record enrollment—over 300 students! The unexpected interest in the course forced Eric and me to move from a classroom to a spacious auditorium.

On the first day of class, Eric surprised me by beginning his lecture with the issue of the university loyalty oath. "This class, The History of Nonviolent Action in America, began even before the course started," Eric said. "Francesco Da Vinci, my assistant, would not sign the loyalty oath because he would not lie and say that he had read the California Constitution. The university oath requires everyone who signs it to have read the entire state constitution, which is one of the longest and most technical constitutions in the world. In my many years of teaching, I've *never* read a state constitution, and I've never met anyone who's read all 354 pages!" The students roared with laughter. "Yet, I signed it," Eric said. "I guess some battles are too tiring for me to fight now. Francesco, however, was willing to sacrifice his teaching salary as a matter of principle. So you see, you can take nonviolent action, but you've got to be prepared to accept the consequences to make a moral point." He looked over at me, and I nodded gratefully. "You must feel proud," Eric said.

"Not really," I quipped. "I really could have used that money!"

45

CHARLIE, MY NINTH DRAFT ATTORNEY

(1971)

"I ain't draft dodging. I ain't burning no flag. I ain't running to Canada. I'm staying right here."

—Muhammad Ali

With the threat of prison closing in, I conferred with my latest draft attorney.

My previous draft lawyers, without exception, declined to stick with my CO case. The fact that I would not take advantage of legal tricks to avoid the draft made me appear hell-bent on prison. At my most recent interview, the vexed attorney asked, "Do you *want* to go to jail?"

"Just because I'm *willing* to go doesn't mean I *want* to go."

"What *do* you want, Mr. Da Vinci?"

"It's simple—I want to stick to the truth."

Silence. "And your religion, if I may ask?"

I pointed to my heart. "A personal one."

"So, you have no organized religion to fall back on, which would give you at least a slightly better chance of being approved as a CO, and you won't even *consider* stalling your draft board?"

"That's right."

He cleared this throat. "Uh . . . to be honest, I'm not really comfortable with this case. Nothing personal, Mr. Da Vinci, but I'd like to refer you to an attorney I know who is a bit of a maverick. Charlie actually *likes* hopeless cases."

The bio on draft attorney Charlie Khoury, a former Annapolis Naval Cadet, gave me the image of an attorney with a buzz cut. But our first meeting shattered that illusion. Sitting across from me at his desk, Charlie was hip-looking with a light beard and a trim Afro. Slight crinkles extended beneath the eyes that studied me intently. “Well, Francesco, I was warned that you don’t know what the word *compromise* means.”

“I know what it means,” I said, “but some things are an impossible compromise.”

“Such as?” he asked.

“I’ve been honest with my draft board in the past, and I’m being honest with them now. I want to stay that way in the future. No legal loopholes.”

Charlie pressed an intercom. “Margaret, please bring in Mr. Da Vinci’s folder.”

The secretary, wearing a floral knee-length Mary Quant dress, came in with my thick folder in hand. Her shoulder-length red hair fell freely on both sides of her shoulders.

Charlie stood and flipped through my file. After a cursory examination, he closed the folder and looked at me with steadfast eyes. “Quite a history. You walked out of your LA induction, your CO claim was twice rejected by your draft board by a vote of four to nothing, you’ve got no supporting religion, and your draft board is in a tough pro-war state.” Charlie paused, sat back down, and fired a shot: “I’d drop the CO routine if I were you.”

It took me a moment to recover and fire back. “It’s not a routine, and no offense, but why would you assume that?”

“A lot of my clients fake their applications to stall things. You open to that?”

“No. I want to keep things direct, and I’m prepared to go to prison. I don’t want to manipulate my way out of the draft.”

Charlie leaned forward on his desk. “Manipulation is a lawyer’s *job*. So why in the hell are you here?”

“To learn what my rights are. I want to update my CO statement, and that’s it.”

He paced, then froze. “In other words, you want us to choose between hanging, drowning, or electrocution! They all have the same result. Well, *I’m* not going to be part of it! You want to stand in front of a firing squad, *fine*, but don’t ask me to help with it!”

“I’m sure you respect my right to follow my conscience.”

“Do you have family?” he asked.

“I’m married.”

“Do you love her?”

“Definitely,” I answered.

“Do you realize that the path you’re on leads to jail? That could mean a few *years* away from your wife.”

“I think I can win this case once the draft board sees how sincere I am.”

“My God, you have *no* idea . . . Here’s what your trial will be like. The jury, average age ninety, will plod in, and the judge will say, ‘All those who are veterans of foreign wars, raise your hand.’ Everyone will raise a hand. Then he’ll say, ‘All those who see COs as traitors, raise a hand.’ Everyone will raise a hand. Then he’ll ask, ‘How many want to throw this pinko draft-dodger in jail, raise a hand. By then, the revved-up jury will unanimously conclude that it's their patriotic *duty* to boot your butt to jail for as long as possible. Do you get the picture? Case closed."

"You're overstating it, don't you think?"

"I'm *understating* it! The prosecuting attorney will make the case against you for walking out on your L.A. induction and paint you as a modern-day Benedict Arnold! Then I'll take issue with what was said, and here's what'll happen." Charlie leaned down menacingly and looked me in the eye. "In order to stall them, I'll say that we never received such and such a form. But in fact," he continued, "you *will* have received that form." He looked at me significantly. "Well?"

"I'd definitely have a problem with that."

"*See!* And there goes our slim-to-none chance for a case right out the window! If you want that, fine! You have every right to hold a gun to your head."

He grabbed a Kleenex with ferocity, and I asked, "Do you have a cold?"

"Yes! If you're saying that might be why I'm so irascible today . . . well . . . you're probably right."

"I think you'd be an *excellent* attorney for me," I said.

He squinted. "I just lambasted you to hell and back. Why would you want *me* to be your attorney?"

"You're not like the others. You don't hold back. You're direct."

"Just how many attorneys have you had?" he asked.

"Eight."

"And you want me to be foolish enough to be number nine?"

"Yes, you're different," I said.

"You're pretty *different* yourself," Charlie said. "*If* I was psychotic enough to take your case, I'd tell you right off that I'm going to counsel you on *all* your options, even ones you'll consider manipulative and dishonest."

"Fair enough."

He hesitated. "This case is 99 percent futile, but for some perverse reason, I'm attracted to it. Maybe it's the challenge." Charlie stroked his beard for several moments, then blurted, "Okay, Da Vinci, I'm in."

I thanked him and left before he could change his mind.

46

THE CONSTELLATION PROJECT
(1971)

"Nonviolence is a flop. The only bigger flop is violence."
—Joan Baez

My work with Nonviolent Action became a welcome distraction from my CO case and the constant threat of prison. The meetings that I often chaired kept growing in size, and I knew that this evening's get-together promised to be especially eventful. The spacious main room of the Peace House was nearly filled with 175 volunteers sitting cross-legged on the floor. They buzzed loudly with excitement. Word had spread that an innovative nonviolent campaign was going to be proposed tonight.

Norie brought the meeting to order, and the clamor of conversations tapered to a hush. "Welcome, everyone," she began. "I'd like to introduce Ben, a Vietnam vet, who has an exciting new project for us to consider."

As everyone applauded, Ben walked to the front of the room. "I'm proposing a nonviolent campaign around the attack aircraft carrier, the USS *Constellation*, which is scheduled to dock here in San Diego before being redeployed to Vietnam. Carriers in 'Nam are conducting the most massive bombing in the history of warfare. That's not to mention the defoliants we hit 'Nam with like Agent Orange and anti-personnel weapons like cluster bombs that are killing and maiming. If we adopt the Constellation Project, we can wake people up to the need to finally end this damn war."

Norie called for a discussion on whether NVA should take on the Constellation Project in addition to our Farm Workers Project and Draft Project. A volunteer voiced skepticism of our ability to expand and said that by taking on a new ambitious campaign like this, we'd be spreading ourselves too thin to be effective.

Vociferous debate erupted. Jim, who had been one of the first volunteers to join NVA, said flatly, "I'm against it. We'll never be able to pull it off. Then we'll end up looking ridiculous and losing our credibility."

"What credibility?" someone quipped. Laughter followed.

Several others sided with Jim. I liked the idea of the project, however, and spoke up. "It's pretty amazing what we've already done," I countered. "We've helped the farm workers with food and clothing. On top of that, we've leafleted hundreds and hundreds of draftees, giving them the option of free draft counseling. So why *not* this? I say we can make it happen."

The professor, Eric, concurred, then the tide shifted in favor of the project. Norie took a vote, and the project passed with a three-fourths majority. I was voted Action Coordinator, and Eric, the visiting professor at UCSD, was voted Research Coordinator.

The first action of The Constellation Project was to pull an all-nighter and hand-write a letter to each of the 5000-member *Connie* crew. The letter explained the purpose of our campaign—to make it clear that we support the crew while protesting their orders. And second, to call for an immediate end to the war that was now in its seventh year. The letter included an invitation to the crew to visit NVA, hang out, and relax.

The next morning, we mailed out the letters to the crew in bulk, but strangely, we did not receive a single reply.

A few ex-Navy guys in NVA contacted their friends on the *Connie* and asked if they had received our mail. They were told that our efforts to communicate with the crew had literally gone up in smoke. Without regard for the postal laws, the *Connie*'s Captain Gerhard had confiscated our letters and burned them on the deck of the USS *Constellation*.

At the next Nonviolent Action meeting, anger ran high. "That was outrageously illegal!" someone hollered.

"It shows you the arrogance of the Captain," a vet added.

Eric suggested that we file a formal complaint with the U.S. Post Office against the US Navy and the Captain of the *Connie* for illegally burning first-class U.S. mail. I signed the formal complaint along with an ex-Navy pilot who had served in Vietnam. The Post Office assured us that they would conduct a fair investigation into the matter.

The result—a mild slap on the Navy's wrist. The report stated that Captain Gerhard "probably" shouldn't have burned the mail and that it "would have been better" if the mail had been returned. Many at NVA were asking, *What would have happened if a civilian had intentionally burned 5,000 letters?*

At the general NVA meeting, Ben quieted the crowd and said, "When the *Connie* arrives in port tomorrow, I'd like to prep everyone on what to expect when we greet the crew. First of all, they're not gonna want to talk about the war. Most will make a beeline for their families and friends or maybe head straight to a bar. Be sensitive to their moods, and don't hassle 'em with heavy talk about the war. If a sailor wants to talk about Vietnam or a personal problem, let *him* make that decision. Those guys don't need any more pressure than they're already under."

"One more thing," Ben said as he picked up a newspaper and held it high. "There's a bogus article in here about vets being spit on by protesters when they get back home. Maybe there are some nut jobs who do stuff like that, but I've never seen it, and I know that I'll never see it from anyone in this group. The government and the press are dividing the vets from the peace movement. They tried to get us to hate the Vietnamese, and that didn't work, so now people in the peace movement are the enemy. They're painting protesters as 'anti-soldier.'" Ben paused and scanned the crowd with a mischievous look. "Actually, when I look around this room, I can see this is a *very* unsavory group!" Laughter broke the tension in the room. "Before we adjourn the meeting, I'd like to remind everyone that the *only* message we want to give to the *Connie* crew tomorrow morning is 'Welcome home.'"

47

MY NEW CO STATEMENT

(April 15, 1971)

"I will not wait 'til I have converted the whole society to my view but will straightaway make a beginning with myself."

—Mahatma Gandhi

Pre-dawn, April 15, 1971, the USS *Constellation* was scheduled to dock in San Diego.

As I neared the main gate at North Island, the song on the radio added to my good mood—"Here Comes the Sun" by Richie Havens. I couldn't wait to join two dozen NVA volunteers in welcoming the crew back home. Suddenly the music was murdered with a special news bulletin: "The USS *Constellation* arrived early this morning, thwarting the anti-war demonstration of a peace group called Nonviolent Action." I almost drove off the road. The newscaster added, "A naval officer stated that the unannounced early arrival had nothing to do with the planned demonstration. However, no other reason was given."

"*Damn!*" I muttered. I figured that the secret change of plans was more than likely the work of undercover agents at NVA that tipped off the Navy about our plans to greet the crew. Steeped in rancor, I asked myself, *Who do the undercover agents at NVA work for—military intelligence, the FBI., the CIA., NSA, all of them?* At the time, I didn't have the slightest idea of the extent to which the CIA and other clandestine agencies had infiltrated civilian life in the U.S. Richard Goodwin, in his book *Remembering America,* stated that even the president of the National Student Association was on the CIA payroll!

In despair, I watched carloads of enthusiastic NVA volunteers arrive to greet the crew of the *Connie*. They carried *Welcome Home* signs and walked gingerly toward me. I hated to break the bad news, but it was time to step up to the plate. "Hold it, everyone!" I said loudly. I motioned to the *Connie* sitting in the bay. "The carrier came in early, *way* before it was supposed to. Sorry to say this, but the Navy zapped us. They arrived hours ahead of time, then told the press that Nonviolent Action had nothing to do with it."

"What bullshit," someone muttered.

"A total crock," said another.

"Their spies must've tipped 'em off," someone else said.

In the silence that followed, I noticed several volunteers looking at each other suspiciously. I needed to say something to stave off the mounting paranoia. "We're not going to let this stop us, are we?"

A few volunteers weakly shook their heads no.

"Hey!" Jim exclaimed. "Look at it this way. We're having an impact. We made them change their plans!"

A few volunteers applauded.

"Moving on," I said, "let's decide who will pick up Congressman Dellums at the airport."

Dellums had flown in to investigate complaints of drug abuse and serious racial problems on the *Connie.* The new congressman had created quite a stir in Washington. He was making what Congressman John Lewis would call "good trouble." Even as a freshman congressman, Dellums wasn't afraid to rock the boat. Just *weeks* into his first term, the former Marine called attention to atrocities committed by American soldiers in Vietnam. He called for a formal investigation into the allegations of war crimes, but Congress chose not to approve the proceedings.

When NVA learned that the congressman would be visiting San Diego, we requested a meeting. Dellums said he had an interest in learning about our Constellation Project, so we offered to pick him up at the airport. "That'll give me a chance to talk with you before I meet with the captain of the *Connie,*" Dellums said. "We're going to have an airing of crew grievances on the carrier."

As I plodded back to my car, I heard a loud, heated argument escalating behind me. I turned in dismay and discovered two volunteers steeped in a shouting match over who would be the one to pick up the congressman at the airport. Already in low spirits, I snapped, "Enough!" They stared at me in shock. "I thought this was a *peace* group? Both of you go."

Despite the setback due to the early arrival of the carrier, I felt determined to find a way to salvage what was left of the day and our pride. In that it was April 15th, we had planned to leaflet last-minute tax filers this evening at the US Post Office. Our leaflets showed how billions of dollars were being devoured by the unnecessary and immoral war in Vietnam. Looking back, the Vietnam war, in financial terms, cost the US $168 billion, or in today's dollars—$1 trillion![1]

---

1. Source: *Vietnam War Facts, Costs and Timeline: How the Vietnam War Affects You Today*, updated 2020.

When a dozen of us from NVA arrived at the US Post Office around 7:30 P.M., there wasn't a single soul in sight. The Post Office, completely dark and locked up, had closed early.

Ben asked a street vendor what was going on. "It's weird," the vendor said. "The Post Office shut down at six when they were supposed to close at midnight. People that had to turn in their tax returns were really pissed off."

Ben turned to me. "The government knew we'd be here. They must've ordered the early shut down."

I scanned the long faces of our volunteers. As they turned to leave, I called, "Hold it! We can still leaflet the people on the sidewalk. Then let's hold a silent vigil." I figured it would help our spirits to be busy and accomplish *something*.

After leafleting, we gathered in a circle, and I said to the group, "Everything went wrong today, I know. But tomorrow, we've got a plane flying over the city with a peace banner that says, *Connie—Stay Home for Peace*. Everyone will see it, and there's no way they can stop us from . . ."

"About the plane . . ." The guy in charge of hiring the plane raised his hand sheepishly.

"What?" I asked.

"I forgot to tell you—the guy who owns the plane we were gonna rent canceled."

"You've got to be kidding."

"No. He changed his mind and said that he wasn't about to do anything unpatriotic. Somebody must've gotten to him."

"Great," I said, shaking my head.

"Score another one for the Navy," Ben said dejectedly.

Jim looked about. "There are definitely spies in NVA, and one of them might be somebody right here that's tipping them off!"

"Yeah," a volunteer said, "and maybe it's you!"

"I've been here since the beginning," Jim protested. "Who the hell are *you* to point a finger!"

"Stop it," I interjected. "We don't know who it is or how many spies there are in NVA, but it doesn't matter unless we let it matter. Let's hold a vigil right now and meditate."

We formed a large circle. Several volunteers stayed back, watching each other with accusing eyes. I motioned to them and said, "C'mon, *everybody* in." We sat down and closed our eyes.

In a morose mood, my 'enlightening' meditation went dark. It concerned recent conversations I had with Vietnam vets who had joined NVA. Most didn't want to talk about the trauma, but some felt compelled to relate the atrocities they had either witnessed or participated in: torture, mutilations, poisoning the water of a village, burning homes, and executions. Of course, there were atrocities on both sides, but the vets only wanted to talk about their own direct experiences. One vet told me that it was no wonder that so many vets "hit drugs hard" because, in battle, they saw things like "intestines spilling from a buddy's stomach, or limbs blown off." I couldn't get these horrific images out of my mind, nor did I want to entirely. If my brothers in Vietnam had to endure them, I would share in the anguish, at least indirectly. What I would *not* allow myself to do was act as if the traumas of our troops were not a problem as long as I didn't see them.

It seemed beyond comprehension how our young vets could cope with the nightmarish stresses of war, particularly a war most either doubted or did not believe in! Recently, a Navy vet had opened up to me as if he needed to get an incident off his chest. He said, "Our patrol boat was just offshore in 'Nam, and there was this family in a fishing boat that looked suspicious to one of the officers. 'Blast it out of the water,' the officer said. I mean, it wasn't like it was a threat. They weren't coming toward us; we were coming to them. When we were closer, we saw there were a few kids on the boat. Again, the officer said, 'Blast it out of the water! Do it!' A few of us looked at each other, but we knew we couldn't disobey an order and not end up in the brig, so we shot the boat to bits . . . and the people. What we did . . . it was way too much. We didn't give 'em a warning. Nothing. We just opened fire. Mangled bodies . . . young, old, covered in blood. We didn't find any weapons in the boat."

In meditation, I wished for an end to the atrocities, for an end to the war, and for the troops to come home. When everyone opened their eyes again, their faces mirrored utter defeat. *Was this the end of the Constellation Project?* I was tempted to say yes. But I told myself that if we gave up on this project, we'd be giving up not only on our efforts to support the crew but on ourselves and our ability to help bring the war to an end.

As the volunteers said goodbye to one another and began to head their separate ways, I shouted, "Wait!" Everyone stopped in their tracks. "I know it feels like everything with the Constellation Project caved in, that there's no sense in staying with it when nothing we do seems to work. I know that. But it's not over . . . unless we think it's over!" I paused, grateful to see I had their full attention. "We knew this project would be tough when we took it on, right? The easier thing would've been to give up before we started. But we didn't. So, I'm asking you, right now, do we do the easy thing and quit, or do we keep fighting to end the war? Is this the day that we give up, or the day that we get back in the fight for peace?"

Ben mumbled, "We fight back."

"I couldn't hear you."

Ben said loudly, "We fight back!"

"What about the rest of you?"

A chant picked up, "We fight back, we fight back!" After a group hug, we headed our separate ways, linked once again in spirit.

On my way home from the Post Office, I reflected on what an utterly demoralizing day it had been. The grueling series of adversities I endured over the last few months started to take their toll and depress me: my defeats as action coordinator of The Constellation Project, my uncertain marriage, and my struggle to become recognized as a conscientious objector.

When I finally returned home that evening, Jane said, "You look so beat."

We embraced, then I went to the bathroom to get ready for bed. A glance in the mirror revealed a shocking weariness etched on my face.

When I hit the bed, I melted into the mattress but was unable to sleep. Wide-eyed, I stared at the cottage cheese ceiling. It was crazy. I was utterly exhausted, yet adrenaline raced through my body. My mind churned like a speeding train. For over nine months, I had been working non-stop at NVA against the war. Now I was working against an aircraft carrier returning to Vietnam. I asked myself, *When are you going to take the time to speak to what you're* for? *Jerry is right when he says, 'No one wants to kill. What the hell are your alternatives to violence?'* Then I remembered what Charlie had said: *'You have the right to update your CO statement.'* What was I waiting for? I thought, *How can you expect your draft board to get what you believe in if you don't update your statement and reaffirm your philosophy of nonviolence? It's in your head. Put it down on paper. Don't let today's defeats stop you. Get the hell out of bed and turn things around!*

As Jane slept, I gave her a light kiss on the cheek and quietly slipped out of bed. In my study, with posters of Gandhi, Einstein, Cesar Chavez, and Dr. King looking on, I went to work on my new CO statement, which poured out in a stream of consciousness. A few hours passed, then shortly before midnight, I finished and dated it—"April 15, 1971."

Satisfied with my updated and final CO application, I thought, *Today didn't turn out too bad after all.* A symbolic exchange had been made. A massive weapon of war, the USS *Constellation* had arrived in San Diego the same day that I had deployed my statement of conscientious objection to all wars.

The next morning, I called Joyce at my Virginia draft board to let her know my new CO claim would be coming in the mail. "I'll be on the lookout for it," she said.

I asked, "About how long before the draft board decides on my statement?"

"Not long at all," she replied. "By the way, I hope it goes well for you."

48

FACING PRISON

(May 1971)

"Under a government which imprisons any unjustly,
the true place for a just man is also a prison."
—Henry David Thoreau

Jane and I checked the mail religiously in anticipation of my new draft card. It would either be marked 1-A, ready for war, or 1-O, conscientious objector. About a month after I updated my CO statement, I finally received the Selective Service envelope that contained the verdict of my draft board. I tore it open and quickly scanned the draft card.

Instead of being reclassified 1-O, I remained 1-A. My draft board had once again rejected my CO claim by a vote of 4-0.

Charlie and I met in his office. "Sorry, pal," he said. I half-expected him to add, *I told you this would happen.* Instead, he moved on to the present. "You have the right to one last appeal. You can write the Virginia State Director of Selective Service. We'll do that, but you should know that this is pretty much a done deal."

"I appreciate the directness."

"I'd have a talk with Jane and let her know that you'll be going to prison for a while."

"What's 'a while'?" I asked.

Charlie looked away, and then his eyes came to mine. "You refused induction. You were interrogated by who knows what government agency at Fort Holabird, and now that you're a prominent activist, they'll want to make an example out of you. I hate to be the bearer of bad news, but I think they're going to give you the maximum sentence—five years."

I nodded that I understood, but inside I felt overwhelmed at the thought of half a decade without Jane. It seemed too much to bear. From Charlie's office, I called NVA and told a volunteer that I wouldn't be coming into the Peace House due to a "personal emergency." There were always a million things to do at NVA, but I needed a break to meditate. I knew if I didn't have peace within, I wouldn't be useful to anyone.

My sadness was mixed with bitterness. *After three years of applying as a CO, how could the draft board not recognize that I was sincere? Jane was right. Obviously, they didn't care.* I had long counseled Jane not to be spiteful toward them. Now I had to take my own advice and shake the animosity I felt toward the draft board members.

I drove from Charlie's office into Southeast San Diego, the ill will I felt still lingering. As I cruised aimlessly in an impoverished neighborhood, I came upon a church with its doors wide open. It seemed a personal invitation.

It struck me as strange that the church was completely empty. I stood alone at the altar, reading the signs posted up high between the arched mosaic windows: MY PEACE IS MY GIFT TO YOU . . . BE KIND TO ONE ANOTHER . . . GOD IS LOVE . . . I HAVE A DREAM . . .

Before me was a life-size statue of Christ, the face painted black. The compassionate eyes reminded me to lose my resentments and to embrace the adage, "Love your enemies." As I meditated on letting go of my bitterness, Buddha's quote came to mind: "Forgive others not because they deserve forgiveness, but because you deserve peace."

That evening I waited for Jane to come home from work to break the news that my prison sentence, according to Charlie, would likely be the maximum of five years.

As usual, she came home, plopped her social work files on the table, and gave me a warm hug.

"How's work?" I asked.

"A lotta paperwork," she answered, "but the faster I get through it, the faster I can help people."

"I'm so proud of you." She smiled, and I started in on what I hated to bring up. "I had a talk with Charlie today . . . about prison."

Jane's face tensed.

"He said he thinks I'll have a long prison term."

"What's long?"

"Charlie could be wrong."

"But?"

"But he thinks five years."

Jane's eyes shined with tears. I held her, half-fearing that she would threaten to leave again, that she couldn't stand the stress anymore. Instead, after a pause, she said, "Somehow . . . I don't know how . . . we'll get through everything."

A week later, on Memorial Day, May 31st, I asked Jane to come with me to the Fort Rosecrans National Cemetery to pay our respects to fallen soldiers.

As we walked up an incline, we paused at a particularly striking vantage point. From where we were standing, two endless lines of tombstones came to a "V" and converged at our feet. I pulled out a paper I had typed up for this Memorial Day visit and shared it with Jane.

"In World War I, 8 million men, women, and children were killed, and 21 million wounded. The direct financial cost was about 200 billion dollars.

"In World War II, the total loss of life is estimated between 70 and 85 million people, an unprecedented level of carnage in the history of 'humanity.' That death toll includes the six million Jews that were killed by the Nazis. But it was not the West that paid the highest price in winning the war. The Soviet Union lost an estimated 26 million Soviet citizens. The financial cost of World War II was more than 1 trillion dollars.

"Other costs, in every war, include amputations, reparations, broken families, lifetime traumas, and the shameful neglect of human needs at home. And almost invariably connected to the violence are widespread policies of racism and religious intolerance.

"There are military cemeteries like this one to honor our soldiers," I said, "as there should be. But where is the cemetery for conscientious objectors? Where's the tribute to COs in history books? Where's the respect for the thousands and thousands of COs that were scorned, tortured, and killed for their stand for nonviolence?"

Jane said, "I'm as guilty as anyone. I didn't even know what a conscientious objector was until I met you."

We slowly walked on, and I said, "We've gone to the Moon, but we still don't know how to live on Earth. You'd think that as time goes by and we become more 'advanced,' we'd outlaw war. We're a planet of humans that haven't learned to be human. Instead, we've become experts at maiming and killing each other. Take napalm, for example."

I explained that napalm was developed in a secret lab at one of our highest institutions of learning—Harvard, in 1942. Most Americans were either ignorant of our use of napalm in Vietnam or in denial about it. How does napalm work? Consider that water boils at 212 degrees Fahrenheit. Napalm, however, sticks to the skin and produces temperatures of 1,500 to 2,200 degrees Fahrenheit. I read about a Vietnamese woman who was struck with it. Both her arms were burned off. This is the macabre ingenuity that our government and military have sponsored. How strange and twisted that we devote our best scientific minds to the task of finding the most effective ways to kill and mutilate each other—all in the name of patriotism. As much as I admired President Kennedy, I was dismayed to learn that he was among those who approved use of napalm.

Other Vietnam war "acceptable" weapons included Agent Orange, cluster bombs, and white phosphorus, which penetrates to the bone.

Jane and I walked up to the hill's peak and looked out over the Fort Rosecrans Cemetery. Solemnly, we took in the view of the endless tombstones. They represented generation upon generation of young lives cut short by the path of war that inevitably leads to cemeteries like this one. I held Jane and said, "This is why I'm a CO."

"I understand," Jane said, "but it seems so hopeless to try to end war."

"Even if it's not possible, I want to be on the side that fought it with nonviolence, that went to war with war."

When we returned home, I mailed Joyce, the clerk at my Virginia draft board, a note that seemed fitting for Memorial Day:

> As you know, Joyce, my CO application was again unjustly rejected. Because Memorial Day and Walt Whitman's birthday fell on the same day this year, I thought I'd ask you to share this poem with the members of my draft board:
>
> > 'Be not dishearten'd—affection shall solve the problem of
> > Freedom yet,
> > Those who love each other shall become invincible—
> >
> > Were you looking to be held together by lawyers?
> > Or by an agreement on a paper? or by arms?
> > Nay, nor the world, nor any living, will so cohere.'
> >
> > —"Over the Carnage Rose Prophetic a Voice," *Leaves of Grass* by Walt Whitman
>
> peace and friendship,
> Francesco

49

THE MOTORBOAT VS. THE AIRCRAFT CARRIER

(September 1971)

"Don't give up the ship!"

—Captain James Lawrence

Despite our setbacks with the Constellation Project, Nonviolent Action was not about to quit. We even expanded the project to include what we called The Motorboat Campaign.

I helped launch the project on a glorious, sunny morning. Under a clear and vibrant sky, Ben, Jim, and I arrived at Brophy's Boat Rentals and chartered a 14-foot motorboat for ten dollars. I paid the rental manager, and he stood there on the dock, eyeing us suspiciously. "You guys experienced on the water?"

"I am," Ben assured him.

"I am, too," Jim chimed.

The manager looked at me. I shrugged and said, "I was drafted."

"I'll take the stern," Ben suggested.

"Translation?" I asked.

"You know, the back of the boat. I'll steer us."

Jim said, "I'll take the bow."

"The bow?" I asked.

"Towards the front of the boat," Jim answered. "The left side facing the front is the port side; the right side facing the front is the starboard side. Don't you know *anything* about boating?"

"I can spell 'boating,' that's about it," I said.

The three of us headed out toward the USS *Constellation* in our small craft to display a canvas peace banner that read: *Connie—Stay Home for Peace!* As we glided along smooth waters towards the gargantuan USS *Constellation* attack aircraft carrier, Ben asked loudly, "Do you know how to swim, Francesco?"

"I tread."

"Just in case," Ben explained, "that cushion you're sitting on is also a life preserver."

"Good to know," I said, thinking, *What have I gotten myself into?*

The closer we came to the *Connie*, the larger the carrier loomed. If you could lay the Empire State Building on its side, it would be about the same size as the carrier.

Along the way, we passed several destroyers, the type of ship my buddy Jerry served on as an officer. The crews of the naval ships stared at us curiously. We flashed them the peace sign, and to our surprise, they returned it. In the mid-sixties, that gesture would have guaranteed strong hostility; today, in 1971, it signaled brotherhood. Ben looked at me with a big grin. "This is way cool!"

Up-close to the USS *Constellation,* we spied a long line of white dots bordering the deck—sailors standing at attention for inspection. "Perfect timing," Jim said. I stood up cautiously, and we unfurled our banner: *Connie—Stay Home for Peace!*

As we slowly cruised along the carrier, the perfectly straight line of sailors in the back row of the inspection began to shift unevenly. A dozen or so men had turned to get a look at our banner and surreptitiously give us the peace sign. After a few runs along the carrier, Ben shouted, "Looks like we've got company!"

Two large naval cutters roared directly toward us, and they were not slowing down! At the last second, the first cutter swerved, creating a huge wave that raced fast toward our craft.

"Quick, turn!" I shouted to Ben.

"No!" Ben shouted back. "We gotta take the wave head-on, or we'll flip. Stay low and hold on!"

Our bow cut into the first wave, and the nose of the motorboat shot up high. For a few moments, we seemed weightless. Then gravity took its course, and we crashed back down with a loud smack against the water. I fell sideways and cut my jaw against the rim of the boat.

"You're bleeding," Jim yelled. "You okay?"

I wiped the blood away. "Yeah, I'm fine." I pointed to the second Navy cutter, which had started charging toward us full-speed. Again, we took our positions and rode out the onslaught of waves. It seemed the captains of the cutters were determined not to stop until they capsized our boat or forced us to leave.

In my mind, retreating was not an option, but I felt responsible for the safety of Ben and Jim. "Do you guys want to go back?" I asked. "No problem, if that's what you want."

"You're the one that's bleeding!" Jim said. "I want to stay if you're up to it."

"I'm fine. What about you, Ben? Do you want to go back?"

"No way!"

Jim suddenly turned and pointed. "Uh-oh," he uttered. Both cutters were speeding directly toward us at high speed, one behind the other.

Ben muttered, "Holy shit." I hoped those wouldn't be the last two words I ever heard.

Suddenly, the cutters swerved in front of us, one after the other, sending rising waves racing toward us. The three of us held on tight. As the first wave hit, our craft catapulted into the air. All I saw was a blurred sky. Then BAM! We crashed down, and by some miracle, landed upright in the water.

Finally, after maybe ten minutes of their attack, the cutters gave up and left. We were a bit banged up, and the motorboat had taken in a lot of water, but the three of us grinned with victory smiles. There was a moment or two of silence, when sailors on the *Connie* suddenly let loose with an outburst of cheers.

"Cool!" Ben exclaimed. "That's pretty brave of 'em to do that." Through binoculars, we saw an officer angrily dispersing those on deck. Sailors scattered like ants under attack, rapidly funneling down exposed stairwells.

"Hey, we've got more company!" Jim said, pointing to another naval cutter. As the cutter slowed and neared, the officer on board spoke through a bullhorn: "Get out of these waters or we're calling the Harbor Police!"

I asked Ben to steer us close. He looked at me skeptically but obliged. Gliding up close to the cutter, I shouted, "I called the Harbor Police this morning." The officer's mouth dropped in shock. "We're completely within our rights," I said. "We're just showing this harmless banner, that's all."

As the officer demanded that we immediately get out of the area, a commotion behind him distracted me. Behind the officer's back, his crew was furtively flashing us the peace sign to show their support.

"Did you hear me? Out of these waters *now*," the officer snapped.

Stubbornly, and knowing we were within our rights, I said, "Okay, we'll leave after one more run. You have my word."

Once again, we cruised the entire length of the *Connie* with our banner held high. A bit closer to the carrier this time, we could see a few disapproving sailors flip us the finger. As I stood at the bow, I noticed a sailor on the top deck. He had some kind of silver metallic object propped up on his shoulder. His right hand shot up in the air, then he quickly leaned back and hurled the object. It turned end over end towards us with a terrifying whistling sound. The closer it came, the louder it screamed. The object came into focus in a split second—a heavy-duty four-way lug wrench flying directly toward me. The metal wrench whizzed just past my head with a *whoosh* sound as it cut into the water and sunk.

Ben, Jim, and I stared into the water, knowing that if the wrench had struck any one of us squarely, it would have been fatal.

The sailor that threw the makeshift weapon ran off. Then Jim broke the somber silence. "I say we pack up and call it a day."

As we headed back to port, a boat packed with tourists was passing nearby. The guide spoke through a bullhorn: "The USS *Constellation* over there is nicknamed 'America's Flagship,' and soon she'll be redeployed to Vietnam."

"Hey, let's show 'em the banner," I said.

"I'm in," Ben said, maneuvering us in close to the tour boat. Jim and I unfurled the banner: *Connie—Stay Home for Peace*. The smiling tourists took it as a photo op, raising their Instamatics and snapping away. We waved goodbye and headed off.

Near the pier, we furiously scooped out the water we had taken in to make our rented craft a bit more presentable. As we glided in and tied the motorboat at the pier, I winced at the sight of the manager of Brophy's Boat Rentals grimly staring down at us. "You guys look like three drowned rats!" His eyes lowered to the several inches of bloody water that remained in the boat. "Yeah, you guys are *real* experienced."

At the next general NVA meeting, we told everyone how the naval cutters had charged our motorboat. Incensed that the Navy had put our lives in danger, the members of NVA voted to file a formal complaint.

The Navy never replied.

A week later, our motorboat crew was back for another run along the *Connie*. This time, if the Navy did anything illegal, we would have it documented. Another motorboat, piloted by national press photographer Bob Fitch, would be following us.

"You again," the manager of Brophy's Boat Rentals said, disgruntled.

"We'll be more careful," I assured him. Ben, Jim, and I climbed in the motorboat as the manager yelled, "*This* time, no water in the boat!"

"Yes, sir!" Jim said, saluting the manager.

As our motorboat glided towards the USS *Constellation,* with Fitch's boat trailing us, we passed a slew of ships—the *Ticonderoga* and *Kitty Hawk* aircraft carriers, several destroyers, harbor excursion boats, and a Coast Guard cutter.

Surprisingly, no naval cutters pursued us. Or perhaps not surprisingly. Likely, undercover agents at NVA had informed the Navy that we would be accompanied by a prominent press photographer.

While displaying our banner near the colossal *Connie*, a navy boat approached in the distance. It was smaller than the cutters that had attacked us, but we weren't taking any chances. We braced ourselves in case they charged. The press photographer in the second boat readied his camera. But instead of speeding up, the naval boat slowed down and came close. An officer shouted, "A lot of people on the *Connie* are *very* upset with you guys bein' out here." He paused, then added, "Screw 'em! We totally support what you're doing. You're good men!"

Ben, Jim, and I exchanged looks of shock, and Ben said, "Thanks, brother."

A crew mate with the officer said, "We gotta look like we're hassling you, but all we're gonna do is circle you a few times. By the way, don't laugh or smile 'cause the brass is watching us."

The officer added, "We were ordered to read you guys the riot act. That's why I've got my back to the ship. Personally, *my* message is to keep up the good work."

"Thanks," I said, poker-faced, "and take care. We really appreciate this."

The officer gave a barely discernible nod, and though I was stoic on the outside, I glowed inside at the mutual respect.

The naval boat revved its engines, circled us a couple of times for show, then left.

Jim yelled to the photographer trailing us that we were going to approach the carrier. As we cruised along the *Connie* and unfurled our banner, Fitch photographed us. One of the striking photos that he snapped that day appeared in the October 4th, 1971 issue of *Newsweek* magazine. It showed me standing at the bow, holding one end of the banner high; Jim held up the other end; and Ben was aft, steering us. Looming in the background was the humongous USS *Constellation* that made our motorboat seem like a toy.

I contacted Bob Fitch and asked, "What does the photo mean to you?"

"I think of it as 'David vs. Goliath.'"

I called my folks a few days later and asked, "When you saw the *Newsweek* photo, what did you think?"

Mom quipped, "I thought, *Where did we go wrong?*"

Two NVA volunteers and I sail toward the USS *Constellation* with our peace banner "CONNIE—STAY HOME FOR PEACE," 1971.

Inspection on the USS *Constellation,* 1971. (Photo: F. Da Vinci)

A happy day. The Navy didn't try to sink our boat this time, 1971. (Courtesy of the Bob Fitch photography archive—Stanford Library)

The photographer called this shot "David vs. Goliath," *Newsweek*, 1971. (Photo: Bob Fitch)

50

SUPPORT FROM SENATOR GEORGE MCGOVERN

(1971)

"When the power of love overcomes the love of power,
the world will know peace."

—Jimi Hendrix

Over 200 volunteers filed into NVA. Norie led the meeting and proposed that we start a letter-writing campaign to Congress about the Constellation Project. She argued that we need to make it crystal-clear that the people have had it with this war, that they want an immediate end to it, and they're not buying Nixon's line that the war is winding down.

Some in NVA expressed doubt about writing Congress, stating that it would be a waste of time. One volunteer argued, "Congress doesn't care about letters. They only care about the next election."

Ben countered with, "We've got nothing to lose and everything to gain by giving it a shot." Norie took a vote and the proposal passed. I was nominated to write the letter that we would send to the most influential members of Congress concerning the war.

About a month later, Norie announced at the general meeting that she had an update about our letter-writing campaign. Only Norie and I knew the surprise in store for the members.

After the packed meeting was called to order, Norie said, "At first, when Francesco wrote Congress about The Constellation Project, not one legislator wanted to be bothered, except to have their assistants say, 'Your letter has been duly noted.' I realize a lot of you thought that writing Congress was a total waste of time. For a little over a month, it seemed that was true.

But today, that changed. Francesco, will you read the letter you received?"

I read it aloud:

> Thank you so much for your letter, Mr. Da Vinci, concerning the planned deployment of the USS *Constellation* to Vietnam. I certainly agree that the problems you described should be investigated [regarding the continuation of the war], and I have asked Secretary of Defense Melvin Laird to respond.

"Wow!" someone exclaimed, which set off a wave of cheers and applause.

> In addition, as you requested, I think we also deserve an explanation as to why the attack carrier must still be deployed in a war which is supposedly winding down. I appreciate your calling this urgent matter to my attention.
>
> With every good wish, I am.
>
> Sincerely,
>
> Senator George McGovern

The room exploded with fervent applause. Norie said loudly, "Can you believe it! NVA's call to end the war has made its way to the halls of Congress and the president's cabinet!" Another roar of applause ripped through the room.

Eric leaned in toward me and said, "This is a turning point in The Constellation Project. You know that if McGovern contacted the Secretary of Defense Laird, it's almost definite that Nixon is being advised. Nonviolent Action is stirring things up in a good way. We're a force to be reckoned with. You should be proud of that, Francesco, and I know I'm damn proud to be part of NVA."

The letter of support from Senator McGovern prompted me to reflect on how far NVA had come in such a short time. It was largely due to the remarkable dedication and work ethic of our volunteers. So many put in such long hours they might as well have made the Peace House their home.

Just before the next general meeting was to start, Ben said, "I've got some great news, Francesco. A little while ago, David Harris, Joan Baez's husband, said he's coming down from the Bay Area and that he's got an outta sight idea on how we can expand the Constellation Project. He didn't give any details, but he said, 'NVA is gonna love it, and the press will eat it up!'"

I'm thanking Sen. George McGovern for his support of Nonviolent Action.

51

EXPANSION OF THE CONSTELLATION PROJECT

(1971)

"Worldly fame is but a breath of wind that blows now this way and now that, and changes name as it changes direction."

—Dante Alighieri

The air was electric. A record number of volunteers arrived for tonight's general meeting at the Peace House. Everyone wanted to hear the new proposal from David Harris.

Even after the spacious meeting room filled to capacity, volunteers continued to pour in, spilling into adjacent rooms. Inside, Eric looked at me with a smile and gave me a thumbs up.

Wearing a work shirt, blue jeans, and rimless glasses, Harris sat on the floor among our several hundred volunteers, intermittently biting his fingernails to nubs as he waited to be introduced. Having been convicted of draft evasion, Harris had served about fifteen months in various minimum and medium-security prisons as a draft resister. I wondered how much stress he had suffered from incarceration, and how he was readjusting to the outside world.

When David took the floor, he complimented NVA on our peace work and said he had an idea that would take the Constellation Project up to the next level. "We hold a city-wide vote that asks San Diegans if they think the USS *Constellation* should be redeployed to Vietnam or stay home. Even though the vote won't be legally binding, it'll be a great exercise in democracy. And it'll give the people of San Diego a voice in the war."

Buzzing excitement broke out in the room. Bob Fitch, the press photographer who documented our motorboat campaign, spoke up. "I've covered major historic social movements for a long time, and I've got a gut feeling that this Constellation Project is going to be another big one."

As soon as I heard the idea, I liked it.

A skeptical student volunteer, however, stood and asked, "What if we try to pull off a vote, and we don't get a decent turnout? The press will have a field day." Other voices echoed the same kind of doubts, viewing the campaign as "unrealistic."

Inspired by the ambitious project, I spoke up in favor of the vote. "We heard these same arguments the first time the idea of The Constellation Project came up, but we *made* it happen. We can make this happen too. I think a Constellation Vote is a brilliant idea, and like David said, it'll be a great exercise in democracy." David nodded in appreciation.

The Constellation Vote proposal was adopted with only a small minority dissenting. Once again, I was nominated and voted in as the Action Coordinator of the project. Eric was made the Research Coordinator. After the meeting, a volunteer enthusiastically told Eric and me, "I've got great news. David plans to stay on at NVA and be a spokesperson for the project."

It turned out that David had been right in his prediction about the Constellation Vote and the press—"They'll eat it up." Local and even national newspapers and magazines began contacting us. They were intrigued that David had become part of NVA and that Joan Baez had announced she would give at least one concert in San Diego to benefit the Constellation Vote. Some of our volunteers, however, had misgivings about David's role in our project.

At one meeting, David was confronted by several NVA members who accused him of "monopolizing media attention" for himself.

David laughed, "I can't help it if I'm a celebrity. I mean, that's a good thing to use, isn't it? It keeps us in the press."

Others argued that David's interviews were only giving the media *his* perspective on the Constellation Vote and that David was consistently omitting any reference or credit to Nonviolent Action. But most in NVA were all too glad to overlook our lack of credit in favor of increased local and national media coverage from the participation of David and Joan.

Attracted by NVA's new fame, our volunteer numbers grew exponentially. With only four months to go before we held the Constellation Vote, everyone dug in and worked incredibly long hours, almost in 24-7 shifts. In fact, most of us became so passionate about the Constellation Vote that the tasks of daily existence like eating and sleeping only seemed impediments to our progress. We were imbued with a driving dedication to awaken the conscience of San Diego.

The ruinous routine of skipping meals in favor of settling for unhealthy snacks, downing way too much coffee, and sleep deprivation made me a bit loopy. One evening David and I stood before 200 plus volunteers at the Peace House, waiting for the meeting to begin. To put it mildly, I was not in good shape.

I happened to notice that everyone in sight was wearing jeans. Drunk with weariness, it hit me as hysterical. At that moment, someone casually mentioned the need to raise money for the Constellation Vote. I said, "Don't worry. David and I will raise the bucks with a jeans commercial."

David looked at me with a raised eyebrow as if wondering if I was serious.

"It'll be great," I assured David and the on-looking volunteers. "Here's a sample." I walked back and forth, modeling my blue jeans, then paused. "Whenever I march in a protest, I wear 501 jeans. Whether they're bell-bottomed or straight, they're sexy, and they get me noticed. I wouldn't dream of wearing anything else. How about you, David?"

"Uh, yeah. They're my top choice, alright."

"See, guys. That's what I'm talkin' about. Don't get left out. Whether you wear 'em at a sit-in or a peace march, 501's are the first choice of the counter-culture. Even if you get your head beat in, you don't mind 'cause you look so damn good!"

52

NONVIOLENT ACTION: A HOUSE DIVIDED

(1971)

"The means may be likened to a seed, the end to a tree,
and there is just the same inviolable connection between the means
and the end as there is between the seed and the tree."

—Mahatma Gandhi

NVA had become a hot item in the press. Only a year before, we couldn't *buy* coverage of our nonviolent campaigns. But today, with the ever-expanding opposition to the war and with David and Joan's participation in the ConstellaZtion Vote, we had become a media magnet.

Our volunteers reveled in the snowball of press coverage. One article described NVA as "on the forefront of the peace movement." While we relished our newfound praise in the press, the gift revealed itself to be a beguiling Trojan Horse. The media made celebrity participation the prime focus; our causes became secondary. More disturbing was the fact that our peace group, predominantly, didn't seem to care that much as long as we were getting noticed.

As new volunteers poured in from various regions of America, I felt ambivalent about our unparalleled growth. On the one hand, it seemed an exciting sign of our burgeoning success; on the other hand, a great many of the new members had absolutely no understanding of our philosophy of nonviolence, nor did they care to learn about it. The main attraction was that NVA had become an "in" place to be.

Another issue surfaced—the greater the membership of NVA, the more intimidated people felt to speak up. Eric and I devised a way to encourage more participation. We would begin with everyone briefly meeting together, then break up the group into smaller subgroups, and finally reunite as a whole. Immediately, there was a change for the better. Those that timidly stayed silent began to voice their opinions in the smaller, more intimate groups. Even those who had *never* made verbal input became vocal, sometimes shockingly so.

With our current unwieldy meetings of over 200 members, I began to long for the early days of NVA when we were a tight-knit group. There was a feeling of family that had long ago evaporated. Then another vital element evaporated—democratic decision-making.

A San Andreas-like fault line developed between two main groups of vets. The larger vet group was democratic. These vets had strong, positive qualities: a relentless dedication to ending the war, a cooperative spirit, dependability, attention to detail, loyalty, and determination. They were open in their intentions and happy to abide by NVA's approval or disapproval of proposed actions. The smaller group was authoritarian with top-down leadership. Their self-appointed leaders operated without the whole group's knowledge or approval of their actions.

Admittedly, I did not possess the worldly skills needed to detect and counter the latter group's increasing control of Nonviolent Action's Constellation Project. Once, in the early stages, Ben warned me about it, but I naively dismissed the subgroup's actions as harmless.

Eventually, Ben, Norie, and Jim opened my eyes with a shocking revelation. They confronted me one day in what amounted to an intervention. Ben blurted, "You're destroying NVA."

That certainly got my attention. I asked how, and he said, "David and some of the vets belong to their own separate peace groups. They don't really care about NVA. They're just using our volunteers for their own projects and taking credit for everything NVA has done. Why do you let it go on?"

Norie backed up Ben's statement and added, "A lot of people at NVA are confused, especially the new volunteers. They keep asking if the Constellation Vote is a project of the vet Concerned Officer's Movement, or if it's David Harris' group, the People's Union."

"She's right," Ben said. "Both the vet group and David's group are using our volunteers to do what *their* groups want, not what NVA wants. On the outside, it looks like all of us are working together, but we're not. NVA volunteers don't know who to listen to, so I tell 'em it's not another group's project; it's NVA's project."

Jim added, "Now everyone under the sun is taking credit for the Constellation Vote along with everything that NVA has built up with blood, sweat, and tears." Ben and Norie nodded in agreement.

"Why are you letting them take the credit for all our hard work?" asked Ben.

"Do we really care about that?" I asked.

"*Yes*," came a chorus of three.

Ben turned to Norie and Jim. "Let me have a word with Francesco." They nodded, and Ben walked me out of the Peace House. "This isn't just about taking credit. It's about respect. Those of us that have been here from the beginning feel betrayed by everyone that's taking false credit for all our sacrifice. I know you're focused on the causes instead of the politics of NVA, but this is important too. And if you don't make it important to you, the people around you who love you and what NVA stands for are going to feel that you let them down."

I sighed. It was a heck of a lot to take in.

"There's another thing we need to deal with," Ben said.

I made a face and asked, "There's more?" Suddenly Ben laughed, which made me chuckle.

"This is the last thing, for now," Ben assured. "It's something you brought up to me, but I didn't get it at the time."

"What's that?"

"Remember, about a month ago, when you told me you thought the women at NVA were being disrespected and that there should be more women leading things, not just Norie? I thought you were way overboard on that. But not now. I started to notice how the guys that are taking over NVA are bossing the women around. Some of these guys yell at the women to do what they want. One girl told a guy giving out orders that she was sick and tired of doing menial stuff like pinning notecards on a bulletin board. The guy got in her face and screamed, 'Just do what you're told!' It was so loud she flinched and ran out of the room. I looked at the guy for at least *some* kind of reaction, but nothing. He went right on like not a damn thing happened."

"I'll talk with Norie," I said, "and see what we can do about it."

Ben walked me to my car, patted my back, and said, "Don't let all this stuff get you down. Shit happens. I don't know how we fix things, but we gotta try, right?"

"Yeah, we gotta try."

On my drive home, I reflected on Nonviolent Action's sad state of affairs, the problems for which I was largely responsible. I had been so intensely focused on the USS *Constellation* and the war that I turned a blind eye to the problems right here at NVA.

I looked inward. Although certain vets and self-appointed leaders had used NVA's volunteers for their agenda, it could not be denied that they had worked tirelessly for an end to the war. Yet, it also could not be denied that they had acted arrogantly and undermined NVA's democratic foundation, taking actions in NVA's name without the larger group's consent. Part of me was pissed off at them, but mostly I was angry at myself for missing what was all too obvious to Norie, Ben, and Jim.

Emotionally, I demonized those that were seizing power and running NVA into the ground. Yet I knew better—*There is no enemy.* I gradually got hold of myself and recognized the need to separate the deed from the doer, to accord my adversaries the same dignity and respect that I would want.

There was an important lesson to be learned—to be especially mindful of my tendency to maintain a laser-beam focus on my peace work and CO stand at the expense of not recognizing problems that were right in front of me. I had done that with Jane, and I had done that with Nonviolent Action. It was high time to make amends.

53

LAUNCH OF THE CONSTELLATION VOTE
(1971)

"The most common way people give up their power
is by thinking they don't have any."

—Alice Walker

I felt compelled to address the problems raised by Ben, Norie, and Jim as soon as possible. But with NVA's Constellation Vote in full swing, I had to hold off until there was less pressure on everyone.

Under the spotlight of national magazines and newspapers, we felt a duty to get the vote right. Then, even more pressure came our way—good pressure. Norie called me shortly before midnight and said breathlessly, "I just got off the phone with CBS in LA. They said they'd like to cover the Constellation Vote on the evening national news! They asked us to send them a *lot* of background material. But . . . uh, here's the catch—they need it by tomorrow morning, or they may not broadcast the story." She paused. "Since you're a writer . . . and since you can type . . . and since everything has to be turned in tomorrow morning . . ."

"Ai yai yai," I said groggily. "Okay, I'll be there as soon as I can."

Jane rolled over in bed and looked at me sympathetically. "Duty calls?"

I nodded sleepily with a smile.

At the Peace House I was greeted by about a dozen volunteers. They looked like they hadn't eaten or slept in ages. "How much do I need to type?" The volunteers averted my gaze. Norie moved aside, revealing a *huge* stack of papers on a foldout table.

"*All* of it?" I asked.

Everyone nodded. I took a seat behind a typewriter that should have been in the Smithsonian, demanded coffee, and pecked away. Going straight through with only bathroom breaks, I finished the next morning as the sun was rising.

As we packed up the material for mailing, a call came in. Norie answered. "Sure, I'll hold," she said. She covered the receiver with her hand, "It's CBS!" The caller came back on the line. "Yes, it's ready," Norie said. "We'll send the material right away. The New York office. Fine." She hung up and grinned. "They want us to mark the package: 'Special Attention: Walter Cronkite'! Cronkite won't do the broadcast himself, but they said it's 'almost definite' that the story will air!"

Cheers broke out. We understood that if one of Cronkite's associates covered the Constellation Project, the entire nation would hear about NVA's call to end the war and bring the troops home.

Originally, we planned to hold The Constellation Vote on a single day. Later we concluded that we could allow more voters to participate if we gave them five days—September 17th to September 21st.

The funds for the Constellation Vote came from the generosity of Joan Baez. She offered to give two benefit concerts organized largely by Lee McComb, a volunteer that had been with NVA nearly from the beginning. Lee told me he wanted to make the concerts multi-media, and knowing that photography was my passion, asked, "Do you have any photos that would make people think of peace?"

I thought, *What could be more inspiring of peace and opposite of war than the innocent faces of children!* So, I offered my portraits of kids that celebrated diversity.

Jane and I attended one of the concerts. As we took our seats in the huge gym at San Diego State University, Jane pointed out an anti-draft poster that added a touch of levity to the event: Girls Say Yes to Guys Who Say No.

While Baez's powerful soprano voice served as a clarion call to end war, my photos of children were projected larger than life. As the concert ended, Jane looked at me and said, "I just decided that all our ambassadors to other countries should be musicians. Forget all the détente and negotiations that drag on for years. Forget sending weapons around the world. From now on, we send artists like Joan Baez or Bob Dylan or Peter, Paul and Mary and let 'em tell our so-called enemies that we don't want war; it's our government that does. Then those countries can send their musicians here with the same message—We, the People, say, 'No more war.'"

"I like it," I said. "Gandhi used to say that the governments of the world hide the people's hearts from each other. Music is doing what Nixon promised he'd do but didn't—it's bringing us together."

Democracy was in bloom.

On the first day of the Constellation Vote—Friday, September 17, 1971, I arrived at the dock as a CBS-TV crew filmed civilians and military personnel voting. There were two choices—vote for the USS *Constellation* to return to the war or vote for it to stay home.

Many of those in favor of the *Connie* returning to Vietnam felt it improper to question the president's policy in Vietnam and believed that NVA, intentionally or unintentionally, was "giving comfort to the enemy."

On the other hand, those in favor of the *Connie* staying home tended to view the non-binding referendum as a call, not just to San Diego, but to the nation—end the war now.

Whether the pro-war or anti-war people would dominate the five-day vote, I felt terribly proud to be part of NVA and what we had accomplished from our humble beginnings.

In anxious anticipation, Jane and I joined dozens of NVA volunteers as they filed into the Peace House to watch the CBS coverage of the Constellation Vote on the evening national news. The broadcast began with reporter Bill Kurtis: "The issue of US involvement in Vietnam is very much alive in San Diego, a predominantly Navy and Marine Corps town . . ."

Clips ran of our volunteers conducting the Constellation Vote. Kurtis continued, "Ballots are pouring in from nearly one hundred polling places around the city." In closing, the reporter said, "Realistically, none of the young people expect the carrier to stay at home, but with the Constellation Vote, they have made their point—to keep the Vietnam War issue alive, especially among young service men."

After the broadcast, I watched volunteers pat each other on the back, shake hands, and hug. It reminded me of scenes in a NASA control room after a successful launch. I thought *I'm happy about today, but NVA is in trouble. What the public doesn't know is that we're a house divided. But at least we had this call of conscience to all of America.*

As I left the Peace House, Norie, Ben, and Jim came up to me with big celebratory grins. I couldn't help but smile back. I was enormously pleased with the broadcast and with the fact that morale at NVA was sky-high. Yet, at the same time, I worried that tonight's victory might be NVA's swan song. I thought *It's all glitter. Who's going to be around once the vote is over? Either NVA gets back to its roots—deciding things together and insisting on equality—or it's going to turn into a distant memory.*

From the Peace House, I went to the ocean to meditate on the problems at NVA and how to counter them. As I pulled into a parking space facing the beach, I noticed a gaping hole in the steel-net fence in front of my car. Through it, I watched the red-yellow sun rapidly sinking behind the ocean's horizon. I wondered, *Is it too late to have an impact at the next NVA general meeting, to make my plea that we get back on track?*

In the dim after-glow of the sunset, I walked barefoot along the beach and stepped up onto my favorite reef. The endless Pacific extended before me, giving me a much-needed sense of peace. In meditation, I gleaned a lesson from my work at NVA—any worthy cause requires eternal vigilance. But that lesson also led to an array of disturbing questions.

Why was the authoritarian way so popular with so many at NVA? How could that undemocratic way of doing things appeal? And why? If authoritarian people and I both want peace, which I'm sure we do, what's the fundamental difference between their approach and mine? Then it dawned on me that what separated authoritarian actions from truly democratic actions was perhaps the central principle of nonviolence—*means and ends.* Nonviolence requires *making the way we do something just as important as what we want.* Gandhi consistently noted that the journey must be as important as the destination.

Standing on the reef and looking out at where the sun had disappeared only moments ago, I felt invigorated by the ocean breeze.

I realized that NVA had lost a priceless framework for governing itself, similar to the framework set forth at the Philadelphia Constitutional Convention of 1787. The Founding Fathers sharply debated our country's future, but in the end, they wisely came up with a system based roughly on the phrase that Benjamin Franklin had contributed to the new America: *E Pluribus Unum,* out of many, one.

The new Constitution evolved to embrace a brilliant and beautiful combination—one nation united yet a federation of separate states. I had viewed NVA as a microcosm of that. We were united as a peace group, yet we made each individual important. As Eric often said, "*Everyone* at NVA is a leader." The same could be said of Quaker meetings—*all* members are , in effect, ministers.

The real power of NVA was derived from all its members, not from a dictatorial minority that considered themselves 'more equal than others' and sacrificed our means of governing for a supposedly good end. I realized I should have reiterated the principle of means and ends at general NVA meetings so that we would stay consistent with what we stood for—*democratic,* nonviolent action.

As the evening's first pale star appeared against the dark blue sky, I felt I had just reaffirmed who I was and what Nonviolent Action had stood for since its birth.

Nonviolent Action faced a critical juncture in its history. It had reached the peak of its glory in the press, yet, at the same time, it had reached the depths of its divisiveness. I knew what I had to do to try and save NVA from self-destructing. Just as I had been confronted by my caring friends—Norie, Ben, and Jim—I would confront NVA as a whole at the next general meeting.

At home, I told Jane I felt that I had a duty to raise issues that threatened NVA from within. "Okay," she said, "but be prepared. No one likes the messenger with bad news."

One year after the Constellation Vote, Joan Baez and I held a press conference calling for an end to the Vietnam war, 1972.

54

LETTING GO OF NONVIOLENT ACTION
(September 1971)

"When you are sorrowful look again in your heart,
and you shall see that in truth you are weeping for that
which has been your delight."
—Kahlil Gibran

At this evening's massive Nonviolent Action meeting, I stood before the crowd of two hundred and fifty plus and took a deep breath. I scanned the young faces of the volunteers that had flocked here from across the country. They were largely innocent faces, excited with our momentum. And here I was, about to pull the rug from under them for reasons I knew they could not understand.

We were at our peak with our famed five-day Constellation Vote. Who would want to question things now? Few, if any. And who would understand my plea that NVA get back to its democratic, humanistic roots and tactics? By confronting the authoritarian and chauvinist leaders in NVA, I would undoubtedly become an outcast to the peace group I had founded.

As Norie was about to call the meeting to order, Ben motioned me aside. He knew my controversial topic and said, "I'm with you all the way on this, buddy." I nodded thanks.

Norie quieted the crowd and waited until the room came to a hush. "Francesco wrote a letter that he'd like you to take a minute to read before he talks with you. He's raising two issues that he feels are crucial to the survival and growth of Nonviolent Action, so please read the letter carefully."

Norie looked at me with a comforting smile as the members skimmed my heartfelt letter. First, I spelled out my belief that NVA would be in danger of self-destructing if decision-making power was not restored to the whole group. Second, I called for the women in NVA to be treated with more respect and given equal leadership roles rather than token tasks.

Tensions ran high as buzzing conversations filled the room, coupled with a sea of disgruntled expressions: *The founder of Nonviolent Action has turned on his own peace group! Traitor!*

I raised my voice so it could be heard to the back of the room. "Nonviolent Action has accomplished *amazing* things since it was formed over a year ago." A sprinkling of applause. "But now it's at a turning point, maybe the point of no return."

Our army of peace activists looked up from their sitting positions on the floor with knitted eyebrows.

"It wasn't easy writing this letter," I began. "I did it because I feel we're no longer practicing a basic principle of nonviolence—making the way we do something just as important as what we want. About the letter you're reading . . . I didn't write it to blame anyone other than myself. The purpose of it is to try and turn NVA around. I know a lot of you think that NVA has never been better. After all, we're now national and international news."

"*Yeah!*" someone exclaimed. A smattering of applause.

"I look out at this crowd, and I think of how far NVA has come. I'm so proud of what we've accomplished. We've helped the farm workers, thousands of draftees, and we've supported the crew of the *Connie*. But somewhere along the way, we got side-tracked. Ironically, we're encouraging everyone in San Diego to vote and use the power of democracy, yet we've become hypocrites to democratic decisions. We used to vote on every issue together. But now a small group of self-appointed leaders are acting in NVA's name without consulting the rest of us, and worse, they're using many of you for their own purposes, and not NVA's." I looked around the silent, jam-packed room.

The reactions of the vets using our volunteers varied. A few sneered at my talk, but one vet actually had tears in his eyes. Apparently, he had no idea that he was seriously damaging NVA by using our volunteers for his peace group without any consent from NVA. I paused and absorbed his pain, then continued. "NVA used to *share* in making decisions. That democratic way of doing things is what made us strong, not the fame."

Silence. I pressed on.

"I've got another issue to raise. Has anyone noticed how badly the women in NVA are treated? Other than Norie, only guys are running things. Does *any* woman here feel this . . . demeaned or disrespected in any way? You don't have to go into it now, but after the meeting, feel free to let Norie and I know how you feel. I know if *I* feel this, you've got to feel it a hundred times more."

A tense silence followed, then one woman said loudly, "We don't mind."

I stared, stunned, as Norie muttered, "Well, you damn well should!"

Though I saw several women look at each other knowingly, not one spoke to the daily disrespect. I paused, not sure how to close my remarks. "For those of you who will be leaving NVA and working for peace in your home states, I have a lesson to pass on. If we want America to be a moral example to the world, then we have to be a moral example to ourselves and each other, here and now. Nonviolence is all about means and ends. Never forget to make the way you do something just as important as what you want." I noticed a few people nod earnestly. "Well . . ." I began, struggling not to let my voice break, "I don't want to end on a negative note, so instead, I'd like to thank each and every one of you for joining Nonviolent Action. You've worked night and day to help the farm workers and the draftees and to help stop the war. You've left a beautiful, amazing legacy. With hard work, we grew into a national nonviolent movement. No one here in San Diego thought we'd last more than a month or two. They said it was *impossible* for us to make a difference. But you know what—we stirred the conscience of the whole country!"

The room broke into applause. I had justifiably torn down their pride, and now I justifiably built it back up. My voice raised with passion. "Someday, when we're old and decrepit, we'll be able to say to ourselves and our children, 'Wasn't that a time, a time we didn't stand by and watch the war rage in our name. Together, as vets and as civilians, we went to war with war. Together, we were peacemakers.' *Never* forget." I waved goodbye and started for the door. Before I could go any further, someone caught me by the arm. It was Norie, her eyes shining with tears. She hugged me and went back to the meeting.

There was only one place to go for peace of mind.

Standing atop the large circular reef, I looked out over the darkening Pacific Ocean. The sky turned gloomy, and the water turbulent. I felt I was in mourning as if about to witness the burial at sea of a loved one.

This afternoon's meeting at the Peace House convinced me that I should leave NVA after the Constellation Vote. *But how can I leave something I love so much?* Ominous dark clouds continued to drift in fast, and I thought, *NVA had its birth, its brief life, and now it's time for me to accept its passing.*

Thunder rumbled in the distance, reminding me of a story about storms in Asia. A monsoon would sweep in and wipe out a whole village. It was a terrible catastrophe, yet the villagers would see it in a positive light. They welcomed the adversity as an opportunity to begin anew. Their hardship served as a reminder that their most valuable possession was a positive, kind spirit. *So it is with NVA,* I thought. *But in our case, the storm came from within.*

As the violent squall continued to envelop the sky, I extended an open hand and let go of Nonviolent Action forever.

55

THE CONSTELLATION VOTE RESULTS

(September 17–21, 1971)

"I am only one, but still I am one.
I cannot do everything, but still I can do something.
And because I cannot do everything
I will not refuse to do the something that I can do."

—Helen Keller

Exuberant and gratified that NVA's Constellation Vote reached the nation via CBS, I thought, *If anyone had told me at the beginning of NVA that we would not only impact our intended audience in San Diego, but we would also impact the country, including the president's cabinet, I would have immediately referred them to my psychiatrist dad.*

I figured our Constellation Vote couldn't possibly get any more media exposure, but I was wrong. Like CBS, ABC-TV called and said they'll do a prime-time evening news feature on the vote and our call to end the war. All I could think of was the California motto—*Eureka!*

From our living room, Jane and I watched the evening news report by Harry Reasoner. The backdrop for Reasoner's report was a map image of Vietnam set next to a silhouette of an attack aircraft carrier that represented the USS *Constellation.* Reasoner began, "In San Diego, California today [September 20, 1971], an antiwar group entered the final phase of a major effort to bring out a popular vote of protest against the return of an American aircraft carrier to Indochina."

From ABC in New York, the shot cut to a reporter in San Diego. In the bay behind the commentator loomed the USS *Constellation.* In coat and tie, the reporter spoke in a brisk, staccato manner: "The USS *Constellation* is a fighting carrier. From these decks, their planes have bombed North Vietnam. But now it's the *ship* that's under attack by war protesters who don't want her to go back to Southeast Asia."

Jane and I looked at each other. "What language!" I exclaimed with a laugh. "We're not attacking the carrier. We're attacking the carrier's orders."

The reporter added, "The campaign, reportedly, is costing $50,000, much of the money raised in concerts by singer Joan Baez." The segment quickly cut to Joan Baez singing "Joe Hill" at San Diego State University: *"From San Diego up to Maine . . ."* Second quick cut! We're back to the reporter on the dock, who commented, "The war protesters realize they really aren't going to change Navy policy, but in the words of one of them, 'the important thing' he said, 'is that we tried.'"

Considering the scope of our task, the five-day voting went amazingly well. NVA had succeeded in making the deployment of another attack aircraft carrier to Vietnam a national issue. Our citywide non-binding vote had been covered by both CBS and ABC national news as well as by foreign press.

When Ben announced the vote results, most of us at NVA were startled: more than 45,000 of the 54,000 citizens who participated voted to keep the *Connie* home! Even the military vote—the *Connie* crew and crews from other ships in port—favored the *Connie* not going to war. The biggest shock—2,575 of those in the military voted for the carrier to return to Vietnam, while 6,951 voted *against* the carrier's departure for war.

At home, I received a call from someone who didn't identify himself at first. "You really shook things up in San Diego," he said.

"Who is this?" I asked.

"It's Hal Bruno from *Newsweek* magazine. I'd like to ask you about the recent Constellation Vote. In your eyes, what was that all about?"

"Well, it was mainly about giving the people of San Diego and the crew of the *Connie* a voice. Even though the vote was non-binding, it gave people a chance to say, *Enough is enough!* The Vietnam War has dragged on for seven years now. Even today, we've got the Secretary of Defense telling us that 'Vietnamization' is running '*ahead* of schedule.' Nonviolent Action has from the beginning called for an immediate end to the war and for the troops to come home."

"Tell me about Nonviolent Action and what it stands for?"

"We're all about helping to build a culture of nonviolence in America."

"How?"

"I can't speak for the whole group, but personally, I think our country needs to change our budget priorities—less on the military, more on people needs. And we urgently need to convert our economic system from a military-industrial war economy to an environmentally friendly peace economy. That'll include changing our tax structure. The wealthy corporations and individuals aren't paying their fair share. Why should a working family pay hundreds in taxes, while a multi-million-dollar corporation pays zero in taxes?"

"Any other changes?"

"Yes. We've got a Secretary of Defense, which earlier in our history used to be called the Secretary of War. Why not establish a Department of Peace that would be devoted to solving international conflicts nonviolently? It's an old idea, but it's still a good one. We go to war way too easily."

"When the *Connie* left for Vietnam on October 1st, did you feel that NVA failed?"

"Not at all. We didn't expect to stop it from going, but we didn't want it to go in our name without participatory democracy being exercised."

"I heard that nine of the sailors refused to sail with the ship. What happened to them?"

"The 'Connie Nine' took sanctuary in Christ the King Church where they were arrested by U.S. Marshals. They were flown to the *Connie* by helicopter and put in the ship's brig. The charge against them was 'shirking important service' when, in fact, they were demonstrating important service. It took courage for them to stand against the war. The Navy ended up sentencing the sailors to thirty days in custody. Later all nine were discharged honorably."

"What's your personal situation with the draft?"

"I'm a conscientious objector, but my Virginia draft board has turned me down twice."

"Would you go to prison for your CO beliefs?"

"I would, and I expect to do just that in the near future."

After a pause, he continued, "When you founded NVA, did you ever dream it would become so big? I mean, I've gotta say that for a grassroots peace organization in such a gung-ho military town, NVA certainly seems to have its act together."

"Thanks, but believe me, we have our share of problems."

"I heard you left the group. What are you going to do now?"

"I'm looking for a job where I can do community work at the local level."

I landed a job as director of a community center in a downtown San Diego barrio. Over the last year and a half, I had focused on national issues like farm workers' rights, the draft, and the war. The NVA meetings were massive. Now I could work with people one on one. Another benefit was working with people spanning the whole spectrum of life: children, teens, and senior citizens. My duties included getting to know the residents in the area, offering health and educational programs, and delivering food to shut-in seniors.

The initial interview for the job had been rough. One of the board members didn't mince words: "I've got strong reservations about hiring you, Mr. Da Vinci. They tell me you're a CO with no military service. This is one damn tough neighborhood. I'm not sure you can handle it."

"I can handle it."

"You're confident about that?"

"Very."

"You're going to be dealing with a lot of tough teens, and they'll need military-style firmness."

"I can give 'em all the firmness and leadership they need," I replied, "but I'm not going to *order* them around. I'm going to work *with* them."

"That can't be done here. They *need* orders. Your background has me very concerned."

I didn't realize just how concerned. Later, Bill, a friend of Jane's on the board, told me he had a private meeting with the executive committee. "In that meeting," Bill said, "the guy who interviewed you warned the rest of the board members that since you're a CO, you might *corrupt* the children."

"You're kidding!"

"I kid you not," Bill said. "I demanded to know why he would say that, and he said, 'Not only is Da Vinci a CO, but his resume shows that his family once took him on a Mediterranean cruise that included a visit to the Soviet Union!' I said, 'So?' and he said, 'It's obvious. We might well be dealing with a communist.'"

"You've got to be putting me on," I said to Bill.

"I swear to you, that's exactly what he said. I told everyone at the meeting, 'Francesco is just as patriotic as anyone else in this room, and probably *more* so.' Then I cracked 'em up. I said that when I was visiting your apartment, I didn't see a single shortwave radio tuned in to Moscow. Everybody laughed except Dr. Strangelove, and you were hired."

The first proposal I made as director of the community center was to disarm it. The tall steel-net fence surrounding the center was bordered by huge spirals of barbed wire. I told the administration, "The people in the neighborhood would probably feel a lot more comfortable using the center if it was more inviting and didn't look so much like an armed fortress."

The administration had a few meetings, then gave me the green light to remove the barbed wire as well as a few threatening signs. I recruited a dozen local teens and asked, "What do you say we humanize the center and cut down the barbed wire? Anybody up for that?"

Roberto, a young Chicano teen with long black, shoulder-length hair, said, "Fantastic! It's the biggest eyesore in the neighborhood! Let's do it!" The teens applauded and cheered.

I handed out the wire-cutters, and in no time, the foreboding fortress had turned eye-friendly. Once the barbed wire was down, I asked, "Would you like to repaint the teen center?"

The teens cheered again. "Okay, let's vote on the color," I suggested.

Roberto looked at me astounded. "We get to vote? *Really*?"

"Of course, you get to vote," I assured him. "You've heard of 'democracy,' haven't you?"

"Yeah, man, but not in the barrio!"

56

THE HOME STRETCH WITH CHARLIE
(1971)

"Fear not the path of truth for the lack of people walking on it."
—Robert F. Kennedy (the last speech he gave)

"Since we only have one appeal left and not much time before you turn 26," Charlie began, "I think it's important that you keep a low profile. The FBI is monitoring you, and probably me because of you. Who's to say if they talked with the draft board about your case."

"Is that legal?"

"Does it matter? Nixon is president and John Mitchell is attorney general."

"About the low profile," I began uneasily, "I should tell you that when we finish today, I've got a TV interview about the peace work of Nonviolent Action. It's only local."

"Only local. Well, that's just *great!*" Charlie exclaimed, throwing his hands in the air. "I've got an idea. While you're on TV, hold up a sign for the FBI that says, 'Come and Get Me!'"

"You didn't expect me to stop working for peace, did you?"

"No, but I did hope for a little common sense. Is it too much to ask you to lay low, just for the home stretch? You stay in the limelight, and you'll be antagonizing them. Sometimes I don't know why the hell I bother advising you."

"I always listen to what you have to say. You make me aware of my legal rights, and you tell me straight up what you think is best for my welfare. I know that, and I appreciate it."

"Like *hell.* Do you really get it? I don't think so. You could be going to jail for half a decade! And knowing you, Da Vinci, I don't think you'll *ever* get out. You question everything and everyone, and that's not going to go over big with prison guards!"

"Einstein said—" I began.

"I know, Albert said to question everything, but he wasn't in jail!" Charlie started pacing, and I moved out of his way. "I used to think that *you* were the one here that was naïve. But it's me! I had *no* idea what I was getting myself into when I took this case. Now I see why there were eight attorneys before me; eight *smart* attorneys who bailed out."

I listened, fearful that Charlie was about to quit my case. "I need you to see this through with me," I interjected. "Like you said, it's the home stretch."

He stood motionless a moment. "I wasn't about to drop you, if that's what you thought, but *strangling* you—now that's a different story. Let's switch roles a minute so you can appreciate what a royal pain in the ass you are, Da Vinci. The other day someone asked about your case and I started *stuttering*! I'm an *attorney*, and your case is causing me to lose the power of speech! I don't believe in hell, but if there is one, I know what your fate will be—you'll have yourself as a client. *God*, I'd love to see that!"

The following week, Charlie called and said, "We need to meet and go over your case."

"Sure, but why now?"

"I wouldn't ask for a meeting if it wasn't important, would I?"

His abrupt tone took me aback. "I guess not."

On the drive over, I couldn't figure out what I had done to make him so angry. I just knew I was in trouble.

Anxiously, I walked into his office. "How's it going, Charlie?"

"Have a seat, Da Vinci."

I took a chair, never taking my eyes off Charlie's face. His eyes widened as if they were going to devour me while his brows pushed downward, hiding his upper eyelids. The lips bore a tight frown. "Congratulations," he said dryly. He leaned in over the magazine rack next to his desk, picked up the current copy of *LIFE* magazine, and held it up. "I see they published your article about the draft."

"It's just a 'Letter to the Editor,'" I said.

"Just a 'Letter to the Editor' in *LIFE* magazine, the *biggest* fucking magazine in the country! *LIFE* comes out *for* the draft, and you have to write 'em and tell 'em that they're 'contradicting the ideals we believe in.' And you close with:

> No matter how you feel about the war, no matter what your politics are, the draft is forcing young men to enter the military against their will. That is clearly involuntary servitude, and involuntary servitude is clearly undemocratic. A true democracy respects the freedom of the individual. If an end to the draft is "ill-considered" then so is freedom.

"You know *damn* well the FBI is watching you, and *still* you have to go out of your way to rile 'em up. You're givin' 'em even more reason to put you away for as long as possible! Don't you get it! They'll use any reason they can to crucify you! I'm sick and tired of watching young guys being abused by the system." Charlie walked over to a window, his face half in light, half in shadow. His jaw clenched tight. His eyes welled up with tears.

"What's going on, Charlie? You okay?"

"Not really. A judge reopened a draft case against my client, a twenty-year old kid who lied on his student deferment form. The kid told his draft board that he was in college, which wasn't true. Because of that, this incredibly sadistic judge threatened the guy with *ten years* in prison. The kid went to pieces and hanged himself."

"I'm sorry."

"I'll never get over the loss of that young man. I'm still raging at the obscenity of what was done, of what's now being repeated by that judge and others." Charlie started pacing with a vengeance. "Rage is good in this work as long as I can channel it. It's what keeps me running. It's what allows me to sleep at night and get up the next morning to fight back." My eyes followed Charlie as he walked briskly across the room, then froze. "You *do* realize how fucking naïve you are, don't you?"

"Maybe." I looked into his eyes that shined bright.

"I don't think you have the slightest idea about the brutal forces that are behind this war and the draft . . . or about what's in store for you. Before you know it, you're gonna get hammered by a judge and then by the guards in the prison that you're sent to. I know the hate that's out there. But you? Just look at you in your white peasant shirt, like a fucking lamb, oblivious to the fact that it's heading straight for the meat-grinder."

Charlie walked over to his world globe and placed a hand on it. "All around the planet, we're waging war after war after war. Can you smell the death? It's from the machine that keeps rolling along, the machine that Eisenhower warned us about—the damn military-industrial complex. He warned us that the military would get in bed with the corporations, that we'd all be fucked if no one did anything about it. And sure enough, we keep intervening all over the world where we've got no damn business. The result is that young guys keep comin' home in boxes, or if they say no to the slaughter, they put 'em in prison. Why? For greed, for money over life. *That's* what it's all about, my principled friend, that's what it's all about."

57

CHARLIE, FRIEND AND ADVERSARY
(1971)

"A true friend is someone who thinks that you are a good egg even though he knows that you are slightly cracked."

—Bernard Meltzer

The moment I entered the foyer of Charlie's office, Margaret, the secretary, said, "You can go in. He's already worn a hole in the carpet."

Charlie paced back and forth, paused, and said, "It's all come down to this—for your last appeal, we're going to ask the Virginia State Director to overturn your draft board's two rejections. If the director doesn't rule in our favor, you go to jail."

"What happens if he overturns in my favor?" I asked.

"That's *very* unrealistic. I want to be clear that this is basically a futile gesture. Still, we've got nothing to lose by going for it."

"Okay, but *if* he did that?"

"Then, you would do two years of alternative service. Your draft board would send you their recommendations, which you could either accept or reject. If you reject them, then you can make three selections of your own."

"What kind of selections?" I asked.

"Hold it a minute," Charlie said. "Let's not waste too much time on this. You're not getting your hopes up on this last appeal, are you? I mean, you *are* prepared to go to prison, aren't you?"

"I am, as much as I can be."

"And Jane?"

"She says she's going to move near the prison."

"Wow. She's pretty amazing," Charlie said.

"She is."

Charlie smiled. "You know, there's one way that'll give you *much* better odds than this last appeal." He rubbed his hands together with the pride of a gourmet chef who knows he is about to create a masterpiece. "Here's what we *should* do, but it's up to you, of course."

I braced myself. *Listen. Don't cut him off.* "What's that?"

"Who's that draft clerk you've been friends with for years, what's her name?"

"Joyce."

"Oh yeah, write Joyce, and make sure you call her by her first name."

"I always do that."

"Fine. In your letter, stress your staunch patriotism to butter her up. Say you'd like nothing more than to *further the national interest.* Be sure to use that phrase." I smirked, and he paused in the pacing. "Just *think* about this, okay? Keep an open mind."

"Okay."

"I mean, this would be a *brilliant* move." He resumed pacing. "You request a physical, so they'll think you're going in. That'll delay things. *Please*, do *not* roll your eyes."

"Okay."

"You're going to turn 26 in only *six months*, Francesco! If you do this, you and Jane can be free of the draft *forever*. If you won't do it for yourself, at least think about doing it for Jane."

"I don't think I'd like to stall them," I said evenly.

"There goes that calm, '*I don't think I'd like to,*' which is total bullshit! As usual, I give you practical ideas on how to stay out of jail, and every damn time you shoot 'em down. You don't even *think* about delaying things a little, am I right?"

"You're right."

"See! Just what I thought!"

"Look, Charlie, from the beginning, we've made this case stand for something positive. We've always been open with the draft board, and I'd like to continue that way, that's all."

"Continue straight to prison?"

"Prison isn't the point. We've never played games with them. We've given them the truth, whether they liked it or not. Stalling would wipe out everything you and I have fought for from the beginning, do you see that?"

He shook his head. "Okay, okay. Let's go the way we were, plowing our way to prison." Charlie slid behind his desk and leaned back with his hands behind his head. "Let's say that, against all the odds, you're granted status as a CO. Out of curiosity, what would be your first pick for alternative service?"

"Anything?"

"Technically anything, but the draft board has got to approve it. Pick a place that you'd genuinely like to work at the most, a job that would be close to your heart."

"That's easy."

"Good. Lay it on me."

"The National Council to Repeal the Draft."

Charlie burst out laughing. "That's good, real good!" When he saw that I wasn't smiling, his laugh took a dive. "You're not serious?"

"I am."

Through gritted teeth, Charlie said, "We don't want to lose them. Excuse me a minute." He took a deep breath. I feared he was having a heart attack.

"You okay, Charlie?"

"Oh yeah. I'm just trying to stifle a few homicidal thoughts." He maniacally glared at me. "There, that's better. What's another pick for your alternative service, one that's not psychotic?"

"Second choice might be the community center where I'm working now."

"That's a good one. It's actually rational. One more."

"Third choice, the American Friends Service Committee—the Quakers."

"The second and third choices aren't bad, but the first one we need to rethink. The best one is the community center." He looked off and then made a loud clap. "Whoa! I just came up with a plan that's *really* good," he exclaimed. "You won't go for it, but listen anyhow. It will be therapeutic for me."

"What's that?"

"You write your draft board a letter saying, 'I've been thinking things over and I've decided that I'm no longer a CO.'" My eyes flared. Charlie glared back. "Indulge me!"

"Sorry."

"The beauty of telling them you're no longer a CO is that you'd be able to delay things past your 26th birthday and be completely ineligible for the draft."

"What happened to our agreement to stick to the truth?"

"I was only kidding about dropping the CO claim," Charlie said, back-pedaling. "Well . . . maybe half-kidding."

"Why do you keep bringing up these legal maneuvers when you *know* I have no interest in faking my way out of the draft?"

"Because they're the *sensible* way out of this mess. I knew you'd say no, but I had to try. That's my job, to give you alternatives."

"True, but let's stay on track, Charlie, the way we've been doing."

Charlie looked off a moment, then slammed his fist down on his desk. "*Dammit*, Francesco, prison is such a waste!"

We stared at each other in silence, and I said, "You know what? Even if I have to go to prison, we win. We're doing the right thing, in the right way. Know what I mean?"

"Yeah, I get it—means and ends and all that good stuff. I figured you'd say something like that. But you can see the sheer *beauty* of saying that you changed your mind about being a CO. It would be the rip-off of the year!"

"It's . . . clever," I mustered.

"Guess only another lawyer could appreciate it. From a legal standpoint, mind you, there's no problem. From a moral standpoint, I can see there might be some stickiness. Well, if you change your mind, that's okay too."

"Got it. By the way, Charlie, lemme give you my new address. Jane and I are moving into a small house in Pacific Beach."

"You'll need to notify Selective Service about any change of address."

When I got home, I wrote my draft board to tell them that I was moving and used the opportunity to protest their rejection of my CO claim.

> To the draft board members:
>
> Although I'm writing to notify you of my new address, I would also like to request that you reevaluate your past rejection of my CO claim. I am truly a conscientious objector opposed to all war, seeking to build, rather than destroy. Yet you deny me the basic rights our Constitution espouses, not to mention the Human Rights division of the United Nations, which internationally supports the right to refuse to kill.
>
> I'm moving to a new address. I'm changing as life does. All I ask of you is to be open. I am still doubtful as to whether you understand my position. What if I were judging one of you as to the sincerity of your own beliefs? Imagine yourself trying to structure your deeply held convictions in forms; then imagine yourself being interviewed by someone of a different generation who holds views almost opposite your own. Then imagine that after you tried to relate to the person, he or she told you that you were insincere, that you were not what you claimed to be. Ask yourself what you would do in such a situation. I struggled with that question and it was settled. The answer I found was quite simple: to remain free in spirit. Now, whether or not I will be sent to prison is relatively unimportant to me, for I will still be following my conscience. Thus, I am not asking you for freedom; what I seek is justice.

58

EIGHT YEARS FACING THE DRAFT
(1971)

"With malice toward none . . ."
—Abraham Lincoln

About two months after I left NVA, Ben called me at home. "Hey, Francesco. This is my last day here at the Peace House, so I thought I'd update you on how crazy things have gotten here. After you went to work at the community center, and after Eric went back to teaching, all hell broke loose."

"What happened?"

"Norie formed a women's rights group, and the women read their demands at a general meeting. But some of the guys just jeered 'em like it was all a big joke. Norie got so pissed off, she bugged out. Then about thirty women got up and followed her out the door—permanently! Ever since that day, the power-hungry guys have been at war with each other."

Bam! A loud noise made me pull the receiver away from my ear.

"Sorry about that," Ben said. "As I speak, there are two guys at each other's throats. Whoa! I thought the fight was over, but they're at it again!" There was another crash. "Hey!" Ben shouted at someone. "Knock it off or take it outside!" He came back on the line. "Man, how crazy is this! I'm in the middle of fistfights at the *Peace* House! I just hope that these guys quit NVA before they kill each other."

Jane and I put together a reunion for a dozen or so of the original NVA volunteers. We met at *The Cove,* the picturesque park in La Jolla, where I had asked Jane to marry me. Everyone showed up except one. "Where's Jim?" I asked.

Ben and Norie looked at each other. "You didn't know?" Ben asked.

Norie explained, "Jim took off to Canada last week. He's living in a commune."

Ben added, "The war has broken up a lot of families."

Norie looked at me with a tortured gaze. I knew she was thinking about her late husband, whom she had lost to the war. Tears welled up in her eyes, and I held her. Then our hug became a group hug.

For one year, Charlie and I had been battling both the draft *and* each other. Today's meeting would be one of our last before learning the outcome of our final appeal to the Virginia State Director of Selective Service.

I entered Charlie's office and sidestepped his rapid pacing. "Hey, Francesco." He paused only momentarily. "Last night, I got a *great* idea in my sleep. This is *very* cool, so don't say anything. Just listen."

Here we go again.

"I know this is a big 'if,' but let's say the amazing thing happens, and on your last appeal, you're granted CO status. Of course, that's totally unrealistic, but *if* that happened, your draft board would tell you to pick your preferences for alternative service. Well, last night, it hit me that your crazy idea to make your first choice The National Council to Repeal the Draft might actually be smart after all!"

"How's that?"

In Machiavellian mode, Charlie stroked his beard. "Here's the plan. You don't put down the community center where you're working as one of your three preferences. Leave it out. That's too reasonable."

"I thought you liked that one?"

"That was then; this is now. Instead, only give 'em your bent pick—the National Council to Repeal the Draft. That'll be totally unacceptable to them. Then we can stall 'em."

"I'm going to put that one down no matter what because it really is my first choice. There's nothing I'd rather do than help end the draft. But, and I mean this Charlie, there's no way I would want us to stall 'em past my 26th birthday."

"It's *only* a month and a half away! You stall 'em a little, and you and Jane are *completely* clear of the draft!"

I took a deep breath. "If I did something like that, it would nag me for the rest of my life. I'm going to stick with this: First choice—the National Council to Repeal the Draft; second choice, the community center where I'm working now; and third choice, the American Friends Service Committee."

"Are you *sure* you don't want to stall? It would be . . ."

"I'm *positive*."

"Okay then," Charlie said. "As usual, we'll do this the hard way."

"There's something I've got to tell you," I began cautiously. "I'm mailing out two holiday cards: one to President Nixon and the other to Joyce at the draft board."

Charlie's lips tightened. "Self-sabotage, but go on."

"The one that I'm sending to President Nixon is a photograph I took which is a reminder of how families are being broken apart by the war."

I handed Charlie the photo, and he quipped, "No doubt Nixon's staff will be delighted to forward it straight to the FBI. And you mentioned a second card, the one to the draft board clerk."

"I'm sending Joyce an art print." I handed Charlie a large color postcard of the Monet painting, *The Road to Honfleur under Snow*. It depicts a horse-drawn cart traveling down a long snow-covered path. "To me, it represents my eight years of facing the draft. In my note, I want to tell Joyce that I have no malice for her."

"Nice gestures," Charlie said evenly. "Actually, sending the cards is a brilliant move . . . *if* your goal is to call attention to your case and snatch defeat from whatever minute chance we have of victory! Do you really *need* to do this, Francesco?"

"Yes, I need to do it."

Charlie resumed pacing, then stopped abruptly. "Okay, send the damn cards to Nixon and Joyce, but I have a small favor to ask."

"Anything."

"Beat it out of my office before I say, 'To *hell* with nonviolence' and live out my favorite fantasy—strangling you!"

From home, I sent out the cards. Inside the Monet print to Joyce, I wrote the following:

> Dear Joyce,
>
> Eight years have passed since I first had to face the draft. That's a long time in a 25-year-old man's life. During that time, I've suffered, learned, and grown a great deal.
>
> I want you to know that I have no malice for you or the draft board members. I'm only against the draft. The draft forces young men to join the military against their will, and trains them for violence against their fellow human beings. I'm sure you and I agree that we want Peace On Earth, but we differ on how to get there.
>
> Many excuse their inaction with the belief that peace is impossible. They continually blame outside forces, and feel there is nothing the individual can do to change things for the better. It took me a long time to stop waiting, a long time to stop blaming, and a long time to realize that Peace On Earth follows peace alone.
>
> peace and friendship,
> Francesco

The next morning, I awoke and recalled a dream about the draft: Joyce slyly looked around her office to make sure no one was watching. Then she pulled my file from the top of a big stack of papers and slipped it at the bottom so that it would be lost forever.

"It's *very* important that you come by my office," Charlie said over the phone, his tone grave.

I took a seat from across his desk and tried to gauge his mood. He seemed somber, without the usual agitation. At first, I was simply curious about his uncharacteristic manner, then I felt unnerved by it, especially since he wasn't in his usual pacing mode.

"There's something I've been meaning to tell you," Charlie said evenly. He looked down. Then his eyes met mine. "As much as I *hate* that you're going to prison, when there's really no need to do that, I want you to know that I respect it . . . 100%. I never told you that before 'cause I didn't want to encourage you."

"I really appreciate that, Charlie. It means a lot to me."

He leaned over his desk and picked up a piece of paper. "This is the phone number for Corey, a CO who served four years in federal prison for refusing induction in LA. I thought it would be a good idea for you to talk to him about what it's like to be behind bars."

I held up the piece of paper he gave me. "Thanks for this . . . and thanks for everything. I . . ."

"I know. Get outta here and talk to the CO. You don't have that much time left on the outside."

Corey and I met for our talk in Balboa Park. As we shook hands, I took in his face. He had short blonde hair, a heavily lined forehead, and curious blue eyes. We started down a long dirt path bordered with tall eucalyptus trees and I asked, "Before you decided to refuse induction, did you ever think about going to Canada?"

"I actually planned on it," Corey said. "I made all the necessary arrangements, then changed my mind at the last minute. In the end, I decided I wouldn't be going to Canada for anything positive. I'd just be going to *avoid* prison."

Our path gently curved down a grassy slope. "Do you think prison was worth it?" I asked.

He hesitated. "Yeah. For me, it was. But there are lots of ways to do your time. Some guys isolate themselves from everyone. I tried to make a community out of it. I liked that I met people there that I would never have met under different circumstances."

"Anything about prison that you didn't expect?"

"Yeah, I assumed that as a CO, I'd be treated like a leper. Instead, I was actually *admired* for being a political prisoner. The prisoners respected COs 'cause they had the balls to stand up to the government."

"It seems crazy that you'd get more respect in there than out here," I said.

Corey laughed. "That *is* crazy, isn't it?"

"Did being in prison affect your personality and the way you are now?"

"Definitely," he answered without hesitation. "There's a saying among ex-Catholics that you can't just walk away from the church. Prison is like that. It stays with you."

As we neared a playground, the sound of children's laughter rang out. Corey flinched sharply. "Anything spooks me now," he said. "'Cause of prison, I'm still tense and on guard all the time." We walked on in silence a bit, then Corey asked, "Are you absolutely clear about going to jail?"

"I am," I answered. "In my mind, prison is the only path left."

"Once you're in, Francesco, never let a single seed of doubt creep into your mind. Otherwise, you're trapped in a living hell. What helped me most was that I'd never think of myself as caged. I stayed free in thought." Corey looked out, then back at me. "It's real important that you *never* let yourself forget that you went in because you did the right thing." I nodded, and he added, "There's one more thing. All over the world are guys like us who give up their freedom so they won't be part of mass murder. You and I are part of that family. So when you're in prison, remember—you're *never* alone."

"Thanks, Corey."

"Of course," Corey said. "You're my brother!"

This Monet print symbolized, for me, my eight-year struggle with the draft. I sent it to Joyce, the clerk of my Virginia draft board, 1971.

The Christmas card I sent to President Nixon in 1971. (Photo: F. Da Vinci)

59

THE FINAL DECISION
(1971)

"When it is dark enough, you can see the stars."
—Ralph Waldo Emerson

The day of reckoning neared. The Virginia State Director of Selective Service would either recognize me as a conscientious objector, or I would be sentenced to prison.

Over the weekend, Jane and I felt the need to visit with Nature and forget about the pressure of the draft, at least for a day. Our destination was a 1000-tree orchard in Julian that had a view of snow-capped mountains in the distance. We had a picnic feast that included two ample pieces of freshly baked cinnamon apple pie from a local café. They were so good we thought they should be illegal!

On the way home, a dark reality began to creep back. I couldn't shake the nightmare of the draft and prison. As we drove along an endless field, I tried to picture life without Jane, a topic I usually pushed to the back of my mind. My eyes began to mist, and I said to Jane, "I've gotta pull over."

She looked deeply into my eyes. "I get it."

I got out of the car, walked about twenty yards into the field, then sat down and folded my head in my arms.

I remembered our wedding day—we were so blissfully happy. How reckless could I be to throw away five years of our life together? At the same time, I knew there was no turning back and that I needed to banish second-guessing. I had proudly taken a stand; a stand that joined me in spirit with the other COs throughout history who faced unnecessary hardships far greater than what I faced. It was not the time to waver. Corey's advice came back loud and clear: 'Never let a single seed of doubt creep into your mind.'

When I broke from my meditation and returned to the car, there was Jane with my camera around her neck. "I snapped a shot of you when you were in the field," she said.

Later, when we looked at the image, Jane said, "It shows your pain, but it also shows the field around you and the mountains in the background, as if you're communicating with Nature, with something wiser than war."

On Monday, after my work at the community center, I came home and anxiously checked the mail. The familiar brown envelope from Selective Service had arrived. I stared at it, knowing that its contents would change my life forever.

Jane was at work.

Over the last few months, I had diligently prepared myself for incarceration, but now that the moment was at hand, all that groundwork seemed to desert me. Against my better judgment, I hoped for justice. I took a deep breath, held it a moment, and let it out. Carefully, I tore open the envelope and discovered it contained only a draft card. I had expected a letter.

My eyes scanned the card and focused on the classification. Instead of the familiar "1-A," meaning ready for war, the classification read, "1-O," meaning conscientious objector! *It couldn't be!*

I read and reread the classification: "1-O."

After over three years of appealing my case, had justice finally been served?

I grabbed the phone, called Charlie, and read the new classification.

"Are you *sure* you read it right?" he asked. "Read it again, carefully."

"I'm positive. It says '1-O,' conscientious objector."

"I don't see how that's . . . Hell, drive it over. I'll take a look. Maybe your eyes are playing tricks, and you're seeing what you want to see."

At Charlie's office, which had become a kind of second home, Charlie studied the card in silence. After a few eternal moments, he looked up. "It's the real deal. The miracle happened, the *miracle* happened! No prison, buddy. You're recognized as a sincere CO!"

We both let out a yell and hugged. When we calmed down, Charlie added, "You'll be serving two years of community service work, probably at the center where you're already working."

"It's really true? The State Director overturned the case in our favor?"

"100 percent true," Charlie said. "This decision is going to help COs everywhere that have a strong personal religion and no traditional religion."

"We did it, Charlie. Somehow we did it."

Charlie pressed the intercom and said to his secretary. "Margaret, you can come in now.

He's dealing with reality after all." Charlie explained, "I told her to wait in case you were . . . uh . . ."

". . . delusional?"

"Yeah, something like that."

Margaret brought in a bottle of champagne and three glasses on a tray.

"So, how's the freedom feel, Francesco?" Charlie asked.

"It's going to take a while to sink in." We raised our glasses, and I said, "To the greatest lawyer on the planet—Charlie Khoury. You met the challenge."

Charlie pointed to his hair. "That challenge gave me most of this gray."

Margaret turned to me. "Every time you left the office, Francesco, I had to listen to the rant. And it wasn't nonviolent!"

"Hey, that's what kept me sane," Charlie protested.

"Mind if I use your phone to call my mom and dad?"

"Help yourself."

I wiped away a tear and called Mom to give her the good news. "That's *wonderful,* dear!" she exclaimed. "Thank goodness! Hold on . . . your dad is right here."

Dad came on the line and asked, "What's up? Your mother said it was good news."

"It is. I won my CO case!"

"That's terrific, Francesco." He hesitated, then said, "I wish I could say I had supported you more."

"Thanks, Dad. Love you."

The next call was to Ralph in Tennessee. "Guess what, buddy. No prison!"

"Fantastic! You calling from Canada?"

"No, no. I won my CO case."

"What? I can't believe it! I don't know how the hell you did it, but way to go!"

"Actually, Charlie is the guy who made it happen. I can't wait to tell Jane. Soon as we get off the line, I'm gonna call her."

"What are you doing on the phone with me? Call her now!"

When I called Jane and gave her the victory news, she screamed so loud I had to pull the receiver away from my ear.

"Let's go out and celebrate."

"We *have* to," Jane exclaimed. "I'll finish up some paperwork and take off early."

"How about dinner at the Hotel Del Coronado," I said. "We'll pretend we can afford it."

"Great. I'll meet you there, sweetheart. Can't wait. Love you. Bye."

I turned to Charlie. "I'll never forget you for hanging in there and never giving up the ship."

After a goodbye hug, Charlie added, "Keep up the good fight."

On the drive to the Hotel Del, I felt overwhelmed with gratitude. I owed Jane, Charlie, and the Virginia State Director of Selective Service so much.

As I drove across the Coronado Bridge, I reflected on my eight years facing the draft. I wondered, *Who was the Virginia State Director of Selective Service that saved me from prison, that backed up my right to say, 'I refuse to kill'?* Silently, I thanked the State Director, who had stood on the side of justice.

Years later, I learned his shocking identity. He was Ernest Fears, Jr.—the *first* African American in all of the U.S. to hold the position of State Director of Selective Service! Mr. Fears' appointment in 1971 had been a major racial breakthrough. Colonel Adams, an information officer for Selective Service, told the press, "This appointment is unprecedented. It makes an old guy like myself feel that there is still hope in this country."

Fears had been the State Director of Selective Service for only eight months when he courageously reversed the draft board's two unanimous rejections of my CO claim. In the eyes of the Nixon Administration and the eyes of my draft board, Fears was supposed to be a role model who didn't rock the boat. Instead, in effect, he told everyone concerned, *You got it wrong. On my watch, I will not look the other way and allow this sincere CO to go to prison.*

Mr. Fears died in 2003, and I deeply regret that I never got the chance to thank him personally for his sense of justice and bravery. I did, however, get in touch with his two sons, telling them, "Your father was a man of courage and principle. He stood against the wind to do the right thing. I'm hoping to honor him in my memoir someday."

At the Hotel Del Coronado, I was seated at a table-for-two when Jane walked in looking more beautiful than ever. I hurried over to her, and we hugged long and tight, ignoring the surrounding guests that stared at our tearful embrace.

"Unbelievable," Jane said. "I still can't get over it." We sat down, and I feasted on the loveliness of her face, glowing softly in the candlelight. Lost in each other's eyes, we held hands. Jane shook her head and said, "Did you *ever* think this might happen?"

"Never. I hoped but never expected."

She looked down. "I want to apologize for something. I'm so sorry . . ." she began.

"For what?"

". . . I'm sorry I gave you such a hard time." She paused. "At first, I thought your CO stand and lack of compromise were flaws in your character, that what you did was out of weakness, out of you being *crazy*. Then I realized that you did those things out of strength and that they were actually *rational.* The draft . . . this war . . . *that's* what's insane! I'm sorry I never told you that." A tear rolled off her cheek.

"There's *nothing* to apologize for, Jane. *I'm* the one who needs to say 'I'm sorry.' I got carried away with the peace work and let our relationship slide *way* too much. It was unfair and selfish. I wasn't listening to you like I should have, and I regret that. I know I caused you a lot of pain."

"You did," she said evenly.

Now I was tearful too. I said, "I don't know how you stayed. Through the whole thing . . . you were a saint."

Silent tension filled the air, then Jane quipped, "I *was* a saint, wasn't I!"

We burst out laughing. Then I said, "Mind if we don't go straight home? I think we should stop somewhere first."

Jane smiled. "I know where."

Of course, she was right. We drove straight to the reef in La Jolla that had been my sanctuary for the last three years. As the sun began to set low over the ocean, Jane said, "You go to the reef first, for time alone. Then I'll come up with you."

From atop the reef, I looked out at the sunset and thought back. It had been a long road since I attended President John F. Kennedy's Inauguration with Jerry; since I got up the nerve to trade my apathy for activism and march for peace; since I took a stand as a conscientious objector and refused induction; since Jane and Charlie stayed by my side in the worst of times; since my peace organization, Nonviolent Action, grew from three people to nearly three hundred and became a national call to conscience; until, at last, "the miracle happened" and I was given recognition as a conscientious objector to war.

Jane took my hand and came up on the reef. A magnificent golden sunset shimmered over the Pacific Ocean.

I closed my eyes, and all I could see, and all I could feel, was freedom.

Shortly before I was to be sentenced to prison for refusing induction, 1971. (Photo: Jane)

Ernest Fears, Jr., honored as the first African American to integrate the position of State Director of Selective Service, 1971.

Freedom, 1971. (Photo: Jane)

Epilogue

LETTER TO THE READER

"... Come, my friends,
'Tis not too late to seek a newer world"
- Tennyson

Dear Reader,

Thank you for reading the story of my conscientious objection to war. Please note that *I Refuse to Kill* is not just my story; it's the story of COs throughout history who suffered greatly to champion nonviolence and remind us to be kind to one another.

May their legacy encourage each of us, and each of our nations, to seek the courage to love.

Peace and friendship,

Francesco Da Vinci TLU

The following is from my statement of conscientious objection to war:

Selective Service Form 150: Describe the nature of your belief, which is the basis of your claim and state why you consider it to be based on religious training and belief.

April 15th, 1971—America
War and violence are as old as human history—so is the desire for peace and love. Everyone is for peace, yet we wage war after war. We are constantly told that to love is unrealistic. To me, the moral and the pragmatic are one. Violence and disregard for life destroy and negate. Love and the sanctity of life create and build. The logical

extension of violence is a world without life. The logical extension of love is a world without war.

The more I learn of love, the more I feel it is impossible to live without it. To love is to live; without love, we only exist. I regard every war as a civil war. Everyone everywhere is my family. It is not so much that I am against war as it is that I am for life. Violence has starved people's thirst for human unity and continual peace. I believe with all my heart and mind that there is an alternative to the futility of war—nonviolence.

The purpose of this writing is not merely to show my conscientious objection to violence, but to show a means of creating a world without war, a means of enhancing lives everywhere, a means of making peace and love living realities rather than ideals that are never attained. I believe, as Martin Luther King said, "The choice is no longer between nonviolence and violence; it is between nonviolence and non-existence."

The basis of my religious belief is the sanctity of life, which is reflected beautifully in the philosophy of nonviolence. Therefore, I chose nonviolence—active love—as my religion, my political philosophy, and my way of life.

Nonviolence is not the absence of violence any more than peace is the absence of war. Nonviolence is a positive method; it calls on our creativity and imagination. On a personal level, nonviolence not only refrains my hand and heart from violence, it calls on me to affirm love. If we regard life as sacred, we cannot be silent in a violent world. We cannot withdraw and only find peace with ourselves. That is abstraction—an abstraction of our own lives and the lives of others. We must translate our principles into action and social service. It is extremely difficult for me to stand up *against* international systems of violence, just as it is difficult for me to stand up *for* human unity. But I know of no better way to do both than by the truth of nonviolence.

Learning and action are inseparable in nonviolence. As we learn the methods of nonviolence, we must breathe life into them by living them. Nonviolence is like music; you study it, but it does not come of its own until you can play it.

The following are my principles of nonviolence:

> If I want peace, I cannot kill for it; if I want love, I cannot hate for it; if I want freedom, I cannot enslave for it. **The means cannot be sacrificed for the ends.** They must be harmonious with each other. Gandhi once wrote, "The means may be likened to a seed, the end to a tree; and there is just the same inviolable connection between the means and the end as there is between the seed and the tree." By this principle, peace cannot be sought; it must be lived. Therefore, our journey is our destination.
>
> **Love is universal.** It compels the recognition of everyone's humanity. Nonviolence knows no human enemy. It does not accept diversity; it celebrates it!

I strive to show empathy and altruism to everyone I encounter. It is easy for me to love those who trust and love, but it is a real test of strength for me to love those who hate. A spirit of understanding allows me to reawaken the love dormant in others. There is no greater protection than love. Violent retaliation only invites further retaliation. If we truly recognize everyone's humanity, then it becomes impossible for us to dehumanize and kill other human beings. Our family is life; our home is the world.

Nonviolence encourages self-reliance. Each of us is tremendously powerful. The existence of any government depends directly on the consent of the governed. Nonviolence encourages independent thinking and challenges blind obedience, especially when blind obedience is required for the purpose of racism and mass murder. Slavery needs slaves as war needs soldiers. Self-reliance gives the individual the strength to question and stand up to authoritarianism.

Nonviolence strives for reconciliation, not domination. It is a powerful method of change that respects the opponent's human dignity. Nonviolence expects and demands dignity, and in the process of struggle, enhances the humanity of both sides. Fear stands in the way of reconciliation. It makes it easier for us to hate and kill. Nonviolence calls on us to constantly face our fears and to affirm love. Hate is out of fear; if we fear, let us fear hate. Love is from courage; if we be courageous, let us love. War cultivates alienation and divisiveness. Peace promotes compassion and unity.

Nonviolence strives to be open. Secrecy encourages suspicion and hate. Openness encourages trust and love. If our actions are out of love, they have no need to be hidden.

Nonviolence seeks truth. I try to practice honesty in my daily life by making my words, thoughts, and actions as harmonious as I possibly can. It is not important that we always act the same. The important thing is to do what we believe at the time and not be silent in the face of injustice and violence. Nonviolence challenges us to be strong and to be willing to speak truth to power.

These principles are my truth. I am a peacemaker, and the meaning of my life is love.

I see all humankind as one family. Therefore, I close in a spirit of racial and religious harmony, in a spirit of *we* rather than a spirit of *us* against *them.* And as we embark to new worlds beyond Earth, let us journey with a reverence for life, rather than a tradition of war. If humanity is to survive and flourish, then each of us must recognize our common enemy—war. As Gandhi said, let each of us 'be the change.'

How long until we seek a newer world based on nonviolence? How long until each of us finds the courage to love?

ABOUT THE AUTHOR

Francesco Da Vinci is a director-producer, photojournalist, peace activist, and public speaker. Previously, for more than 20 years, he was a celebrity portrait photographer with Getty Images. Publication of Francesco's work included *The New York Times, The Los Angeles Times, Harper's Bazaar* (UK), *The Washington Post, Newsweek, Time,* and *LIFE Magazine.*

Currently, Francesco lives and works in Los Angeles, where he is developing a documentary film based on *I Refuse to Kill.* The film will promote social justice, nonviolence, and service to others.

In 2023, Francesco received a nomination for the U.S. Peace Prize.

www.ingramcontent.com/pod-product-compliance
Ingram Content Group UK Ltd.
Pitfield, Milton Keynes, MK11 3LW, UK
UKHW041857190726
13854UKWH00002B/955

9 798218 929985